D1602446

The Spanish
Civil War at Sea

The Spanish Civil War at Sea

Dark and Dangerous Waters

Michael Alpert

Pen & Sword
MILITARY

First published in Great Britain in 2021 by
Pen & Sword Military
An imprint of
Pen & Sword Books Ltd
Yorkshire – Philadelphia

ISBN 978 1 52676 436 2

Typeset by Mac Style
Printed and bound in the UK by CPI Group (UK) Ltd, Croydon, CR0
4YY

Pen & Sword Books Limited incorporates the imprints of Atlas,
Archaeology, Aviation, Discovery, Family History, Fiction, History,
Maritime, Military, Military Classics, Politics, Select, Transport,
True Crime, Air World, Frontline Publishing, Leo Cooper, Remember
When, Seaforth Publishing, The Praetorian Press, Wharncliffe
Local History, Wharncliffe Transport, Wharncliffe True Crime
and White Owl.

For a complete list of Pen & Sword titles please contact

PEN & SWORD BOOKS LIMITED
47 Church Street, Barnsley, South Yorkshire, S70 2AS, England
E-mail: enquiries@pen-and-sword.co.uk
Website: www.pen-and-sword.co.uk

Or

PEN AND SWORD BOOKS
1950 Lawrence Rd, Havertown, PA 19083, USA
E-mail: Uspen-and-sword@casematepublishers.com
Website: www.penandswordbooks.com

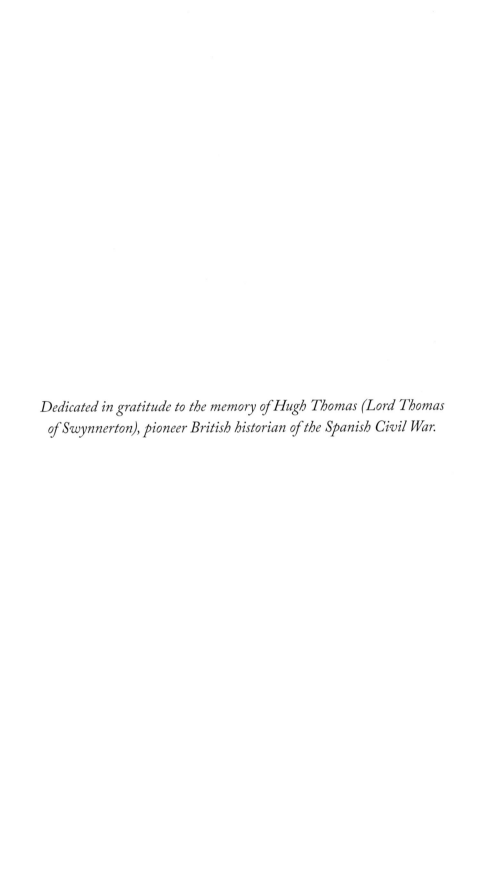

Dedicated in gratitude to the memory of Hugh Thomas (Lord Thomas of Swynnerton), pioneer British historian of the Spanish Civil War.

Contents

Preface

The Spanish Civil War of 1936–1939 has been of permanent interest since Hugh Thomas published his seminal *The Spanish Civil War* in 1961.[1] Yet there has been little in English devoted to the war at sea. Compared with the massive land armies of the Spanish war, relatively few Spaniards served at sea, so there has been virtually no memoir literature. Nor are there any foreign accounts about the war at sea by, for example, journalists or members of the International Brigades which fought in Spain. The two major Spanish works on the subject are by senior Spanish naval officers, Ricardo Cerezo and Fernando and Salvador Moreno, the sons of Admiral Francisco Moreno who commanded the Insurgent fleet during the civil war.[2] These multi-volume works, though somewhat indigestible, are very useful because of their immense detail and direct quotation of original and documentary sources. Apart from Admiral James Cable's book specifically on the 1937 blockade of Bilbao, the only work written in English, though published in a poorly edited Spanish translation, is Admiral Peter Gretton's *El factor olvidado: la Marina Británica y la Guerra Civil Española* (Madrid, San Martín, 1984).

However, the naval aspects of the Spanish Civil War were of more international and specifically British importance than the land war, given the significance and size of the Royal Navy and the British Merchant Marine at the time. Almost all the war material sent to Spain, together with most of the other essential supplies of a country at war, arrived by sea. This was so whether cargoes came from Nazi Germany and Fascist Italy, which massively aided the Insurgents under General Franco, or from the Soviet Union or wherever else the Spanish Republic which Franco was striving to overthrow could buy arms to bring through the Mediterranean, over the Atlantic, or through the English Channel and the Bay of Biscay. Many ships were transferred to the British flag in order to enjoy the protection of the Royal Navy. While the increase in the size of the British Merchant Marine was desirable, much opinion in

Parliament and the press questioned whether ships which had nothing British about them save the Red Ensign should be able to call on Royal Navy protection when trying to break a Spanish Insurgent blockade for the sake of the profits to be made.

As for other countries, Italy saw the Spanish war as a way to challenge the Royal Navy's dominance in the Western Mediterranean, and to wrest control from France of the sea route from North Africa to Europe. For the Nazi regime, helping Franco to win would weaken France but would also offer the chance to stake Germany's right to be a respected naval power.

Because of these rivalries, the Spanish Civil War was seen from London and Paris as potentially liable to provoke a major international war if foreign supporters competed to supply one or other side with armaments. At the same time the Spanish war offered an opportunity to organise a simulacrum of international cooperation with a view to avoiding an international conflict. This was reflected in the pan-European Non-Intervention Agreement of August, 1936, and the International Naval Patrol of April 1937.

To a great extent, the British and French aim of corralling the Spanish Civil War so that it did not directly cause an international conflict was achieved. However, it is arguable that the dictators learned that because their interference in Spain, where they had no justified national interests, was tolerated, the democracies would allow them to extend their aggressive behaviour.

International reaction to the Spanish war took the form of keeping the sea safe for commercial traffic and at the same time enforcing – or rather pretending to enforce – the 'Non-Intervention' Agreement not to allow the shipment of arms to Spain. Thus questions of the legal status of the belligerents, of the identity of ships, of the right to blockade and interfere with legitimate traffic and of the extent of territorial waters became the frequent subject of Question Time in the House of Commons and regular discussion in the press. Royal Navy warships provided information to the Admiralty and thence the British government, while a future Director of Intelligence in the Far East, Lieutenant Commander Alan Hillgarth, became the Admiralty's 'eyes and ears' in what is today the holiday resort of Palma on Majorca but which became a major Insurgent naval base between 1936 and 1939.

Today a majority of the readers of this book will have visited Spain, and will recognise the places it mentions, such as the Málaga and Catalan coasts (the 'Costa del Sol' and the 'Costa Brava') and the Balearic Islands of Majorca, Minorca and Ibiza (where Soviet aircraft bombed a German warship in error), but few of their forbears would have visited Spain before the Spanish Civil War. Most people's knowledge of Spain in the nineteen-thirties was limited to the Inquisition, the opera *Carmen* and of course the Spanish Armada. In many British people's eyes, the Spanish Civil War was being fought in a remote, exotic land between two groups of 'Dagoes', one of which, the Republicans, were seen as at least trying to modernise and democratise their country, while the Francoists were admired only by those who referred to them as 'defenders of Western civilisation against Bolshevism'. Officers of the Royal Navy, reflecting their social class, referred in their messages about Spain to 'Reds', while German sources often speak of the 'Whites'. Such terms harked back to the Russian Revolution, which was a living memory for people over their mid-thirties, many of whom feared Communism and social revolution more than fascism and Nazism.

In this book readers interested in naval questions will read about a war which saw at its beginning a mutiny which was considered, at least by Royal Navy officers, as one more of the mutinies of the early twentieth century, like those of the Russian battleship *Potemkin* in 1905, the German Navy at Kiel in 1918, the French navy in the Black Sea in 1919, and the refusal of duties by Royal Navy crews at Invergordon in 1931. Yet, paradoxically, the mutiny in the Spanish navy in July 1936 was one in which the mutineers asked their government for orders after having deposed and often murdered officers who were rebelling against that very government.

Both sections of the divided navy of Spain had to remake themselves. In this, the Insurgent Navy, which had few ships but plenty of skilled and enthusiastic officers, concentrated on essential targets and fought efficiently with its exiguous resources without guidance from a non-existent Ministry of Marine or even for some time a naval staff, while the much larger Republican fleet, under the orders of a chaotic government and an inexperienced staff, did not rise to the occasion because it lacked a coherent strategy, and was short of all manner of essential supplies. Nor did it have enough officers, and those it had were unsure of their authority, unreliable and suspected. The Republican fleet thus failed to take full advantage of its apparent superiority.

In brief, the Spanish war saw the struggle of each fleet to deny control of the sea to the other, the vital importance of the sea as a route for essential supplies, its connection with the international crisis and the problem of the appeasement of Germany and Italy against the background of the fear of Communist expansion.

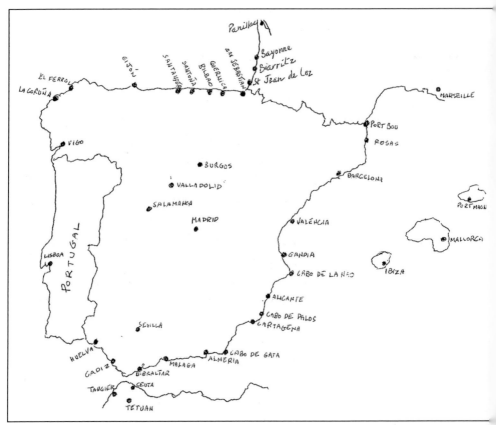

Coasts of Spain and Western France.

Chapter 1

Setting the Scene

I The Spanish Civil War in the Context of the Aims and Objectives of Modern Naval Warfare

Naval policy aims to construct a fleet balanced, in terms of the number and power of its ships, according to the tasks it is required to undertake. In a civil war, however, each side may control only part of the national fleet. In this case, the ships may have to carry out tasks for which they are not designed and either or both sides may have to acquire ships from other countries.

Nevertheless, the principles of naval warfare remain valid for civil wars. Eliminating the enemy may not be the main aim, which is rather to obstruct his sea routes and blockade his ports. The object is to prevent troop movements, arms traffic, the import of goods, specifically essential raw materials and food, and exports which provide international credit.[1]

During the Spanish Civil War of 1936–1939, in which the Insurgents under General Francisco Franco overthrew the Spanish Republic, most of the war material for both sides came by sea, especially so for the Insurgents or Nationalists as they came to be known in Britain. This brought to the forefront the question of blockade and of the protection by foreign navies of merchant shipping, especially the Royal Navy. General Franco's navy used blockade, with all its risks, to the utmost of its abilities and with ever-greater success, while the Republican Government gave up blockade after the first few weeks. How far each side achieved its aims and why the Republican navy failed to obstruct Insurgent sea routes is a fundamental question in investigating the result of the Spanish Civil War and answerable in terms of the international situation at the time.

Much of the international importance of the Spanish conflict lay in the roles of several foreign navies and merchant marines, as they brought material to one side and the other. German, Spanish and Italian merchant ships carried arms to Franco under the protection of warships. Soviet and

Spanish merchant shipping arrived with weapons for the Republic, while the large numbers of British merchant ships sailing to Spain, mostly carrying non-military imports and exports, required protection from the Royal Navy.

II The Royal Navy

The heavy presence of warships around the coasts of Spain was liable, it was feared, to provoke a major European war. Britain in particular, tried hard to ensure that the Spanish war did not lead to a general conflict. In this, the role of the British Foreign Office and Royal Navy in trying to prevent arms shipments to Spain but to protect legitimate trade by sea was primordial.

In the Spanish war the activity of German warships and the participation of Italian submarines in particular created a heavy burden for the Royal Navy, which in the latter 1930s was competing for funds with the other armed services. After 1919 heavy financial cuts were imposed on the Royal Navy. To this were added the effects of the decisions of the 1921–1922 Washington conference. Faced with the threat of an arms race, pacifism at home and economic stringency, the Royal Navy was also to be limited in its parity with other navies.[2] The British government adopted the so-called 'Ten-Year Rule', which assumed that Britain would not be faced by a major war over a self-perpetuating ten year period. This was seen as a correct policy in a decade which hoped that 'the war to end wars', as the 1914–1918 conflict became known, would indeed mean an epoch of international peace, in which disputes would be arbitrated by the League of Nations, German militarism had been vanquished, France's security was guaranteed by the Locarno agreement of 1924 and the Great Powers had renounced war as an instrument of national policy.

However, the British Far East Empire remained the major concern of the Royal Navy. The Annual Report of the chiefs of staff for 1927 had laid down the principle that no anxieties in the Mediterranean could be allowed to interfere with the dispatch of a fleet to the Far East if required.[3] Restated in 1929, the Royal Navy's duty was established as to ensure freedom of passage to all parts of the empire.

The question of the role of the Royal Navy affected policy in Europe also. Ships sailing to the Far East steamed through the Strait of Gibraltar and via Malta and Alexandria and Suez. But the Far East was the greatest concern. In 1930, Ramsey MacDonald, the Prime Minister and Chairman of the International Naval Conference wrote to the King:

[...] Great Britain must not take on further responsibilities and must not be put in the position of having to act mechanically and without freedom of judgement should trouble arise in Europe.[4]

In 1931 the Admiralty complained that the Royal Navy had been seriously weakened, both relatively to other countries and in absolute terms.[5] It was questionable whether the navy could provide cover against Japan while retaining a deterrent force sufficient to prevent the strongest European naval power (presumably Italy) from obtaining control over areas essential to British export and import trade, at a time when Britain imported half of its food. In early 1934, after Hitler's takeover and Germany's withdrawal from the Disarmament Conference, the Defence Requirements Committee gave as its view that Germany was now the greatest danger in Europe. While this stimulated the urgency of spending on the army and the air force, Neville Chamberlain, the Chancellor of the Exchequer, was unwilling to disburse the huge sums needed for capital ship construction.[6]

By the end of 1933, however, the Ten-Year Rule had been allowed to lapse. The Committee for Imperial Defence began to prepare a programme to meet the worst deficiencies. As the months passed the European threat increased, leading France and the Soviet Union to sign a treaty of mutual assistance in the face of Hitler's repudiation of the Treaty of Versailles, his remilitarisation of the Rhineland in March 1936 and the establishment of the German-Italian Axis of November 1936, just at the moment when both countries were taking a major part on Franco's side in Spain.

Rearmament was not a mere question of throwing money at shipbuilding yards. In the 1920s and during the Depression of the 1930s plant had been allowed to decay, skilled labour had been lost to areas which offered work to the unemployed, and firms had closed. Furthermore, the Labour Party had opposed the defence White Paper of 1 March 1935. The Axis threat was obvious. Germany had reintroduced conscription in February 1935. As one naval historian sums up pithily

The spectre of a hostile Germany, Italy and Japan [...] was to condition all British naval thinking and planning for the next five years.[7]

Those years would include Mussolini's campaign to take over the kingdom of Abyssinia and the Spanish Civil War. In the former, if effective sanctions, such as blocking the Suez Canal to Italian forces, were to be effective, Malta and Alexandria might well suffer attack and, while the Royal Navy was confident that it could deal with any threat from the Italian navy, Britain could not afford losses. As Sir Robert Vansittart, the Permanent Under Secretary at the Foreign Office, wrote to the Foreign Secretary, Sir Samuel Hoare and to Admiral Chatfield, the First Sea Lord and Chief of Naval Staff

This country has been so weakened of recent years that we are in no position to take a strong line in the Mediterranean [...] we should be very cautious as to how far and in what manner we force the pace with an unreliable France and an unready England.[8]

Thus it is probable that Britain's weak reaction to the Italian invasion of Abyssinia of 1935 encouraged Mussolini to involve Italy in aiding Franco in 1936, in particular at sea and with shipments of armaments and men.

III The Spanish Navy in the Twentieth Century

In 1898 two Spanish fleets had been destroyed during the war with the United States. Spain had not been a belligerent in the First World War.

Antonio Maura became Prime Minister in January 1907. His personal interest (he had founded the *Liga Marítima Española* or Spanish Navy League in 1900), and his majority in the Spanish parliament or *Cortes* opened the way for a national plan to re-equip the navy. The Navy Minister, José Ferrándiz, announced a plan to build a new fleet, with a budget of two hundred million pesetas (roughly six million pounds sterling) over the next eight years. Most of the sum would be spent on three battleships. The vessels would be built by the *Sociedad Española de Constructores Navales* (SECN), in which the British companies Vickers Armstrong and Brown and Thorneycroft had interests.

The three battleships were based on the *Dreadnought* model. With a displacement of 15,000 tons, with eight 305 mm and twenty 101 mm guns, they represented a huge increase in the firepower of the Spanish navy. The *Alfonso XIII* entered service in 1915 and the *Jaime I* in 1921. Nevertheless, Britain had already built the 25,000 ton super-Dreadnought with guns of 380 mm calibre, so that by the civil war of 1936–1939 the Spanish ships were completely outdated. The third battleship, the *España*, had ran aground off Chile and been abandoned in 1921. The *Alfonso XIII*, renamed *España* in 1931, and the *Jaime I*, would be lost during the civil war.[9]

Admiral Augusto Miranda, Navy Minister between 1913 and 1917, planned to bring the Ferrándiz project up to date. In February 1915 a decision was taken to build four fast cruisers, two of which, the *Méndez Núñez* and the *Almirante Cervera*, would serve in the civil war of 1936–1939, together with six destroyers, the *Alsedo*, *Lazaga*, and *Velasco*, and three of the newer *Churruca* type. Nearly one-third of the Miranda budget was destined for twenty-eight submarines, of which there had been none in the Spanish navy. By the civil war there would be twelve in service. Miranda aimed to deliver the new warships by 1922, but inflation and delays in the purchase of essential material because of the First World War led to long extensions in delivery dates.

IV An Always Outdated Fleet

The cruisers, destroyers, and submarines planned by Miranda would be handed over between 1921 and 1925 but would often still await their artillery, torpedo tubes and other essential equipment. However, the new cruisers had doubled their horsepower and the destroyers had seen theirs increase by thirty per cent. The new cruisers *Príncipe Alfonso*, later renamed *Libertad*, and *Almirante Cervera*, could develop a speed of thirty three knots and carried guns of 152.4 mm and 101.6 mm calibre, but their armour was minimal. The *Churruca* type destroyers, which would characterise the Republican fleet in the civil war, displaced 1,650 tons, could develop 36 knots and were armed with five 120 mm guns and a 76 mm anti-aircraft weapon, as well as six torpedo tubes. The submarines were armed with four 450 mm torpedo tubes and could deliver 10.5 knots submerged.[10]

V The Spanish Navy and the Moroccan Wars

The only war experiences of the Spanish navy in the twentieth century until the civil war were those arising from the Riff wars against the Moroccan tribes between 1922 and 1926. The victorious landings at Alhucemas in September 1925 required the cooperation of the fleet and a great deal of detailed logistics, particularly in view of Spanish cooperation with the French navy in what was a major amphibious operation. Two Spanish battleships, three cruisers, three destroyers and six gunboats, as well as smaller ships and landing-craft, took part. Twenty ships acted as troop and material transports. The air force bombed the area heavily while the navy had to carry out manoeuvres new to it, such as feints of landings, approaches to the coast using smoke screens and diversionary shelling. Fortunately the sea was calm, but dense fog at night created difficulties. Fleet operations continued for twenty-six days. Nevertheless, the inferiority of the enemy and the absence of hostile submarines and mines meant that any lessons which could be derived and applied to the war of 1936–1939, apart from training and practice in shelling and observation from the sea, were of little value.

VI The Ships and Men who Fought the Civil War

The rapid international development of warships, the protection of the shipbuilding industry, Spain's responsibilities in Morocco and rivalry with other navies in the Mediterranean, led the government of General Primo de Rivera, which came to power on 23 September 1923, to sign major contracts for warships. The ships would be the cruiser *Miguel de Cervantes*, which entered service in 1930, and three more destroyers of the *Churruca* class, the *José Luis Díez*, the *Ferrándiz* and the *Lepanto*, which would enter service between 1928 and 1930. However, these ships were only slightly advanced over those of the Miranda Plan. The *Miguel de Cervantes*, for example, was inadequately armoured and its 152 mm calibre artillery was below the standard 203 mm for cruisers. Nevertheless, Spain was coming close to possessing an up to date fleet when a new budget was approved in 1926 for three 10,000 ton cruisers, twelve type C submarines and a further three modern destroyers. Minelayers and minesweepers would also be acquired, and seaplane bases would be established at Port

Mahon on the Balearic island of Minorca, at San Javier near the major naval base at Cartagena in south-east Spain, and at Vigo in north-west Spain. A plan was drawn up for harbour defences and for extensive work in the bases at Cartagena, El Ferrol and San Fernando (Cádiz).[11] The economic boom of the 1920s would provide the 877.6 million pesetas or approximately £30 million that were to be spent.

The most important ships to be built were two 10,000 ton cruisers, the *Canarias* and the *Baleares*. Developing 90,000 horsepower, they could achieve a speed of 33 knots, and had a extended range without refuelling if cruising at economical speed. Their ability to stay at sea for long periods would prove highly valuable in the civil war of 1936–1939. Armed with eight 203 mm, eight 120 and eight 40 mm guns, these two cruisers were far more powerful than the cruisers *Libertad* and *Miguel de Cervantes*. The three further destroyers were the *Churruca*, the *Alcalá Galiano* and the *Almirante Valdés*, which would enter service in 1932, while the last two to be ready by the civil war of 1936 were the *Almirante Antequera* and the *Almirante Miranda*. The *Gravina* was ready in September 1936 and four more of the same type, the *Escaño,* the *Císcar,* the *Jorge Juan, and the Almirante Ulloa,* would enter service during the civil war.

As for the men, the Spanish navy was not a happy service. There was mutual antipathy and suspicion between officers of the General Corps or *Cuerpo General,* who commanded the ships, and the specialist branches of engineers and gunnery, both among officers and the various branches and ranks of petty officers.[12] Ferrándiz's reorganisation had established various corps of specialist petty-officers but these men, however senior and skilled, could not become officers. This is a fundamental point, and contrasts with the very different atmosphere in the Spanish army, where senior non-commissioned officers could achieve officer rank.

The schism in the navy, which the Republic of 1931 would attempt to heal, is an important question and would be reflected in what the officers considered the revolutionary attitude of the petty officers.

VII The Second Republic: Demagogy or Progress?

On 14 April 1931, following the departure of Alfonso XIII, the Spanish Republic was established. Monarchist symbols were hastily removed and names of ships were changed. The battleship *Alfonso XIII* was renamed

España, the cruiser *Reina Victoria Eugenia* would be called *República* and the cruiser *Príncipe Alfonso* received the name *Libertad*. Was this mere demagogy? Moving for the moment from the Spanish scene, the twentieth century had already witnessed disturbances in national navies. In 1905 the crew of the Russian battleship *Potemkin* had mutinied because of the ill treatment of the seamen by the officers. The example of the *Potemkin* led to mutinies in the Russian naval base of Kronstadt which in March 1921 would declare itself autonomous, refuse to accept the orders of the Bolshevik government, and be crushed. Early November 1918 saw mutinies among the highly politicised men of the German fleet. The workers in the Kiel naval base made common cause with the mutineers. In the context of the Russian Revolution, some condemned the strikers and mutineers as treacherous 'Reds'. Nevertheless, a better relationship between the officers, the technical branches and the seamen might have avoided the mutinies. Another mutiny took place in 1919 on French warships in the Black Sea which were trying to contain the Bolsheviks. One of the leaders of this mutiny was André Marty, an engineer officer who twenty years later would command the base of the International Brigades who went to Spain to defend the Republic in the civil war.[13] The Royal Navy, the most respected in the world, was not free of disturbance either. In 1931, seamen at the Invergordon base, angered by a large reduction in pay arising from the financial crisis and budget cuts, refused to perform duties. The incident led to widespread alarm.[14]

In this context of these mutinies, the Spanish navy did not seem to harbour a mass of revolutionaries eager to subvert the regime. Nor were the naval officers affected by the unrest among Spanish army officers from 1916 onward. Unlike the army, the navy was not highly over-officered and did not demonstrate the same level of politicisation as army officers. These factors, which had traditionally encouraged military coups, were absent in the navy where, ideally, the ambition was to be far away at sea, in a situation where marching out of barracks into the street in a city, most of which had army garrisons, and declaring a military takeover, was impossible.

Nevertheless, unrest was spreading among the specialised men and the petty officers in particular. Just before the Republic was declared in 1931, Admiral Carvia, the Navy Minister, warned the senior officers that he had received a large number of anonymous and even insulting communications from the senior petty officers complaining that they could not advance in their careers.[15] It was their status which most seems to have troubled these often technically-specialised men. An illuminating comment was later made by a wireless warrant officer (as senior petty officers became under the Republic), Benjamín Balboa, who would play a major part in encouraging mutiny between 18 July and 21 July 1936 which saw the beginning of the civil war. Writing in the anarchist newspaper *CNT-Maritima* on 23 October 1937, Balboa remarked that the non-technical officers did not respect the specialised skills of warrant officers like himself and that a 'beardless midshipman' could accuse a technically-skilled senior petty officer of being a 'communist' and have him expelled from the navy or kept on shore with reduced pay.

The Republic of 1931 did not publish plans to open the Naval Academy to worthy petty officers. There was no desire to alter the hierarchical structure of the navy. There would be no purge of monarchists in the navy and no 'socialist' navy, despite what the administrations of 1931–1933 could have done if they had wanted, given the overwhelming Left Republican and Socialist majority in the *Cortes* and the spirit of the time which might even have approved the abolition of the armed services. Legislation in 1931–1933 did not even try to republicanise the navy, but merely to satisfy the aspirations of some of its personnel, which might have happened in any navy.

Some long-overdue reforms were introduced. From then on, only ships' commanders could impose punishments. Saturday shore leave was extended. Sailors would be paid for rations which had not been consumed, and guard-duty was relaxed. Such modifications were not particularly revolutionary and had been introduced in foreign navies. They were neither demagogic and certainly not intended to reduce the authority of the officers, but merely to remove areas of friction in order to increase operative efficiency.

VIII Reorganisation

Parallel to the major reorganisation of the army in 1931–1933, attempts were made to encourage early retirement, to reduce the total number of naval officers and in general, to remove the high status in civilian life of the generals and admirals. The admirals in command of the major naval bases lost a great deal of their jurisdiction, which was now to be limited to the dockyard, the harbour and naval installations on land. The loss of their traditional authority over questions of civilian law and order naturally aroused concern. Indeed, such measures might be considered demagogic, and intended merely to reduce the prestige of the military and naval authorities, who considered that Spain was not yet ready for removing their jurisdiction. This measure was probably one of those which might be considered disruptive rather than representing an urgent reform.

However, the new Republic wanted to bring the armed services up to date, not to carry out major change. The various adjustments made in the internal organisation of the Spanish navy were not introduced by a demagogic minister, but followed the recommendations of a commission which included Captain Francisco Moreno, Director of the Naval Academy and a future commander of the Insurgent navy during the civil war. The reforms included an attempt to improve the careers of the 679 senior and skilled petty officers, now to be called class one, two or three warrant officers.

As the aggressive attitude of Mussolini's Fascist Italy led to growing tension in the Mediterranean area, the only war experience of the Spanish navy before the outbreak of civil war in 1936 was internal. It concerned the use of ships to transport troops and to shell the northern coast. In order to suppress an armed uprising in the mining province of Asturias, the cruiser *Almirante Cervera* shelled the coal basin and forced revolutionary miners to surrender, while the cruiser *Miguel de Cervantes* carried troops and munitions to the port of Gijón. Lessons in logistics were learned, but since the enemy had no navy, little more. Given what later pro-Franco historians would say about revolutionary infiltration in the navy, if such had occurred, it was none too successful, for only two seamen deserted during this counter-revolutionary action.

IX On the Eve of Civil War

To what extent can one speak of plots of mutiny among the sailors and petty officers on the one hand and on the other of anti-government insurgency among the commanding officers of the navy even before many of the army garrisons declared a state of war against the government of Spain in July 1936?

Significant communist or revolutionary cells do not seem to have been present in the navy. The Spanish Communist Party was small and weak. The word 'communist' was used by conservatives as a word to describe any kind of progressive view. Nor was there a history of indiscipline in the navy even after during the social and industrial agitation in Spain in the months since the electoral victory of the Popular Front in February 1936. To support the thesis of a planned mutiny among the crews, a claim supported by senior naval officers who have written accounts of naval operations in the civil war, the very fact of the maintenance of discipline would have to be interpreted as part of a planned plot. Such a plot would include a decision by the crews and petty officers to isolate the professional part of the Spanish army in Morocco.[16] The other element in the alleged planning of mutiny has been freemasonry, in its particular Spanish form of a liberal and progressive attitude, the bogeyman of Spanish reactionaries. There were said to be 315 members of masonic lodges in the navy.[17] Captain Angel Rizo Bayona, Director of Merchant Marine in the Navy Ministry, had established what he called 'floating lodges' in some of the ships, whose task was to keep an eye on possible disloyalty of the officers.[18]

On 24 March 1936 the newly-elected Popular Front government permitted men who had been expelled from the navy for subversive activities to return to their posts. It may well be that some of these men were resentful and politically aware petty officers, but whether these groups existed to plan revolutionary subversion or to keep an eye on the officers whom they suspected of disloyalty to the Republic is a moot point. That there were such groups or cells is evident from the private papers of Benjamín Balboa, the radio warrant officer who would warn the crews against their officers once the army officers had begun their insurrection. Balboa sent warnings to the Navy Ministry, but the only result was a disciplinary charge against him. All that can be concluded is that the 'cells' observed the activities, described as 'monarchist', of the officers, their disrespect for the Republic and their foot-dragging in putting into effect changes which would recognise the improved status of the petty officers.[19] It would be mistaken to assume that the Navy Minister or the Republic in general took much notice of men such as Balboa who risked expulsion from the navy or long prison sentences.

The groups of long-service and resentful petty officers were probably different from the 'troikas' or three-man committees mentioned in a confidential note from one of the secret services linked with the Interior Ministry. Dated 5 August 1933, this note reported that the *troika* was centred on the occasional recruit who had a socialist or communist connection in civilian life. The local committee of the Communist Party would contact him and persuade him to join a 'cell'. However, it would be strange if the extensive activity described by the governmental informer could possibly have taken place among recruits on a ship subjected to close discipline and observation. The only important aspect of the note was the information that subversive or revolutionary and anti-military leaflets were being distributed, though to what extent is unknown. Nevertheless, the same report underlined that, at least until the Asturias revolution of October 1934, almost all seamen's conduct and discipline were unimpeachable.[20]

In the army, and even more so in the air force, a different tradition had contributed to creating some liberal and republican sectors among the officers. In 1934 the *Unión Militar Republicana* had emerged in order to counter the influence of the conservative and monarchist *Unión Militar Española*. A petty officer in the naval engineer corps, Eugenio Rodríguez Sierra, was a member of the UMR, which fused with another progressive officers' association to form the *Unión Militar Republicana y Antifascista*.[21] A very important part in the events of 18 July 1936 and the following days was played by Manuel Vázquez Seco, the most senior warrant officer in the Corps of Radio-Telegraphists, and the more junior Benjamín Balboa, whom Vázquez Seco had managed to have posted to the main communications centre of the navy in Madrid.[22]

The Popular Front government of the Spanish Republic, elected in February 1936, alarmed right wing and conservative opinion. Many feared that it would carry out the reforms that the 1931–1933 governments had partly undertaken, and that it would do so by revolutionary means. The government, for its part, suspected with some justification that the armed forces were planning subversion and even insurrection against it. Ministers of the army and navy appointed trusted officers to sensitive commands and surrounded themselves with men of republican sympathies. Some of these were the very few naval officers who would lead the Republican navy in the civil war. One of them, Commander (*capitán de fragata*) Fernando Navarro Capdevila, was appointed to chair the Navy Minister's advisory committee. Other rare naval officers of progressive sympathies were Lieutenant Commander (*capitán de corbeta*) Federico Monreal, his brother Luis and Lieutenant (*teniente de navío*) Pedro Prado.

At this stage, there was little evidence of conspiracy or revolution on the part of the seamen and the petty officers, but the sailors' committees undoubtedly existed and their purpose was to observe the officers and to nip a possible officers' uprising in the bud.

Concrete evidence of a conspiracy among the officers is also lacking. However, what might be described as the social and corporate arrogance of the *Cuerpo General*, that is the non-specialist and non-technical officers who commanded the ships, is admitted even by Franco's own naval commander in chief, Admiral Cervera, who stated during the civil war that the hatred between the different navy ranks was due to 'so many social events, dances, music, cocktail parties and so forth' ('*tantas reuniones de sociedad, baile, música, copeo etc.*)'.[23] Franco himself, in a speech delivered to officers at a fleet review on 31 May 1938, said

> The watchword for officers is to ensure that they are liked and respected, because if this had always been the case, if there had been affection, we should have had more of a navy. (*La consigna para los jefes es hacerse querer y respetar, porque si esto hubiera pasado siempre, si hubiera habido cariño, habríamos tenido más marina.*)[24]

Later, in private conversation with his cousin and confidant, General Franco said that the *Cuerpo General* had always opposed raising the professional status of the skilled petty officers and that

> They (referring to the *Cuerpo General*) considered themselves superior and looked down on everyone else. (*Aquel se consideraba superior y miraba a los demás por encima del hombro.*)[25]

Franco had originally wanted to be a naval officer, but admission to the naval academy was closed at the time. This perhaps conditioned his view. The *Cuerpo General* came from a limited social milieu and the naval officers' very upper class upbringing contrasts with the pattern among army officers. The typical army officer came from a lower middle class origin and was not infrequently the son of a non-commissioned officer or had been promoted from the ranks. Sometimes the fathers and grandfathers of army officers had defended liberal regimes in the nineteenth century. In the navy, the friction between the *Cuerpo General* and the officers of the technical arms, as well as the seamen and petty officers, who were grateful to the Republic which had tried to give them greater status and were thus highly sensitive to the slightest hint of disloyalty to the regime, might lead to an explosion at a critical moment.

Was there in fact a conspiracy against the Republic among the *Cuerpo General*, the few hundred officers who actually commanded the ships of the Spanish navy? Most of them must have been uncomfortable in the political and social atmosphere of Spain in 1936. The entire ambience of the Republic was that of a wind of change in structures, in hierarchies, and in the scales of values in religion and family. These changes threatened social disruption and were directed by a new set of politicians whose intellectual and questioning criteria clashed with the mindset of the naval officers, who viewed the Republic as hostile and disdainful. Spanish naval officers considered the Republic, and in particular its present Popular Front regime, as temporary, while they saw their loyalty as owed to an entity which they called 'Spain', characterised not by the Republic, but by the monarchy which had been overwhelmed by popular vote in 1931 but which the naval officers thought had been betrayed.

This hostility, disdain or at the least indifference, had already been evident in the insulting expression of monarchist sentiments when the President of the Republic had visited naval bases in 1932, and in opposition to the possibly tactless order of the Navy Minister in the same year that photographs of the king should be removed from the walls and pro-monarchist books from the library, and that left-wing newspapers should be allowed into the naval bases.[26] The officers would have seen this order as an attack on cherished values, just as the preservation of monarchist material would have been seen by the Republican minister as disloyalty. Army and navy officers feared the destruction of their values and some would be ready to take part in a coup, as was traditional behaviour at least among army officers. Pro-Franco writers have tended to give little credence to a plot by naval officers to rise against the Republic but use the word 'conspiracy' to describe the actions of the pro-Republican onboard committees.[27] The contradiction is that, if the navy officers were so convinced that mutiny was being planned, they ought to have been more prepared to face it than they seem to have been.

X Planning the Uprising

During the annual *Fallas* festivals, held in Valencia in March 1936, army plotters spoke to navy officers who were on shore leave during cruises and exercises, asking them to remain neutral and not try to block troop transports crossing the Strait of Gibraltar from Morocco to the Peninsula.[28] Captain (*Capitán de Navío*) Francisco Moreno Fernández, in command of the two cruisers, the *Canarias* and the *Baleares*, under construction at El Ferrol, and his brother, Commander (*Capitán de fragata*) Salvador Moreno Fernández, a later Minister of the Navy in Franco's governments, took part in these talks. How interested the naval officers were in army plots to overthrow the government is uncertain. These two officers were most worried about the security of the base at El Ferrol if the revolution which was widely feared came about or, perhaps, if it were provoked by a military insurrection.

In April 1936, Brigadier-General Emilio Mola, based in the northern city of Pamplona, took the post of 'Director' of the planned army uprising, and drew up his first set of instructions for the planned military coup. In its third paragraph Mola wrote that it would be necessary 'to seek the support of the navy and even its collaboration where necessary'.[29] This would apply to the naval bases and to the shipping of troops over the Strait of Gibraltar. At the same time, instructions were sent out to the bases to deal with any sort of mutiny. Such an event was feared for the First of May holiday when demonstrations were expected in the cities where the bases were located, El Ferrol, Cartagena and Cádiz. The instructions show that there was undoubtedly a genuine fear of left-wing insurrection, but they also demonstrated that the naval authorities were preparing to guarantee the success of a military insurrection. The illicit sailors' committee of the cruiser *República*, in dock at Cádiz, immediately informed the government of the measures being taken there.

During naval exercises in the spring of 1936 in waters around the Canary Islands, General Franco, who was in local military command, offered a reception to the naval officers. His words were unequivocal:

The Motherland is in difficulties, and when this happens, its armed forces, the army and the navy, are obliged to save her, from both exterior and interior enemies: and within the army and the navy it is the officers who are responsible for carrying out this sacred mission.

(La Patria está en peligro, y cuando esto sucede, el brazo armado de la patria, el Ejército y la Marina, quedan obligados a salvarla, tanto de los enemigos exteriores como de los interiores; y dentro del Ejército y de la Marina son los jefes y los oficiales los encargados de que esta misión sagrada se cumpla.)[30]

The reference to 'internal enemies' was highly significant, because it quoted the basic Army Law of 29 November 1878, whose Article 2 proclaimed that

The first and most important mission of the Army is to maintain the independence of Spain and to defend it from external and internal enemies.

(La primera y más importante misión del Ejército es sostener la independencia de la Patria, y defenderla de enemigos exteriores e interiores.)

The justification for the uprising of 18 July 1936 against the Republic without the government's having declared a state of war as was required by the constitution, was precisely this article. That Franco should use it in speaking to the naval officers was clearly intentional.

The petty officers and the civil authorities of Santa Cruz de Tenerife, where the reception was held, sent reports to Madrid on what had been said. Franco's words had been received with applause and excitement. One local right-wing newspaper had gone as far as describing the reaction of the officers of the *Jaime I* as 'an apotheosis of cries of approval'.[31]

Before their cruise to the Canaries, some ships had visited the Spanish enclaves on the Moroccan coast, Ceuta and Melilla, where the commanders discussed how to help the army coup with senior officers of the Legion, the thirty-four thousand professional, mostly Spanish, troops of the Army of Africa, who would have to be shipped across the Strait.[32]

Yet these events prove only that the navy officers knew that the army was planning an uprising, not that the navy itself was intending one. Nevertheless, the navy officers must have been aware of the role planned for the navy to take firm control of the bases of Cartagena, Cádiz and El Ferrol, not to put obstacles in the way of the transport of troops across the Strait of Gibraltar, and to shell the harbours of northern Spain if the uprising failed there. The 'Director' of the uprising, General Mola, circulated the following, in his *Instrucción* of 25 May 1936:

> Seek the support of the navy where this is necessary, and even its collaboration.

More specifically, Mola considered that

> The collaboration of the navy in Galicia (north west Spain), which should oppose the landing of forces hostile to the 'Movement' [as the uprising had begun to be called] is indispensable.[33]

On 20 June 1936, encouraged by the apparent support of the naval officers, Mola circulated his Instructions for Naval Forces (*Instrucciones para fuerzas de la Marina de Guerra*). In brief, these were to put the bases under firm control, to patrol the northern coast, especially Asturias, where ships were to shell the mining basin, and to ensure that naval forces off the Moroccan coast were ready to support the transfer of troops by sea.

But who among the naval officers intended to collaborate in an uprising against the Republic and at what level of cooperation with the army plotters? The naval officers who have written on the subject, Captain Cerezo and Admirals Fernando and Salvador Moreno de Reyna, tend to minimise or deny even the awareness of the plot among most of their colleagues in 1936 and prefer to underline the threat of mutiny among the lower ranks. Yet there was undeniably a conspiratorial network in the naval command, and personal contact at lower rank level was maintained between them and the military plotters. Not to hinder troops commanded by insurrectionary army officers would be an act of clear support for an uprising against the government. Taking measures to prevent or crush a mutiny in the naval bases would at the same time support a military uprising.

How far the conspiracy had taken root among the ships' officers in general is hard to verify. In the case of the battleship *Jaime I*, on 14 July 1936 the Navy Minister, José Giral, who was in receipt of regular messages from the crews about the activity of the officers, dismissed the captain and his second-in-command for at least potential disloyalty. In other cases, ships' commanders assured themselves of the determination of their officer subordinates to defy the government and support the army coup.

It is fair to say that the naval officers were, in their majority, aware and supportive of the planned uprising, even if they were not in possession of many of the details. The insurrection was intended to be violent and more or less immediately successful, not to lead to a war which lasted nearly three years. The navy officers needed only to assure the army that their ships would not obstruct the movement of troops from Morocco to the Peninsula, and would ensure the support of the naval bases for the coup.

Much of the information about the actions of the ships' commanders comes from the *Informe Colomina*, the report drawn up in 1940 to investigate what had happened on the ships in July 1936. The report includes testimony which throws a light on what the situation actually was in the Spanish navy. At midnight on Sunday 19 July 1936, Lieutenant Commander (*Capitán de Corbeta*) Rivera addressed the crew of his ship to calm them about his intentions. A senior petty officer asked a midshipman 'Do you doubt us?' presumably referring to what the commander had said about the loyalty of the crew. The midshipman replied 'You must have given us some reason to so do'. The petty officer retorted that the army uprising, already almost two days' old, had no other reason than to bring Fascism to Spain, to which the midshipman replied: 'You know that isn't true; it's just to fight against Communism, which we shall have if the uprising fails.' The petty officer answered: 'We don't want Communism or Fascism, and we shall give our blood to defend the Republic from one and the other.'[34]

This is an extraordinary and moving text which expresses the emotions of both sides. The crews did not yearn for communism, certainly not the Stalinist kind, but not even the revolutionary anarchism more characteristic of the Spanish working-class movement. On the other hand the officers were not really Fascists. This conversation of two men on a minor ship of the Spanish navy reflects the tragedy of the conflict which was about to lay Spain waste.

Chapter 2

The Die is Cast

I Giral Takes Precautions. The Spanish Fleet Mutinies

On Monday 13 July, 1936, following the night when left-wing members of the armed police (*guardia de asalto*) assassinated the right-wing leader José Calvo Sotelo in revenge for the killing of left-wing army officers who had been instructing socialist militia, the atmosphere was sufficiently tense for the Navy Minister, José Giral, to remove certain officers from their commands. These included the chief of staff at the base at El Ferrol, the commander of the destroyer *Ferrándiz*,

The Largo Caballero government 4 September 1936–17 May, 1937. Third from left is Juan Negrín, Minister of Finance, Prime Minister from 17 May 1937 and Minister of National Defence from 5 April 1938 until the end of the war. Left of Negrín is José Giral, Navy Minister in 1936 and Prime Minister from 19 July 1936 to 4 September 1936. Third from right is Indalecio Prieto, Minister of Navy and Air Force, 19 July 1936 until 17 May 1937, then Minister of National Defence until 5 April 1938. (*Source of image: Narodove Archivium Cyfrowe in Wikimedia, author unknown/World History Archive 'no restrictions apply'*)

the chief of staff of the first destroyer flotilla, two submarine commanders and the artillery commander in the Cartagena naval base.[1] The minister had received information which assured him of the unreliability of these men. The next day, Giral sent the following message to the admirals in command of the bases:

> In view of the seriousness of the situation, you will take every possible precaution to avoid extremists of one or other kind propagandising among naval personnel. You will act with all possible energy against any agents you discover and inform me. Kindly advise me of the reliability of all personnel under your orders.[2]

When Giral dictated the words 'one or other kind' (*una u otra naturaleza*), he presumably meant either an uprising from the left, that is the crews, or from the right, which could mean only the officers. However, whether or

General Franco in 1930. Source: Biblioteca Virtual de Defensa. (*The Creative Commons CC0 1.0 Universal Public Domain Dedication (CC0)*).

not the commanders at El Ferrol feared a mutiny, they replied that they had complete confidence in the men and that there was no reason to doubt their reliability. In the other major base, Cartagena, the commanders were less sure. The Vice-Admiral, Francisco Márquez, and the commander of the destroyer flotillas, Rear-Admiral Navía, replied that they taken precautions as the Minister had ordered. Similar replies came from the smaller bases of Port Mahon (Minorca) and Cádiz.

On Wednesday 15 July 1936, Giral issued orders which were to lead to the first signs of insurrection among the naval commanders. Messages to ships at anchor at Cartagena ordered the destroyers *Churruca*, *Lepanto*, and *Ferrándiz* to make at once for Cádiz, Almería and Barcelona respectively. If there were to be unrest in the military garrisons of those ports or among the working class, the presence of warships would help maintain order provided that the government could be sure that the ships' commanders would not make common cause with insurrectionary army officers. Fear of this had led to the recent dismissal of Captain Galán of the *Ferrándiz*.

Galán's dismissal had had consequences. His second in command and all the other officers had refused to take over command of the ship. When finally Vice-Admiral Márquez in Cartagena received a direct order, command of the destroyer was assumed, in the face of the hostility of the ship's officers, by the commander of the first destroyer flotilla, and the *Ferrándiz* sailed for Barcelona as ordered.

Meanwhile, the *Churruca* was sailing for Cádiz, receiving as it went a message from Madrid : 'I hope that you will obey orders unhesitatingly and with loyalty and zeal.' (*Espero de su lealtad y celo cumplirá órdenes sin vacilar*.)[3] The tone of this message suggested some doubt about whether in fact the ship's commander would obey orders. The suspicion was justified, for the *Churruca* called at Algeciras, on the other side of the bay from Gibraltar. Here the officers discussed matters with the garrison in this port which would be a vital landing place for troops arriving from Morocco.

II Balboa Controls the Radio Waves

Warrant officer and radio telegraphist Benjamín Balboa was on duty on Friday 17 July at the navy's communications centre in Ciudad Lineal, a newly developed suburb to the east of Madrid. His task was to maintain

Benjamín Balboa sitting at his transmitter in the naval communications centre warning the crews that the officers of the Spanish Navy were planning to support the military insurrection.

wireless contact with the naval bases and ships. In the navy since his teens, Balboa was now thirty-five years old and an ardent supporter of the progressive ideas for which the Republic stood.

Balboa would ensure that most of the crews of the Spanish navy remained loyal to the Republic. He received news of the military uprising from radio stations in Morocco. Many of the ships were at sea, with orders to watch the Moroccan coast and the Strait of Gibraltar and to prevent attempts to move troops from Africa to Spain. He himself had sent the orders and knew that the government was aware of the potential disloyalty of the naval officers. He was concerned that the crews might not realise what their officers were planning.[4]

The following morning, Saturday 18 July 1936, before Franco left the Canaries to fly to Tetuán, capital of Spanish Morocco, to take command of the Army of Africa, he sent a message to the Spanish enclave of Melilla, situated on the Moroccan coast, congratulating the garrison for rising against the Republic. Later the message was received in Madrid. At once Balboa informed the members of the new emergency structure which had been put together at the Navy Ministry in order to take control of the critical situation which seemed to be developing. He spoke to Lieutenant Pedro Prado, ADC to the Minister, José Giral. To do so, he used a telephone which was not automatically connected to the one which the commander of the communications centre, Lieutenant Commander Ibáñez, had in his quarters, which were on the same site. Ibáñez was a supporter of the planned insurrection. Balboa ought, according to regulations, to have told his superior of Franco's message, which in normal circumstances should have gone up the levels of command to the chief of naval staff, Vice Admiral Salas. Balboa had, however, told the Minister's ADC directly. Ibáñez reproved Balboa, but when the former tried to retransmit the message to all the garrisons as he had been requested by Franco, Balboa arrested him at gunpoint.

Now, two or three sleepless nights awaited Balboa, as, buoyed up by coffee and cigarettes, he maintained constant contact with the radio operators on the ships at sea, a small corps of men, many of whom he knew personally given his twenty years of service. If the officers decided to join the uprising they would keep tight control over communications, so Balboa's first message ordered the radio operators to transmit their ships' positions every two hours in an uncoded message. If a ship did not transmit or did so in code Balboa would know that the officers had been able to overcome the crew and had thus risen in rebellion.

III Mutiny Aboard the Destroyers

That morning, Saturday 18 July 1936, with army garrisons rising all over Spain, orders were flashed from the Navy Ministry to the northern naval base of El Ferrol – where Franco had been born and which was renamed El Ferrol del Caudillo after his victory in the civil war – that the two available cruisers, the *Miguel de Cervantes* and the *Libertad* (the *Almirante Cervera* was under repair), should raise steam at once and sail south to Algeciras, one of the ports where troops from Morocco could be landed. The destroyer *Ferrándiz*, which had been ordered to Barcelona, was recalled to the southern naval base of Cartagena. The battleship *Jaime I*, coaling in the north western port of Vigo, was ordered down to the Strait of Gibraltar. The gunboat *Dato*, in harbour at Ceuta, opposite Gibraltar, was ordered to patrol the Strait. Commander Azcárate, from a well-known and traditionally republican family, was ordered to take over the Cádiz base. He had headed the communications centre at the base and had probably informed Balboa of the disloyalty of the command there. It was too late. The insurgent naval officers arrested Azcárate and his immediate subordinate, subjected them to drumhead court-martial, and executed them. Many such officers, loyal to the Republic in the army and air force as well as the navy, suffered the same fate.

The destroyer *Almirante Antequera* was by now on its way to Málaga, another port where troops might be disembarked. At anchor in Cartagena were the destroyers *José Luis Díez*, *Alcalá Galiano*, and *Almirante Miranda*. Five submarines were ordered to watch the coast between Cape Gata and Gibraltar and to stop any vessel carrying troops from Morocco, while the destroyers *Almirante Valdés*, *Sánchez Barcáiztegui* and *Lepanto* were ordered to shell military installations at Ceuta.[5]

This was the moment when the ships' commanders were faced with a crucial decision. If they obeyed the orders from Madrid they would prevent troops being brought from Morocco to the Peninsula and effectively cause the coup to fail. If they disobeyed their orders they would be aiding if not joining the military insurrection. Two of the ships' commanders, Taviel on the *Almirante Valdés* and Bastarreche on the *Sánchez Barcáiztegui*, decided to make for Melilla, at the eastern end of Spanish Morocco which had been taken over by its insurrectionary garrison. Dropping anchor, they discussed the situation with the army officers. In contrast, the *Lepanto*, under Captain Valentín Fuentes, who was loyal, refused to drop anchor in Melilla.

In an attempt to persuade the crews to follow their example, the insurrectionary commanders harangued the sailors. However, Balboa's messages had got through. The crews refused to obey and sailed the destroyers out of Melilla harbour, though the commander of the *Almirante Valdés* tried unsuccessfully to run his ship aground. The mutinous crews then arrested the commanders and sailed for Cartagena. The destroyer *Churruca*, meanwhile, had been ordered to sail for Ceuta and join the gunboat *Dato* as it watched for any military transport which might try to leave the port and cross the Strait. It was clear by now that the insurrectionary military were in control of Ceuta, so the *Churruca* and the *Dato* were ordered to shell the town, an order which the commanders refused to obey without apparent reaction from the crew. Then commanders next took the step of entering the port, embarking troops and sailing for the Peninsula.

That same evening, Commander Fernando Navarro, head of the Navy Minister's *Secretaría Técnica*, or advisory committee, had assumed command of the destroyer *Ferrándiz*, after having been sent urgently by air from Madrid to quell a feared uprising by the officers of the destroyers. Landing at the naval air base of San Javier, near Cartagena, he had been arrested by rebel officers.[6] In Cartagena, the military governor, General Martínez Cabrera, as well as admirals Márquez and Molíns, refused to declare a state of war, that is to come out in rebellion, and insisted that the officers at San Javier release Navarro. The mutiny of the crew of the destroyer *Sánchez Barcáiztegui*, and the decidedly pro-government stance of the air force commander, Major Ortiz, of the nearby Los Alcázares base, were other reasons why the Republic retained control of the Cartagena naval base.

On land, throughout the weekend of the 18 and 19, and Monday 20 July 1936, the military, dominant from the outset in Morocco, took over in large parts of the north and west of Spain, the Canary Islands and Majorca, and several cities and ports in southern Spain, among them Seville, Granada, Córdoba, Cádiz and Algeciras. In contrast, army attempts at uprising failed disastrously in the three largest cities of Madrid, Barcelona, and Valencia, together with large areas of eastern Spain and the Mediterranean coastline.

From the naval communications centre in Madrid, Benjamín Balboa kept in permanent contact with the radio operators of the fleet. Though the officers must have maintained some control, they were not able or perhaps did not realise the importance of overseeing the messages that the radio operators were receiving regularly from Madrid. The reports over previous weeks from ships' commanders that discipline was being maintained indicate that inciting mutiny through the radio would not have been easy. On receiving messages from Balboa, the operator would have to refer, not as regulations required, to an officer, but to a petty or warrant officer whose views he knew. Balboa's messages, warning that the officers were not to be trusted, had to be received and repeated. How would the crews, now at sea, know for sure that there had been insurrections among the army officers? Perhaps the ships were receiving orders to cooperate with the army to suppress left-wing uprisings such as had been feared. Should all the crews imitate the mutineers of the *Almirante Valdés* and the *Sánchez Barcáiztegui*? What authority did Balboa have? The radio-telegraphists would mull over these and other questions as the cruisers sailed south from El Ferrol down the coast of Portugal to the Strait of Gibraltar, and as the *Churruca*, the *Laya* and the submarines cruised the Strait, while the radio operators on the battleship *España* and the cruiser *Almirante Cervera* in the harbour of El Ferrol and those of the gunboats *Lauria* and *Cánovas*, whose commanders had decided to rebel against the Republic, were ordered to block all messages from Balboa.

IV In the Strait of Gibraltar

The first result of Balboa's warnings was mutiny on the destroyer *Churruca*. This ship had taken on troops at Ceuta and sailed to Cádiz where they had disembarked in the early morning of Sunday 19 July, assuring that city, base and port for the Insurgents. At sea once more, the radio operator received this message from Balboa:

> The whole of Spain is watching our glorious fleet [...] you are the only ship which has struck a discordant note (*Toda España está pendiente de nuestra gloriosa Marina* [...] *Sólo ese buque ha dado la nota discordante.*)

His message had a result. At 0815 hours the crew of the *Churruca* arrested their officers.

Lieutenant Commander Manuel Súnico, who commanded the gunboat *Dato*, the other ship which had landed troops in the Peninsula, this time at Algeciras, was more aware than many of the other ships' commanding officers of the danger of the crew realising what they were doing, because he had discussed matters at some length at Ceuta with Lieutenant Colonel Yagüe of the Legion. The other gunboat, the *Laya*, patrolling the Strait at its narrowest point between Ceuta and Gibraltar, was taken over by its mutinous crew in the evening of Sunday 19 July 1936.

V In Cartagena

In Cartagena, the second main naval base, on 18 July, Lieutenant Commander Cano, of the destroyer *Alsedo*, was ordered to take his ship along the coast to Almería and keep watch over the entrance to the port, lest the Insurgents should try to land troops there. Army officers from the garrison came out to discuss matters with Cano, who was later ordered to sail to Málaga. There he and his officers were summoned to the destroyer *Sánchez Barcáiztegui* to appear in front of its new captain, Federico Monreal, who had just arrived from the ministry in Madrid, and were arrested. The *Alsedo*'s sister ship, the *Lazaga*, was in Cartagena being fitted with new boiler tubes. Its officers had given hospitality to Captain Galán, who had been one of the first destroyer captains to be dismissed from command. The *Lazaga* sent messages to Murcia and Valencia, along the Mediterranean coast, claiming untruthfully and without success, that the state of war had been declared in Cartagena. In the base itself, the top military and naval commanders hesitated as they waited to hear from the headquarters of the Third Army Region at Valencia. Were the regiments stationed in Spain's third city going to rise against the government of the Republic? They were not.

By the evening of 18 July, the mutinies on board the *Almirante Valdés*, the *Sánchez Barcáiztegui* and the *Lepanto* had come to the knowledge of naval headquarters. The Insurgent officers at the San Javier naval air base surrendered early on 19 July, while the dockyard at Cartagena was surrounded by armed civilians and armed police. The *Almirante Valdés* with its mutinous crew sailed into harbour at 1700 hours to loud cheers. Cartagena had been saved for the Republic. At mid-morning of Monday 20 July, Admiral Molíns ordered the commander and officers to disembark from the *Lazaga*. The previous night the crew of the destroyer *José Luis Díez*, warned by radio from Madrid of what the officers were planning, had mutinied and arrested their Captain. A similar reaction took place on the destroyer *Alcalá Galiano* though with some delay because its commander had managed to keep news from the crew by shutting down the radio receiver, but the crew did in fact challenge him about his intentions. He replied

I want you to know […] that this commander obeys no orders other than those of the Republic (*Quiero que sepan ustedes […] que este mando no obedece más órdenes que las de la República.*)[7]

Perhaps he had blocked communications because he thought, wrongly, that the Madrid radio station had been taken over by Insurgents, but if this was so, his defence was sadly of no use when he was court-martialled and shot.

To sum up the situation in the two bases in southern Spain, Cádiz and Cartagena, in the former the Insurgents had been successful when during the night of 18–19 July the *Churruca* had brought a unit of Moorish *regulares* from Ceuta, but some smaller ships had mutinied and taken the side of the government, leaving the coastguard cutter *Uad Kert*, the gunboat *Dato* and a torpedo boat in the service of the Insurgents, who also kept the cruiser *República*, though this ship was in the process of major repairs. The Insurgents could count also on two gunboats, the *Canalejas* and the *Lauria*, whose mutinous crews had been crushed by marine infantry and surrendered on Tuesday 22 July, and two other gunboats, the *Alcázar* and the *Larache*, which did not mutiny. None of these ships, however, possessed the firepower to oppose the destroyers which had declared for the Republic. On land, Admirals Gámez and Ruiz, together with the colonel of marines and the military governor of the province, had acted in agreement and decisively to quell any attempt by the sailors of the base and the civilian population to oppose the uprising.

In Cartagena the uprising had failed because of the indecision of Admirals Molíns and Márquez, and the loyalty to the Republic of the military commander, General Martínez Cabrera, which would cost him his life at the end of the war, and of the commander of the air base. Here, all the destroyers remained under the flag of the Spanish Republic: the *Churruca*, the *Ferrándiz*, the *Lepanto*, the *Almirante Valdés*, the *Sánchez Barcáiztegui*, the *José Luis Díez*, and the *Alcalá Galiano*, as well as the two older destroyers *Lazaga* and *Alsedo*, and six still being built: the *Almirante Miranda*, the *Gravina*, the *Císcar*, the *Jorge Juan*, the *Escaño* and the *Ulloa*. In all, the Republic retained ten destroyers, most of which were modern, and six more at an advanced stage of construction (See Appendix I for a list of warships and their characteristics, as retained by both sides.)

In the Canary Islands, where General Franco had proclaimed the uprising on the morning of 18 July 1936, the coastguard cutter *Arcila*, whose second in command was Gabriel Pita da Veiga, who would many years later become Navy Minister in one of Franco's cabinets, gave hospitality to the Insurgent general's wife and baby daughter while Franco flew to Morocco. The following day, they embarked on a German steamship, the *Waldi*, on its way to Lisbon where they would be safe if the Glorious National Uprising, as it became officially known, failed.[8]

VI Twelve Submarines

While the submarines *C2* and *B5*, in harbour at Cartagena, were now available for service with the Republican navy, the crews of the *C1*, *C3* and *C4*, patrolling the coast, mutinied, evidently distrusting their officers who had ordered the boats to submerge every time a ship came into view, apparently unwilling to challenge and investigate whether it was carrying troops from Morocco. The *C6* returned to Málaga to take on supplies, and the officers were arrested. The crew of the *B6* mutinied on 21 July. Most of the officers sympathised with the ideals behind the insurrection and had agreed to do what they could to sabotage the single torpedo that each boat carried and to throw a vital part of its one gun overboard.[9]

Submarine *B1* was being repaired at Port Mahon and three more of the older B series were cruising in the area. The crews mutinied and sailed for Minorca where the military uprising had failed. Thus the Republic retained all twelve submarines of the Spanish navy, though the B series was outdated and some of the C series were in poor condition and with hardly any loyal officers.

VII Battleships and Cruisers

On Sunday, 19 July, the cruiser *Libertad* was off Cádiz on its urgent voyage from El Ferrol south to the Strait of Gibraltar. The haste of their departure and the rumours circulating about the military uprising, which was taking place that day in the Madrid garrison, created tension and uncertainty in the crew. Despite the precautions of the officers, the radio-telegraphists received messages from Benjamín Balboa, who told them about the mutinies taking place already on some of the destroyers and urged them to take over the *Libertad* before 'untrustworthy personnel do something treacherous.' ('[*A*]*ntes de que el personal dudoso nos haga una traición*').

At 1540 hours the *Libertad* received the order to shell Cádiz, which was now in Insurgent hands. As the officers ordered the small 47 mm guns rather than the large 152.2 artillery to be made ready, and seemed to be delaying giving orders to fire by questioning the visibility and the identification of the targets, the crew mutinied. That evening, however, short of fuel, alarmed by false messages arriving from Cádiz, attacks from a seaplane and the potential threat from coastal batteries, the improvised leadership of the cruiser made for Tangiers, on the Moroccan side of the Strait and under an international regime.

Meanwhile the cruiser *Miguel de Cervantes*, with Admiral de Mier on board, left El Ferrol at 1930 hours on 18 July, cleared the long estuary and set sail for Cartagena. Inexplicably, the officers did not supervise the radio-telegraphists, and Balboa's messages, informing of the mutiny aboard the *Libertad*, spread rapidly among the crew. These were his inspiring or provocative, depending on one's point of view, words as they came through the ether from Madrid and were taken down by the radio-telegraphist:

Comrades: the moment has arrived to combat treason. Do not allow it to take the first step. However senior the officers, they cannot be allowed to argue about orders from the government and refuse to obey them. I am fully convinced of their treason [...] We must take up arms and defend, if we must, liberty, equality and fraternity which those elements which perjure their own honour intend to snatch from us. I know that you will do your duty like men. Long live the revolution. Long live the Republic. Benjamín Balboa.

(*Compañeros, ha llegado el momento de presentar batalla a la traición. Que ésta no dé un paso más adelante. No puede admitirse, por elevadas que sean las jerarquías, que se discutan primero y no se cumplan después las órdenes del Gobierno. Estoy plenamente convencido de su traición [...] empuñemos las armas para defender con ellas si es preciso la libertad, la igualdad y la fraternidad que pretenden arrebatarnos todos los elementos perjuros a su propio honor. Sé que cumpliréis con vuestro deber como hombres. Viva la revolución. Viva la República. Benjamín Balboa*).[10]

The mutiny on the *Miguel de Cervantes* began at 0530 the following morning, when the ship was off Lisbon. Steered by a petty officer, the cruiser made for Tangiers where it anchored on 20 July.

The *Jaime I*, one of the Spanish navy's two battleships, was under a new commander, Captain Joaquín García del Valle, and a new second in command, Commander Bernardo Navarro, who had replaced officers whose loyalty had been suspected by the Navy Minister. At 0200 hours on 20 July the ship set sail. Many of the officers, however, intended to take over the battleship, an event which Balboa warned the crew to forestall. The mutiny began the following day. Two officers were killed in an exchange of fire. Their bodies were consigned to the deep following an order signed by Lieutenant Prado, ADC to the Navy Minister in Madrid: 'Lower the bodies into the sea with sober respect, and note position'. (*'Con sobriedad respetuosa den fondo a los cadáveres, anotando situación.'*)[11] On 21 July, the *Jaime I*, navigated by a petty officer, anchored in Tangiers harbour.

VIII El Ferrol

Now only three large vessels remained in the base at El Ferrol: the battleship *España*, the cruiser *Almirante Cervera*, and the destroyer *Velasco*. Two ultra-modern cruisers, however, the *Canarias* and the *Baleares*, were nearing completion.

In El Ferrol, as at Cartagena and Cádiz, there had been plans to take over the base if the feared left-wing disorders occurred. The recently dismissed chief of staff of the naval base, Admiral Manuel de Vierna, Captain Francisco Moreno and his brother Commander Salvador Moreno, together with most of the officers, were aware that a military uprising was in preparation, with the approval, if not the collaboration, of the military governor. The recently appointed commander of the base, Vice-Admiral Núñez Quijano, who must have sensed that the officers were conspiring, probably preferred not to enquire too closely. Franco's message from the Canaries to the fleet and the army garrisons was received on 18 July. The level of readiness and resolution of the senior officers in El Ferrol was so high that the radio-telegraphists were at once put under guard, to prevent them receiving messages from Madrid. For the moment, Admiral Núñez Quijano did not declare a state of war. On 19 July a radio message from Madrid dismissed him and appointed Rear-Admiral Azarola, deputy commander of the Base and a supporter of Republican legality, who would pay for his loyalty with his life.[12]

On the cruiser *Almirante Cervera*, which was in dry dock in El Ferrol, the crew tried but failed to take the ship to sea. They were forced to surrender when bombed by naval aircraft from the base at Marín, where the officers, among them Lieutenant Commander Pedro Nieto, a future minister in Franco's later governments, had risen against the government. The crew of the battleship *España* mutinied, but was forced to surrender by the threat of bombing from the air.

The success of the uprising in El Ferrol, in contrast to its failure in Cartagena, was due to the determination of the senior officers, the blocking of Balboa's messages to the crews urging them to mutiny, and the absence of the large ships *Libertad* and *Miguel de Cervantes*, while the *España* and the *Almirante Cervera* were not in a condition to go to sea where the crew would have been able to overcome the officers. Furthermore, the local air base, the army commanders and the police forces were favourable to the uprising.

IX Barcelona

The officers of the seaplane base in the capital of Catalonia were determined to rise against the Republic. They assembled, together with the naval officers in the city, on the night of 17 July as soon as they heard news of the army uprising in Morocco, prepared the seaplanes for action and set up machine-guns on the perimeter of the base. When the Insurgent general Manuel Goded, one of the youngest and most respected of the army leaders, arrived from Majorca with a seaplane squadron at 1330 hours on Monday 20, the day set for the large army garrison of Barcelona to rebel, the officers gave him the Roman salute rather than the customary military one.[13]

Reports such as this one, made years after the events, may not be entirely true, but it is evident that there had been preparation for an uprising. However, later that day, when it was evident that the insurrection in Barcelona had failed, Goded surrendered. He would be court-martialled and shot.

X The Cruiser *Mendez Nuñez*

This older cruiser was anchored off the coast of Spanish Guinea in West Africa where it had been sent to deal with local disturbances. On 21 July, the ship was ordered to return speedily to Spain. During the voyage, the crew kept a wary eye on the captain who was receiving messages from the Insurgents to make for the Canary Islands and to arrest the radio-telegraphist and thus block messages from Balboa. The crew, however, ordered the captain to obey messages from Madrid and sail the ship to Málaga or Cartagena. Two of the officers dived overboard, abandoning the ship at Dakar, before the *Méndez Núñez* finally reached Málaga on 21 September, becoming the last vessel of the Spanish fleet to join the Republican navy.

XI When the Smoke Cleared: Insurgents and Republicans

The Republican navy, its battleship, three cruisers and many destroyers clearly dominated the Strait of Gibraltar and the Mediterranean coastline. In addition, the Republican navy had taken control of all twelve submarines in service. Of these, the C series were in good condition, although they lacked essential equipment and their periscopes were unreliable. The B series were antiquated and unable to travel at more than shallow depth.

In contrast, along the Cantabrian coast in the north and based at El Ferrol, the minute Insurgent fleet was in complete control. Apart from small vessels such as coastguard cutters, torpedo boats and gunboats, the Insurgents had available the battleship *España*, the cruiser *Almirante Cervera*, and the destroyer *Velasco*. Under construction were two up-to-date cruisers, the *Baleares* and the *Canarias*. Very soon, this small fleet was to begin its task.

The battleship *España*, though designed before 1912, was armed with eight 305 mm guns, which would allow it at least to act as a powerful mobile artillery platform. Despite the lengthy repair programme that it was undergoing in dock at El Ferrol, the *España* raised anchor on 12 August, less than one month after the uprising. As it left El Ferrol the rudder suffered a malfunction, but not so seriously as to prevent the ship from continuing its course. This was perhaps the first example of the professional determination of its officers, Commander Luis de Vierna and Lieutenant Commander Pedro Nieto, seconded by seven junior officers, and the discipline of its new crew, many of whom had not been to sea before. Improvisation and determination were the key.

Forty-eight hours after the sailors' mutiny had been repressed, the cruiser *Almirante Cervera* left El Ferrol under the orders of Commander Salvador Moreno with only 280 of its 564 crew members, reinforced by untrained volunteers, and only fifteen of its thirty officers.[14] The destroyer *Velasco*, though in better condition than its Republican sisters *Alsedo* and *Lazaga* because its turbines had recently been reconditioned, was out of date, but given the absence of any opposition in the Cantabrian Sea, it could function usefully, especially since its crew had not mutinied and it could sail with a full complement.

The crushing of the mutineers in El Ferrol and the intensive, though inevitably superficial, training of volunteer seamen, was possible only because the Insurgent fleet had abundant officers and facilities for its only three warships of importance. In contrast, the never to be solved problem of the large Republican fleet was precisely the absence of experienced senior officers. Not only were there insufficient officers, but many of them were not trustworthy or were not trusted. The inexcusable massacre of so many of their comrades which took place after the uprising had been crushed affected their esprit de corps with a sense of confusion which was reflected sometimes in their lack of decision and as an unwillingness to take an aggressive stance towards the enemy, who were their erstwhile comrades and fellow-officers. In the Republican navy, born out of a mutiny caused by resentment, the question was whether a different kind of discipline could be developed rather than imposed.

A navy depends on its bases and its control of the nearest shore if it sails close to the coast as was the case in this early part of the Spanish war. The Republican navy's only base was Cartagena, which had the serious disadvantage of not having a dry dock large enough for cruisers. The natural harbour and the inner dock were small, forcing warships to anchor close to each other. Cartagena was particularly exposed to submarine and aerial attack, and the base was repeatedly bombed in the latter part of the war. The destroyers had to sail out to sea every night.[15] On the other hand, Cartagena was defended against shelling from the sea by 380 mm coastal artillery and there were two nearby airfields, Los Alcázares and the seaplane base of San Javier.

Port Mahon, on Minorca, under Republican command, had powerful artillery defences but it lacked anti-submarine protection. The Insurgents had no submarines but Fascist Italy would in time remedy this problem. Since the Insurgents also held Ibiza and the important port of Palma on Majorca, Port Mahon was of little value to the Republican fleet.

The advantage of Málaga as a secondary Republican naval base was that it was much closer to the Strait of Gibraltar than Cartagena, but it lacked adequate anti-aircraft defence, coastal artillery and anti-submarine protection. As for the other ports on the Mediterranean coast, such as Alicante, without protection they were of little value to the Republican navy.

All this was important because on the Cantabrian coast, most of which, from the French frontier as far west as Oviedo, was retained in Republican hands, the Insurgent Francoists had the best naval base, El Ferrol, with all the installations required for servicing and repairing the largest ships. Situated at the end of an estuary, it was proof against attack from the air, surface ships and submarines, and was heavily equipped with coastal artillery. Its disadvantage was its distance from the theatres of naval operations in the Strait of Gibraltar and the Mediterranean. The Nationalist (as they insisted on being called) Insurgents, however, had taken the important ports of Cádiz and Palma very early on, which gave them bases in those zones.

Cádiz, in the extreme south of Spain, had coastal artillery, a floating dock and a dry dock as well as workshops for naval guns. There was coastal artillery at El Hacho near Ceuta on the northern coast of Morocco and at Algeciras, on the other side of Gibraltar Bay, all in Insurgent hands.

Thus, the Republican navy far outnumbered the Insurgents in number of ships, but it had few safe harbours beyond Cartagena. In contrast, in the vital Strait of Gibraltar the Insurgents had Cádiz, Algeciras and ports on the Moroccan coast, and in the next few days Republican ships would find themselves barred from Gibraltar and from Tangiers. Their task, nevertheless, was to safeguard the Strait of Gibraltar, prevent troops coming over it from Morocco, and to attack the Insurgent-held ports on either side of that narrow strip of water. It was an essential strategy that the Republican ships would fail to carry out.

XIII The Repression

In both of the zones into which Spain was now split the repression within the armed forces was savage and immediate. In the government or Republican zone some 350 naval officers were killed, a few in the uprising, others after court martial, but mostly in uncontrolled massacres in prisons. In the area where the insurrection triumphed, 176 men lost their lives, including a handful of officers, but mostly warrant officers, petty officers and seamen who were shot after court-martial.[16]

In the Republican zone, where the authorities largely lost control, the behaviour of the mutinous crews did not usually lead to the death on the ships of insurgent officers, unless there was an exchange of fire. Lieutenant Prado's message to the mutineers of the *Jaime I* to lower the bodies into the sea respectfully was obeyed. Benjamín Balboa, on the other hand, radioed to the crew of the destroyer *Churruca*, who had mutinied after been tricked into taking soldiers to the Peninsula from Morocco, urging that they should 'throw the villains overboard' ('*tirar por la borde a esa plebe*'). His rhetoric was understandable in the circumstances but was not heeded by the crew, who handed the insurgent officers over to the authorities and without exception sent messages to the government assuring it of their loyalty and asking for orders. Most of the insurgent officers were imprisoned on a ship in Málaga harbour. On 23 July, 1936, the Navy Ministry sent a telegram to the new commander of the fleet:

> Ministry of Marine to Fleet Commander:
> Convene urgent courts-martial arising from the revolutionary circumstances covering Spain with blood. A prosecutor and judges have been appointed and will arrive by air.[17]

Matters could not however be resolved so simply, as Lieutenant Prado noted on 27 July, after the officers had been captive for a week. He had flown down to Málaga, where the larger part of the imprisoned officers were confined. The relative guilt of the Insurgent officers would have to be weighed by court-martial. Yet the mutinous sailors were so enraged that there was a risk that they might refuse to accept officers as members of courts-martial and would set up a revolutionary tribunal which would order all the imprisoned officers to be executed. Could the sailors appoint members to the courts martial so that at least the proper procedures would be followed? This was not remotely legal.[18] In those extraordinary circumstances a senior judge of the Navy's judicial corps established a new body called the Legal Evaluation Body of the Fleet (*Asesoría Jurídica de la Flota*). A decree of 2 August legalised appointments, enabling any sailor, petty or warrant officer to be raised to the temporary rank which corresponded to the function he was to perform. Thus the law was changed to conform to the new situation.

One of the men appointed was José Balboa, brother of the radio-telegraphist Benjamín Balboa, who was given the temporary rank of *capitán de navío*, equal to that of Captain in the Royal Navy or an army colonel. A parliamentary deputy and leading advocate was also appointed, together with a naval clerk who was given officer's rank. The problem was that José Balboa was the brother of the man who had most responsibility for exciting the crews to mutiny, and the civilian lawyer belonged to the fundamentally revolutionary Syndicalist Party. Would the structure of the courts-martial which would judge the officers stand up to legal scrutiny? Yet the alternative was mass murder without even the simulacrum of legal process.

The courts martial convened on 17 August 1936, sentencing several officers to death, a penalty carried out on 21 August. More trials followed. In all, thirty-five officers were sentenced to death by these courts-martial. However, the majority of the officers who lost their lives were murdered by mobs of sailors.

The murders began on 3 August when troops from the garrison at Port Mahon, capital of Minorca, broke into the prison and killed 23 naval officers. On the same day, on the cruiser *Libertad*, probably after the imprisoned officers became violent, their captors killed several of them, and, not lowering the bodies into the sea with respect, as they had been ordered to do on the *Jaime I*, threw them overboard.

Rumours had spread that in ports where the insurrection had been successful the victors had killed the families of sailors.[19] This may explain, though it does not justify, the state of mind of many sailors who were on guard in the prison ships and other places where the officers were incarcerated. On the cruiser *Miguel de Cervantes*, anchored in Málaga, sailors insisted on carrying out death sentences immediately they had been passed by court-martial. Fourteen captives were murdered on the destroyer *Almirante Valdés*. But worse was to come. A large number of naval officers were imprisoned on two ships harboured in Málaga, which had sailed out to sea on 14 August precisely because the prisoners were thought to be safer away from the harbour where mobs from the anarchist city might assault the ships on which the officers were confined. The arrival of the *Jaime I* on the afternoon of that day, having been bombed by German aircraft in Franco's service, was the signal for the mass murder of 198 men, about half of whom were naval officers.[20]

Apart from the 35 sentences imposed by courts-martial, these appalling massacres on the ships, at Port Mahon, in Cartagena, Madrid and other cities, and in fighting at the bases and elsewhere, led to the deaths of 355 men, over three-quarters of them from the *Cuerpo General* of the Spanish navy.[21]

XII Crews

Given the mutiny in the base of El Ferrol, followed by the executions, imprisonment or dismissal of so many sailors and petty officers, there was obvious difficulty in crewing even the mere three warships left to the Insurgents, but the imminent entry into service of the two new cruisers, the *Canarias* and the *Baleares*, and the fleet of merchant ships and armed fishing vessels that the Insurgents would bring swiftly into service, would need large numbers of men. Training had to be cut short and volunteers recruited, some of whom were members of the Fascist *Falange*. As for officers, the forty-nine cadets who had been on their training voyage in the sailing ship *Galatea* reached El Ferrol on 28 August 1936 and were allotted to the *España*, the *Almirante Cervera* and the *Velasco*.

The difficulty for the Republican ships was evident from the outset. They lacked senior, efficient and reliable officers. For months after the mutinies, the official journal, the *Diario Oficial del Ministerio de Marina*, listed the names of naval officers who had either been killed in the struggles aboard the ships, murdered while under arrest or were known to be serving with the Insurgents. A few men retained their commands but even so, one submarine captain went over to the other side and two sank their boats. Besides the submariners other men were rescued from prison by the offer of commands, but their level of loyalty to the Republic was always in doubt. Furthermore the self-justifications of some of these officers before the courts-martial to which they were subjected after the war make it even more difficult to judge them. The official list published by the Republican government in 1938, with the ranks to which the officers had now been promoted, shows that, at this date, the Republican navy had a total of only fifty-seven officers of the *Cuerpo General* in its service. They were, according to rank:

Two rear-admirals
Two captains (*capitán de navío*, equivalent to Captain RN)
Six commanders (*capitán de fragata*)
Twenty lieutenant commanders (*capitán de corbeta*)
Twenty-five lieutenants (*teniente de navío*)
Two sub-lieutenants (*alférez de fragata*)[22]

Besides these men, the total of officers from the artillery and engineers branches of the service was only 29 of the 89 that there had been in these corps before the uprising and the mutiny. Again, some had been killed and others were in the Insurgent zone.

Of very senior officers, one rear-admiral was compulsorily retired and another was about to reach retirement age, while others remained in bureaucratic positions. Thus the warships of the Republic would be commanded by junior officers, warrant officers and in one case a cadet. There was a complete absence of experienced staff officers.

Chapter 3

Tangiers and Gibraltar.
Franco Crosses the Strait

I Tangiers

Spanish Republican warships, among them the battleship *Jaime I* and the cruisers *Libertad* and *Miguel de Cervantes*, steamed into Tangiers on Sunday 19 July, 1936. The Insurgents held the ports of Algeciras, Cádiz and Ceuta, so Tangiers and Gibraltar were the only harbours in the Strait open to the ships loyal to the Republic. The tactical advantages of being able to refuel at either port would be great, because Tangiers and Gibraltar were on either side of the Strait which troops coming from Morocco would have to cross, whereas Cartagena, now the only naval base of the Republic, was 266 miles away.

The next day, Monday 20 July 1936, the Navy Ministry sent a message from Madrid to the ships, which were badly in need of fuel, food and fresh water, confirming that the Statute which governed Tangiers allowed Spanish ships to take on whatever they needed from that city.[1]

The previous day, when the telegraphist of the *Libertad* had radioed Madrid that the crew had taken over the ship, he had transmitted 'The oil is coming to an end…there are 170 tons left and food for two days.' The *Miguel de Cervantes* dropped anchor in the harbour of Tangiers and also radioed 'Committee *Cervantes* to Navy Ministry. We need to take on fuel. Respectful greetings. *Viva la República!*'

José Giral, now Prime Minister of the Republic as well as Minister of the Navy, at once ordered submarine *B2* to sail from Port Mahon to Valencia and escort a tanker from there to Tangiers.[2] Once at sea the *B2* crew mutinied and sailed the submarine back to Minorca, where only one of its officers survived the massacre of prisoners.[3]

The acting commander of the fleet, Lieutenant Commander Federico Monreal, arrived urgently in Tangiers and ordered food and fuel to be strictly rationed. No washing was to be allowed. The summer heat and the close quarters in which crew lived aboard ship meant that bodies and clothes would give a bad impression to any visitor and particularly to British naval officers.

Tangiers was under international control according to the Treaty of Paris of 1924, which Spain had ratified. Any form of military activity was prohibited within the international zone, which was governed by a Control Commission composed of the consuls-general of Spain, France, Italy, Belgium, Holland, Britain and Portugal.

On Monday 20 July, following the battleship and the two cruisers, three destroyers and some other minor warships of the Spanish Republican fleet entered Tangiers harbour, crowded with French, Portuguese, Italian and British warships which, fearful of the threat of a mutinous fleet to their interests, had also appeared.

For the first time, British naval authorities saw the situation for themselves. The crew of the destroyer HMS *Whitehall* witnessed tumultuous cheering from the Spanish crews as each ship arrived. A search through binoculars revealed a uniformed officer only on the hydrographic survey ship *Tofiño*, still under the orders of Commander Federico Aznar. The captain of the *Whitehall* sent an officer to the *Tofiño*. After a conversation with Aznar, the commander of the *Whitehall* reported that the Republican fleet was under the direction of a Soviet led by a warrant officer.[4] Did Aznar realise the consequences of what he was telling the British officer? Perhaps, overcome emotionally by the extraordinary circumstances and apprehensive of his own crew, he confided in the British officer without realising that the latter's visit was not one of mere protocol but intended to discover what was actually happening, and that whatever he said would be reported to the Admiralty and to the Foreign Office. Aznar's words suggested to London that a mutiny was under way.

General Franco, from his headquarters forty miles away in Tetuán, capital of the Spanish zone of Morocco, reacted immediately and fiercely to what he insisted was the illegal presence of Republican warships in Tangiers harbour.[5] He argued that the crews were mutineers who planned to shell Gibraltar, as well as Cádiz, Algeciras, and Ceuta and Melilla on the Moroccan coast. He omitted to say that the garrisons in those ports were in rebellion against the recognised government of Spain. His mention of Gibraltar was gratuitous. There was no reason to think that the Republican fleet would shell the Rock.

The control commission at Tangiers was concerned that Franco might try to attack the Republican warships, perhaps from the air, with damage to the town and its inhabitants. It feared also that mutinous and undisciplined sailors might disembark and create havoc in the streets of Tangiers, where many of the population were Spanish. The consuls telegraphed their respective countries asking them to exert pressure on the Madrid government to withdraw its ships.

As it happened, the Shell company refused to sell fuel to what it considered mutineers and so, later that night, the Republican warships raised anchor and crossed the Strait to try to obtain fuel in Gibraltar. At 2100 hours on 21 July six ships dropped anchor in the bay of Gibraltar.[6] Others followed. By Wednesday 22 July the rest of the Republican ships which had sailed from El Ferrol were at anchor in the outer commercial harbour of the Rock.

II Gibraltar

The British government now had to take decisions about events in Spanish and Gibraltarian waters. The Rock symbolised the power of the Empire. Soldiers, sailors and colonial administrators saw it on their way to Malta, Suez and the East. Nevertheless, Gibraltar was vulnerable from Spain and Morocco. It had no landing strip yet and thus no air defence. If passage through the Strait were hindered, the strategic value of the Rock to Britain would become questionable.

Information on what was happening in the area was unclear in London. The policy of Non-Intervention in the war in Spain, which would later become a fundamental British stance, was yet to be formulated. For both Republicans and Insurgents control of the Strait was essential because of the presence in Morocco of professional, well-equipped and well-led Spanish and native troops. But control depended on at least a neutral attitude on the part of local authorities on both sides of the Strait. The Republican fleet had been denied facilities in Tangiers. In Gibraltar, the military and naval authorities, as well as the commercial community, would be, to say the least, unhelpful.

Splinters from anti-aircraft fire from one of the Republican ships shooting at hostile aircraft caused alarm in Gibraltar, as did bombs from Franco's aircraft which fell near British ships. The Governor asked the

British Consul General in Tangiers to protest to Franco. Would the general keep his aircraft away from Gibraltar? What is more, bombs had been dropped on a British merchant ship, the *Gibel-Dris*. Franco, concerned that Gibraltar might fire at his few and slow aircraft, sent his apologies.[7]

Julio López Oliván, the Spanish ambassador in London, had enquired whether the Republican warships might buy fuel in Gibraltar. He received a reply from the Foreign Office Under-Secretary, Lord Cranbourne. The British government considered the matter purely commercial, which, while probably untrue, was the best answer at the time. If Britain were to follow the rules of neutrality and supply just enough fuel to enable the ships to reach Málaga, the nearest port still in Republican hands, the Foreign Office feared that this might imply recognising the status of the Republic as a belligerent in international law. This would give it the right to stop, search and remove the cargoes of neutral ships. Furthermore it might be felt politically necessary to give the same privilege to Franco. From the beginning of the war Britain decided to deny this right to both sides even though the Republican government was the internationally recognised authority in Spain. But was it really in charge? Information reaching London seemed to indicate that the Spanish navy was in a state of mutiny. Thus it was essential to investigate exactly what had happened on the ships. Before the latter had anchored in Gibraltar, Franco had sent a message to the military governor on the Rock.

[...] ships of the Spanish navy have left Tangiers and are making for Gibraltar to take on fuel. The position of the crews is of open communism. The officers have been imprisoned if not killed or wounded [...] it is not in the interests of Spain that oil should be supplied or that they should be allowed to take on fuel in British waters. I request Your Excellency to communicate the situation to His Majesty's government, so that an end can be put as soon as possible to the anarchic state which the presence of these ships causes in the Mediterranean.

(...*Barcos de la Marina española se dirigen de Tánger a esa plaza intentando petrolear. El estado de sus dotaciones es de franco comunismo, los jefes y los oficiales fueron apresados cuando no muertos y heridos* [...] *no conviniendo a los intereses de España le facilite petróleo ni se les permita petrolear en aguas inglesas a esos buques, ruego V.E llegar Gobierno S.M. británica estas circunstancias, con el fin de que cuanto antes termine el estado anárquico que la presencia de estos buques fomenta en el Mediterráneo.)*[8]

A British naval officer was rowed to the battleship *Jaime I.* Asking to see the captain, he was kept waiting. Finally, he reported, 'an individual appeared, dressed as a Commander [...] who had forgotten to put on his socks.'[9] This was *Capitán de fragata* Fernando Navarro who indeed had the same rank as a Royal Navy commander. The informality of his appearance may have arisen from the lack of water to wash bodies and clothes, and to Navarro's odyssey, for he had flown hastily from Madrid to San Javier naval air base, where he was put under arrest, then freed, sailed to Tangiers and thence to Gibraltar all in the space of four days. He could scarcely be expected to display Royal Navy standards of personal presentation.

The British government had left the matter of selling fuel to the Republican warships to the decision of the companies. The day after the vessels anchored in the bay, senior warrant officer José Antonio Paz disembarked. He was a member of the Union of Republican Officers (UMRA) and of the Spanish Communist Party.[10] As such, he was in an influential position on board the battleship *Jaime I.* The *Gibraltar Chronicle* had reported that officers were imprisoned on the ships, although the British officials in Gibraltar would not necessarily have known this for sure. Nevertheless, signals had been intercepted from the ships to Madrid which suggested that Spanish officers had been thrown overboard. So when Paz, accompanied by the Spanish vice-consul in Gibraltar, went the rounds of the fuel companies, trying to buy coal and oil, he encountered hesitation, unwillingness and refusal. The Oil Fuel Depot Ltd. was willing, but insisted that it had first to consult its principals in London, the Asiatic Petroleum Company.[11] The fact that the Governor of Gibraltar knew this and reported the information to London indicates that selling fuel to the Republican ships was seen as a political issue. The Asiatic Fuel Company prevaricated, saying that it had to consult the government. The fuel suppliers did not want to do anything contrary to the wish of the Gibraltar authorities, who knew that, without fuel, the Republican warships would not be able to obey their orders and bombard Insurgent ports such as Ceuta, Algeciras and Melilla, where British citizens lived and owned property.[12]

Finally, as the ships waited to see if fuel would be supplied, a Spanish tanker, the *Ophir*, arrived with sufficient fuel to reach Málaga.

In brief, the Gibraltar naval authorities did not know or were not told about the reason for the mutiny, which was the disloyalty of the naval officers to the Spanish government. The Governor of Gibraltar informed London that he did not believe that the Republican ships anchored in the bay were obeying the Madrid government, and claimed that they were 'communist' and thus revolutionary. But, while they were certainly revolutionary, they were hardly communist, and indeed loyal to the government and the Republic.

In any case, the local firms, represented by Lionel Imossi, a leading member of the Gibraltar Chamber of Commerce, told the Spanish vice-consul that no fuel would be sold unless the officers were released.[13] The official British position, following recommendations telegraphed to London from Gibraltar, was to discourage the sale of fuel. Consequently, the Republican warships raised anchor and left Gibraltar for Málaga.[14]

The events at Tangiers and Gibraltar at the beginning of the Spanish Civil War reflect a constant British stance throughout the conflict. The legal situation was clear. As a Foreign Office official noted, the government of the Republic was internationally recognised and had the right and even the obligation to crush an armed rebellion.[15] Yet the general fear of revolution and the belief that one had been planned in Spain inclined people in authority in Gibraltar and in London to believe that the feared revolution had already begun with the mutiny aboard the Spanish fleet, and that it was as grave as those of the *Potemkin* and at Kiel, even though the mass murders of the Spanish naval officers had not yet occurred.

Yet at the same time, it was Franco who seemed to be using most force in the Strait. Despite protests and threats of reprisals from the Gibraltarian authorities, Insurgent aircraft represented a real danger. The Republican ships, anchored in the northern part of the bay off Puente Mayorga as they waited for fuel, were bombed by Franco's aircraft. Fearful of damage to British lives and property, the Gibraltarian authorities insisted on the immediate departure of the Republican warships.

III Franco Crosses the Strait

The ships of the Republican navy were well-placed to block the Strait of Gibraltar and prevent Franco from transferring his Moorish and European professional troops across to the Peninsula. The Insurgents held the large Andalusian cities of Seville, Córdoba and Granada and the important ports in the Strait, although most of the eastern and southern part of Spain was still in the hands of the Republican government. If Franco could not move his troops from Morocco the military uprising would fail. So far only very small ships had taken a few hundred men from Morocco to Cádiz, Algeciras and the small harbour of Tarifa. Franco's air staff had used three Fokker F-VIII bombers and a seaplane which had fallen into his hands, but these could transport only tiny numbers of men.

To protect ships carrying men across the Strait, the Insurgents had some twenty-six aircraft of widely varying types and capabilities at their disposal, among them Bréguet bombers and Nieuport fighters. However, it remained to be seen if these aircraft could mount a successful attack on the Republican fleet. In the meantime they maintained a constant and harassing presence, sufficient to alarm the inexperienced and officerless crews who had received little if any training in how to deal with attacks from the air. On 26 July, as the *Jaime I* and the *Libertad* shelled the Spanish enclave of Melilla, at the eastern end of the Spanish protectorate of Morocco, they radioed in a panic, using somewhat non-regulatory language and the familiar form of address

> 'These blokes are roasting us: if you don't come to our aid soon we shall surrender [...]the entire fleet must come at once. Three Bréguets are bombing me. (*Estos tíos nos asan: si no acudís pronto en nuestro auxilio nos entregamos [...] urge salir toda la Escuadra en mi auxilio.Tres Bréguets me bombardean.*)[16]

The Bréguet bombers, based on a French model of 1922 manufactured in Spain, carried an observer with a machine-gun. However, in order to attack a ship, the pilot would have to put the aircraft on its side for the observer to tilt the gun at an angle sufficient to aim. Hitting a moving ship with bombs was difficult, but the skill of the professional airmen and the lack of training of the ships' crews meant that the battleship *Jaime I* and the cruiser *Libertad* were forced to zigzag.[17] A lone aircraft flying out of Ceuta bombed the Republican submarine *C3* three miles off Europa Point. As Gibraltarians watched, the aircraft flew very low while the submarine fired its gun and then tried to dive. Finally it submerged, but poor maintenance forced it to emerge to recharge its batteries and wait for a tow to Málaga.[18]

There was a general view in the Royal Navy that aircraft could not score hits on moving ships.[19] Nevertheless, on 5 August, the day that several transports carried Franco's troops across the Strait, his aircraft would seriously damage some Republican ships. Low morale, shortage of fuel, a lack of skill and of officers would render the ships incapable of imposing an effective blockade. They would be put to flight by the aircraft of the Insurgents, commanded by General Kindelán, Franco's air force chief, and the few officers in Morocco who had organised the servicing and repair of the heterogeneous seaplanes, bombers and fighters that Franco had assembled.[20]

Yet it was still doubtful if these aircraft would be enough to protect a large convoy of troopships as they crossed the Strait to Spain. The risk seemed unjustified to most of the senior officers who counselled Franco. But the situation changed from 28 July when foreign aircraft reached Spanish Morocco.

A Junkers 52 belonging to the German airline Lufthansa had been sequestered by the Spanish military on Grand Canary and flown to Morocco.[21] On Thursday and Friday 23 and 24 July it was flown to Berlin carrying two envoys from the tiny expatriate German colony in Tetuán. On 25 July the envoys met Hitler, who promised to send some twenty-five Junkers 52s and fighter escorts. Germany was interested in the strategic position of the area of conflict, which was close to important French and British sea routes. Spain was a valuable source of raw materials, among them iron, copper, and tungsten. While there was little likelihood of a Popular Front Spain joining France in a war against Germany, Hitler's aims in Spain were to weaken France by placing a right wing military dictatorship in Madrid.

On 28 July the first Junkers 52 arrived from Germany. Within a few days another nine Junkers 52s had flown from Germany to Tetuán and more would follow, accompanied by fighters and the necessary ground services.[22] The Junkers would carry out the first substantial airlift in history, each flight transporting 35 troops between Tetuán and the air base of Tablada near Seville.

Although the Germans did not play a role in the convoy of 5 August, on 30 July nine Italian Savoia-Marchetti S-81bombers (twelve had been sent but three crashed) also reached Tetuán.[23] These aircraft, with their five machine guns, and bombs of fifty or one hundred kgs, were the most modern in the world and the most recent in the service of the Italian air force. They had been ordered to put themselves at Franco's service without restriction.

Very soon after the insurrection and even before German aircraft had reached Franco, on 23 July, 1936, Admiral Raeder, C-in-C of the German navy, ordered Vice-Admiral Rolf Carls to sail for Spanish waters with the pocket-battleships *Deutschland* and *Admiral Scheer*. Later the *Admiral Graf Spee* left harbour, followed by the light cruisers *Leipzig* and *Köln* and the destroyers *Möve*, *Seeadler*, *Albatros* and *Leopard*, and later *Falke*, *Greif*, *Jaguar* and *Kondor*. This was a substantial fleet, more than enough to protect the fifteen thousand German nationals whom it evacuated from Spain, which was its ostensible purpose.[24] On 3 August Admiral Carls paid a formal visit to Ceuta and then to Tetuán where he had a long talk with Franco. The Insurgent general thanked Carls for German support. Spanish views on both sides were that the presence of the *Deutschland* anchored off Ceuta impeded the Republican ships from bombarding the port and city, using naval signals intelligence techniques which put considerable effort into reading Spanish Republican naval communications.[25] *The Times*'s correspondent reported on 29 July that on the 25 the *Libertad* and the *Jaime I* had shelled Ceuta for fifty-five minutes but had not caused significant damage.[26] Was this because of the German ships or because, with no clear line of command, and led by junior officers, the Republican warships had not learned to direct their fire accurately?

On 5 August, 1936, the day of the crossing of the Strait by Franco's small but significant convoy, there were other concerns occupying the attention of the Navy Ministry in Madrid. Three destroyers, the *Sánchez Barcáiztegui*, the *Churruca* and the *Ferrándiz* were in dock under repair and most of the rest of the fleet was at a distance from the Strait. This was a grave error, allowing Franco to send the convoy at a time when the Republican fleet was dispersed. It illustrates the absence on the part of the Republican authorities of full information and their lack of decision. In addition, Franco was convinced that aircraft could harass moving ships because the crews of the Republican warships were inexpert, their firing

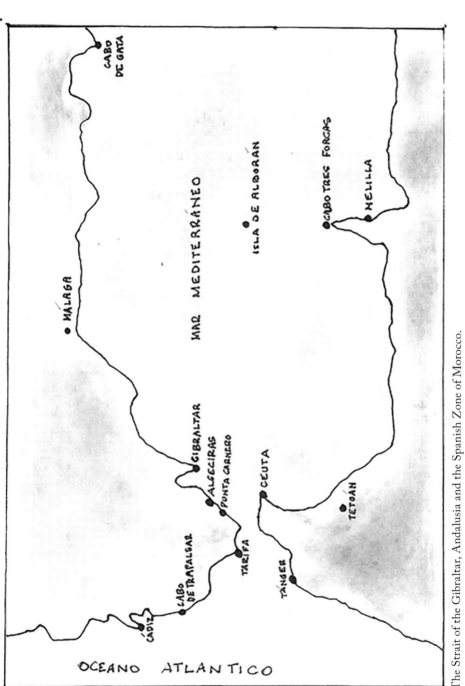

The Strait of the Gibraltar, Andalusia and the Spanish Zone of Morocco.

was inaccurate, they had little, if any, training in anti-aircraft defence and they would panic under attack.

Moreover, by 5 August the nine SM-81 Italian bombers were ready for service, once the special lead tetraethyl high octane fuel which they required had arrived from Italy.

The convoy which was to cross from Morocco to Spain consisted of three passenger steamers, escorted by the gunboat *Dato*, a torpedo boat and a customs cutter. Three thousand men were to embark, together with a large quantity of armament. The task of the twenty-six aircraft which Franco could put into the air was to maintain constant patrols at varying heights and to bottle up the submarine *C4*, the survey ship *Tofiño* and two destroyers which were still at Tangiers,[27] and the battleship *Jaime I*, which was in Málaga together with the cruisers *Libertad* and *Miguel de Cervantes*.

On the morning of 5 August, heavy winds were blowing and thick fog covered the Strait. Very early, two Italian Savoias reconnoitred Tangiers. At seven that morning the Bréguet bombers and a Dornier seaplane bombed the destroyer *Lepanto*, scoring a hit on the port side which killed one sailor and wounded five. The *Lepanto* made for Gibraltar, where it was allowed to disembark the wounded men but not to bury the dead sailor, for fear of political demonstrations from the Gibraltarian population and the refugees from the savage military repression that had been carried out by insurgent troops over the land frontier at La Línea. Instead of consigning the corpse to the sea, the *Lepanto* made for Málaga, escorted by the *Churruca*. Harassed by aircraft, the two destroyers fired back until they exhausted their ammunition. Another destroyer, the *Almirante Valdés*, was also hit by a 100 kg bomb and seriously damaged. In the absence of Republican aircraft, the destroyers were unable to defend themselves, perhaps through lack of discipline, but more probably through lack of training in how to combat attack from the air.

Whatever the theories about the difficulties of bombing moving ships, on 5 August not only the *Lepanto* and the *Valdés* were hit but also two cargo ships, the British *Medon* and the Dutch *Zoundwijk*, while five bombs fell near the Italian cable layer *Città di Milano*, all between 0830 and 1930 hours.

Seeing the capabilities of his aircraft in hampering the Republican warships in the Strait, Franco decided to dispatch the convoy of troops, but his caution made him wait until what he judged the best moment when the Republican ships were most widely dispersed. Finally, at 1630 hours, four transports, the *Ciudad de Algeciras*, the *Ciudad de Ceuta*, the *Arango* and the *Bonet*, sailed in line astern, led by the coastguard cutter *Uad Kert* and the gunboat *Dato*. The tug *Benot* had to return because of the rough seas. These transports carried two and a half battalions, a 105 mm battery, four mortars, signals material, vehicles, 1200 grenades and two million rifle cartridges.[28]

At about 1700 hours the Republican destroyer *Alcalá Galiano*, under the command of sub-lieutenant Diego Marón, appeared from the west, where it had not been seen by Franco's aircraft, in order to replace the damaged *Lepanto* and the other destroyers which were protecting it on its way to Málaga. Summoned at high speed, it covered the fifty kilometres which separated it from Franco's troop-carriers in an hour. However, the *Alcalá Galiano* arrived too late, when the convoy was already approaching Algeciras. The destroyer fired at the *Ciudad de Algeciras* at a range of 10,000 metres but failed to score a hit. The principle of concentration of force came into play when the 101.6 mm guns of the *Dato*, the 4.7s of the torpedo boat and the 76 mm single weapon of the *Uad Kert* all fired at the destroyer. Firing from the west, two shells from the *Alcalá Galiano* fell in Gibraltar, interrupting a peaceful evening game of cricket, as *The Times* reported next day. By this time, all Franco's aircraft were attacking the destroyer, which suffered eighteen dead and twenty-eight men severely wounded. Once it had exhausted its anti-aircraft ammunition, the destroyer was unable to defend itself.[29] Consequently reports from the Republican destroyers spoke of hours of continuous bombing by several aircraft at once. Evidently, the crews and their junior commanders did not have the training or indeed sufficient reserves of ammunition to withstand the assault by concentrated numbers of aircraft.

Yet, despite the apparent impotence of the Republican fleet, complete freedom for Franco's forces to cross the Strait could not be assured until the Insurgent cruisers *Almirante Cervera* and the new *Canarias* sailed south from El Ferrol. Nevertheless, the crossing of the '*Convoy de la Victoria*' as Insurgent propaganda would call it, was more than purely anecdotal. An aggressive and well-organised assembly of aircraft, closely cooperating with the Francoist naval and army leaders – an interarm cooperation which was glaringly absent on the Republican side – showed that the

Republican attempt at blockade was a paper tiger. The question is why the Republican command did not reinforce the *Alcalá Galiano* with the rest of the fleet. While it is true that the *Lepanto* and the *Almirante Valdés* had been hit by bombs, the absence of at least one of the cruisers and the destroyers *Ferrándiz*, *Gravina* and *Sánchez Barcáiztegui* is not easily explained. Could Intelligence have been so defective that the Republican naval command did not know that the convoy was going to leave Ceuta? Since early morning twenty-six aircraft had been flying over the area, which should have indicated that something was going to happen. The answer may be that the successful hits on the *Lepanto* and the *Valdés*, which did not manage to manoeuvre to escape the bombing, and the presence of the Italian bombers, had a depressing effect on the Republican naval command. The latter was bereft of clear leadership from Madrid, determined not to lose more ships and fearful of the effect that efficient bombing was having on the morale of crews. The crews, for their part, had little confidence in their commanders, and probably felt unable to fight desperately to control the Strait without enjoying protective cover from Republican aircraft.

The Republican reaction to the successful convoy came on 7 August when, from 0600 hours, Republican aircraft bombed the port of Algeciras. At 0800 hours the battleship *Jaime I*, the cruiser *Libertad* and two destroyers opened fire five miles off Punta Carnero, just south of the port. Valiantly, the battleship ventured to within two thousand metres of the city, risking fire from the coastal batteries. The battleship's aim was poor, however, and the shells fell beyond the city, although the *Jaime I* set the gunboat *Dato* on fire and destroyed the coastal cutter *Uad Kert*. At the same time, the shelling of Cádiz by the cruiser *Miguel de Cervantes* showed that, properly led (and probably because the gunnery officers were on board and free) the ships of the Republican navy represented a serious problem for Franco. So, when the German Junkers 52 transport aircraft reported that they had been fired on by Republican ships as they carried troops across the Strait, the Germans attacked the Republican fleet. On 13 August, two Junkers 52 bombed the *Jaime I*, which was anchored just outside Málaga. This was the first aggressive action by the German aircraft in the Spanish war.[30] That same day, Mr Monck-Mason, British consul at Tetuán, very supportive of the Insurgents and disdainful of what he called the 'mob', reported to London that there were more than twenty large Junkers bombers on the local airfield. His spy had told him that 550 men had already been flown from Morocco to Spain.[31]

IV Foreign Navies Arrive in Spanish Waters

Ships of the Royal Navy had been arriving in Gibraltar on their way back from Alexandria and Malta where they had been stationed during the Abyssinian crisis. Now that this had subsided, the Navy was returning to the United Kingdom for long-delayed leave and training.[32] As the crisis in Spain erupted however, on 19 July 1936 the destroyers *Whitehall* and *White Swan* were ordered to remain at Gibraltar. Among the tasks of the Royal Navy would be the evacuation of British civilians. By 21 July six destroyers and three cruisers were on station. The Admiralty sent ships to El Ferrol, Corunna and Vigo, though the British consuls in those ports and cities, where the insurrection had triumphed, reported that British citizens were in no danger. The destroyer *Shamrock*, however, evacuated many British subjects from Málaga where the breakdown of authority meant that the safety of middle-class people, clergy, and the wealthy and professional classes could not be assured.[33] Other British ships, arriving hastily from Malta, were sent to Barcelona, Valencia, Alicante, and Almería, on the Mediterranean coast, as well as Bilbao, San Sebastián and Gijón in the north. By the end of the first week of the war five Royal Navy cruisers and fourteen destroyers were evacuating British and other refugees and sometimes Spaniards whose lives were in danger from the revolutionary *incontrolables* who were looting and murdering civilians.[34] Evacuations represented a major effort by the Royal Navy. Its figure for civilians evacuated by the end of October 1936 was 11,195, of whom only 35 per cent were British nationals. British cruisers of the County class which had large deck spaces, and repair ships with large working spaces were used as depots in the chief ports, while destroyers sailed up and down the coasts picking up small parties. Evacuees were taken to Marseilles. In one case the cruiser *Devonshire* sailed from Barcelona to Marseilles with over five hundred civilians, while the battle-cruiser *Repulse* evacuated five hundred, mostly British, refugees from Palma, the only time that a sizeable number of people were taken off Francoist territory, in this case because of the fear of air raids and a possible landing of Republican forces from the mainland.[35] On the larger ships, every possible sheltered space, including the captain's cabin, was used. Even dogs were accommodated in the hangar which had recently been fitted to the *Repulse*. Great attempts were made to attend to the comfort of the refugees. In addition, sick people could use the facilities of the Mediterranean Fleet's hospital ship, the *Maine*, which anchored at Valencia after sailing from Malta. This ship took on refugees arriving from Madrid and called at Barcelona on its way to Marseilles. She made three trips and carried 1,109 people to safety.[36] Many nations, Holland or the Scandinavian countries for example, were not in a position to send warships to evacuate their nationals and relied on the Royal Navy. Argentina, however, sent its cruiser *25 de Mayo*, which had arrived in Alicante harbour by 26 August, 1936, and took over a hundred refugees to Genoa the following day. Up till 15 December 1936 it made four more trips, one to Lisbon and three to Marseilles, with 451 people aboard, 110 of whom were Spaniards. A second Argentinian ship, the destroyer *Tucumán*, reached Alicante on 5 November 1936 and stayed there until 7 June, 1937, carrying a total of 1,486, mostly Spanish, refugees out of danger. One person rescued was Ramón Serrano Súñer, Franco's brother-in-law, who would go on to hold the highest offices in the General's cabinets.[37]

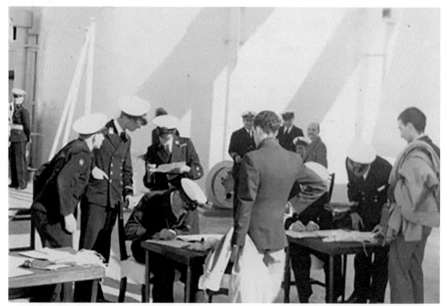

Spanish refugees from the Republican Zone being registered aboard HMS *Hood*. (*Evans Collection, courtesy of Nick Evans*)

V Blockading Merchant Ships

A basic principle of sea warfare is to harass the enemy's merchant traffic, blockade his ports and hinder the arrival of armaments and the foodstuffs and raw materials to enable him to carry on fighting. However, if the merchant ships are registered with neutral countries questions of international law arise. These would be of primary importance in the Spanish war.

Almost all Spain's imports and exports travelled by sea. In 1935 18,500 ships entered Spanish harbours and 17,481 left.[38] Spain's food and manufacturing production was insufficient to fight a war, which meant that traffic by sea would be extremely important. For Franco's Insurgents it was vital to hinder the merchant traffic arriving at northern ports such as Bilbao, Santander and Gijón, and at Mediterranean harbours such as Barcelona, Valencia and Alicante. In the first month of the war, in the Strait of Gibraltar, the Republican navy had not only to prevent the crossing of men and war material from Morocco, but also to make sure that merchant ships did not bring goods and especially war material into the ports that the Insurgents controlled: Cádiz, Seville and Algeciras on the Spanish side of the Strait, and Ceuta and Melilla on the Moroccan side.

At that early stage in the Spanish war, the power of the Insurgents in southern Spain was in the air rather than at sea. The long history of Francoist bombings of merchant ships began as early as 22 July 1936 when Insurgent aircraft dropped bombs near the British P&O liner *Chitral* as well as the destroyer *Shamrock*, which was carrying British refugees from Málaga to Gibraltar. The bombing evoked a protest from the British rear-admiral in local command, who called it 'irresponsible and intentional'.[39] The first adjective was accurate; the second less so, because Franco's pilots had little training in recognising ships from the air. The Spanish Insurgent general had to offer excuses through his air chief General Kindelán. This was the occasion when Kindelán, well received by the British authorities on the Rock, was allowed to use the central telephone exchange to communicate with Lisbon, Berlin and Rome.[40]

On 22 July and following days, the Spanish government declared the Moroccan Protectorate, the southern and Atlantic coasts of Spain and all ports in the hands of the Insurgents to be war zones. This was not a warning of blockade for the moment but advice that merchant shipping entered them at their own risk.

The Admiralty radioed British warships in the area at once:

> Any definite hostile attacks by aircraft on a British ship whether by bomb or other weapon are to be resisted by force without previous warning should this take place outside Spanish territorial waters. Similar acts by Insurgent men of war outside Spanish territorial waters should be resisted if persisted in after remonstrance [. ...] Spanish territorial waters are to be taken as extending three miles from shore. British ships are to be warned to keep outside Spanish territorial waters and British men of war are to avoid as far as possible being berthed or anchoring near Spanish men of war.[41]

Any attack on the high seas, that is outside the three mile limit, would be resisted. In other words, the Admiralty was advising British merchant shipping not to enter Spanish Republican or Insurgent ports, but if Spanish warships of either side were to attack a British merchant ship a British warship should resist, but only 'after remonstrance' in the case of an Insurgent warship.

The first clash came on 3 August when the Republican destroyer *Almirante Valdés* shelled the German merchant ship *Sevilla*, which was unloading at Larache, on the Atlantic coast of Morocco, and forced it out to sea where it anchored in the international port of Tangiers. On the night of 5–6 August, the German *Usaramo*, this time escorted by the pocket-battleship *Deutschland*, arrived unhindered at Cádiz, loaded with war material, including Junkers bombers and Heinkel fighters as well as the men of the German expeditionary force which Hitler had agreed to send to Franco.

The Spanish government's formal declaration of blockade came on 13 August 1936 in the official Navy Ministry journal, the *Diario Oficial del Ministerio de Marina*. The blockade covered waters around the Canaries, Spanish Sahara, Morocco and the Atlantic, the coasts around the Balearic Islands and the north-western province of Galicia.

From the beginning Britain refused to recognise the blockade. Looked at from today's perspective, this appears to reflect British prejudice against the Republic, and there is little doubt that the naval authorities would find it even humilitaing to accept that a warship crewed by what the Royal Navy considered murderous mutineers should be allowed to stop and search a ship flying the Red Ensign on the high seas without the Royal Navy being able to intervene. On the other hand there was evidence that information about the movements of the Republican ships were communicated to the Insurgents.[42] The facilities given in Gibraltar to the Insurgent General Kindelán compared with the obstructive attitude towards the Republican ships anchored in the Bay on 21 July confirm that the Gibraltarian authorities took a favourable view of the Insurgents, whom they supplied with foodstuffs and tobacco.[43] Another reason for Britain not to recognise the Republican government's blockade of Insurgent-held ports was that it was not effective because the Republic did not have the ships to make it so. Nevertheless, the Admiralty's instructions were equivocal. The Royal Navy had to protect commercial traffic but not to encourage merchant ships who wanted to force the blockade, if there was a real risk of intervention by a Republican warship. On 16 August the British *Marklyn* was stopped and inspected by the Republican submarine *C2* as it neared Melilla. British destroyers escorted it into the port.The British protest was very mild compared with the reaction when the German *Kamerun* was stopped off Cádiz by the Republican cruiser *Libertad* on 18 August.[44] The *Kamerun* was carrying petrol and lubricants with documents stating that the ship was destined for Genoa, but it seemed obvious that the *Kamerun* was taking the material for the German aircraft by now in Seville. The captain of the *Libertad* obliged the German merchant to continue his course without anchoring at Cádiz. The German torpedo boat *Leopard* took over the escort and the *Kamerun* sailed from the Strait into the Mediterranean followed closely by the Republican submarine *C3*. As yet, Spain still enjoyed diplomatic relations with Germany. The Spanish government did not want to force a crisis, so the fleet was ordered to maintain a vigilant watch but to avoid using force unless merchant ships entered Spanish territorial waters whose shores were under the control of the Insurgents. Even so, Republican ships were ordered not to fire on merchant ships. Germany protested through her chargé d'affaires who was still in post in Madrid, insisting that it did not accept the Spanish blockade. He claimed that the *Kamerun* had been stopped outside the area of blockade, and added that the captains of the battleship *Admiral*

Scheer and the cruiser *Köln* had been ordered to respond energetically to the use of force.[45] Nevertheless, German merchant ships were told not to try to unload cargoes in ports held by the Spanish insurgents.[46] Despite bellicose statements from the Nazi propaganda minister, Josef Goebbels, German warships had not been ordered to fire on Spanish Republican warships which were enforcing the blockade. For the moment, consequently, German ships carrying war material would avoid Spanish territorial waters and unload their cargoes in Lisbon, where, fortunately for Franco, Antonio d'Oliveira Salazar, leader of the sympathetic right wing *Estado Novo*, in the words of a German diplomatic official in Lisbon, 'removed all difficulties within a very short time' and sent the cargoes to Spain by rail. On 20 August, the *Kamerun*, protected by the *Köln*, entered harbour at Lisbon, together with another merchant ship, the *Wigbert*.[47] Italian merchant ships, for their part, were protected by warships of the same nationality as they carried aircraft, fuel, arms and munitions from La Spezia to Melilla.

German and Italian ships might justifiably be suspected of carrying war materials for the German and Italian aircraft which were by that time in Spain aiding the Insurgents. However, Republican warships twice stopped the British *Gibel-Zerjón*, which was a packet steamer of the Bland line making the regular crossing from Gibraltar to Melilla. There is some evidence to suggest that Bland's provided some help to the Insurgents, certainly at least in continuing the supply of coal.[48] The *Gibel-Zerjón* was stopped by the cruiser *Miguel de Cervantes* on Sunday 23 August. The Governor of Gibraltar and his officials left church hurriedly to dispatch the battle-cruiser *Repulse* to support the destroyers *Codrington* and *Wolsey*, whose firepower was less that that of the Spanish cruiser. With the aid of the battalion of Gordon Highlanders which the *Repulse* was taking home from Egypt, the cruiser collected most of its crew from the bars of Gibraltar, sailed at full steam, intervened and secured the release of the steamer. The captain of the *Miguel de Cervantes* was told that the British government did not recognise Spanish territorial waters as extending for more than three miles out.[49] The *Gibel Zerjón* was again detained on 14 September and this time released by the destroyer *Arrow*.

Given the presence in the Strait of so many Republican ships of the same class, especially the destroyers which were easily confused with British ships of the same class, accidents were likely to occur. On 17

August an Insurgent aircraft attempted to bomb the British destroyer HMS *Blanche*, confusing it with the Republican *José Luis Díez*, which had been reported in the same area shortly before. It would not be the first time that Spanish observers would mistake neutral ships for Spanish ones.

V In Other Seas

While the Republican fleet was trying to prevent Franco bringing his troops over the Strait of Gibraltar, the Madrid government's seeming lack of strategic direction allowed it to ignore the northern coast. Were the Spanish government's channels of information so feeble that it was unaware of German shipments to El Ferrol and Vigo? Or perhaps, in order to preserve some possibility of international support, did the Republic hesitate to exercise its sovereign rights to stop merchant shipping which it thought was bringing arms to its enemies? The fact is that almost nothing was done along the Cantabrian coast until September 1936, several weeks after the insurrection.

In the Mediterranean, in mid-August 1936, the Republican destroyers *Almirante Antequera* and *Almirante Miranda*, accompanied by smaller vessels, were detached to escort an expedition of nine thousand ill-organised and undisciplined militia from Valencia, led by air force captain Alfredo Bayo, to try to reconquer Majorca for the Republic. While fire from the destroyers protected the landings, no substantial advance was made from the beachhead, thus allowing the small garrison to react. Not till 2 September did the battleship *Jaime I* and the cruiser *Libertad* appear, but by then Italian aircraft had decided the result of the operation. Thus Palma, which should have been bombarded and bombed from the air from the beginning, was lost to the Republic, and the city and the island of Majorca became an important naval and air base for the Insurgents.[50]

Chapter 4

Reorganisation

I First Stage: Finding Men to Command Ships

Given the loss, deaths and arrests of so many senior naval officers, the Spanish Republican government, headed by the Navy Minister, José Giral, immediately appointed new commanders of the fleet. On 21 July 1936, Lieutenant Commander Federico Monreal, having held the post for one day, handed over command to Commander Fernando Navarro, who had arrived urgently from Madrid. Both these officers had been on the staff of the Navy Ministry, precisely because their loyalty to the Republic was undoubted.

Instructions were sent immediately from Madrid and communicated to the crews. The situation was improvised; many officers were not trusted by the men, so these *Instrucciones generales* were important. How would the government adjust to the unprecedented situation where the ships were manned by mutinous crews who had nevertheless declared themselves loyal to the government and the Republic? The language of the first orders reflected the revolutionary situation, with words and phrases such as 'delegate' and 'antifascist comrades'. *'Viva la República'* would be a permitted greeting, and all ranks were to have the same rations. On 21 July, from the cruiser *Libertad* which was to be the flagship, Monreal transmitted an order to the ships at anchor in Tangiers, announcing that Commander Navarro had arrived to take over command. The fleet would be run, appropriately for the revolutionary situation in which it found itself, by a committee on each vessel, provided that it enjoyed the confidence of the crew. The committee would appoint a guard to be responsible for security and good order on board. Only the committee and the guard would have weapons. In the last part of his order, Monreal said that he hoped he did not need to say that the crews would preserve discipline, respect for superiors, good behaviour and absolute obedience to orders, obeying 'blindly' (*'ciegamente'*) Commander Navarro, 'who represents the Government of the Republic and of Spain itself as it fights in defence of the Constitution'.[1]

Thus the sailors' committees were recognised as having authority, although the final part of the order makes it clear that the hierarchy of command was to be respected and indeed suggested that this would be a responsibility of the committee.

The moment was delicate. Although Lieutenant Commander Monreal stated that he was sure he did not need to underline the need for discipline, in fact he had to do so. Considering the disappearance of most of the officers this was only to be expected. In the absence of a chain of command, it would have been unwise to try to abolish the sailors' committees.

As Navarro took over command of the fleet of over twenty warships on 21 July, he must have been most unsure of how to proceed. The committees, which were to have the full confidence of the crews and presumably to be elected by them, were recognised as part of the command structure of the new Republican navy, though for the moment their role was limited to maintaining discipline in a situation in which the normal chain of command had disappeared.

Officers such as Navarro came from families with profound Republican sentiments and were in high positions in the Navy Ministry, but they must have had little idea of how to deal with the present situation. Navarro, now fifty-two years old, needed the advice of the much more junior Lieutenant Pedro Prado, the newly appointed Chief of Operations, whom he considered politically important, especially concerning how to deal with the sailors' committees. So, on the same day, Navarro radioed the ministry in Madrid, 'I consider the presence of Lieutenant Prado on this ship [the *Libertad*] essential so that he may attend as necessary to the new way in which this cruiser and the fleet are to be run.'[2]

Prado, however, had another essential task: to create an Operations headquarters in the new naval base at Málaga. On 20 July, when the government had dissolved the Naval Staff, it had left only the Operations Section, under Lieutenant Prado. Five other officers had been appointed to the section, but all had refused the posts.[3] Lieutenant Antonio Ruiz had been appointed to command the Cartagena naval base and a senior warrant officer, Nicanor Menéndez, would head the base at Port Mahon.

Commanders for the ships also had to be appointed. These had to be men who knew the crews and whom the latter trusted. The only captains who retained their posts were Commander Valentín Fuentes of the destroyer *Lepanto*, and Commander José García Freire, of the destroyer *Lazaga*. However, given that the latter remained in the navy after Franco's victory in 1939, and in fact later reached the rank of admiral, his presence on the bridge of a Republican ship can be assumed to have been counter-productive, and he was soon removed from command.[4] Doubt about the loyalty of officers was clashing with the sheer shortage of competent men.

The following officers were placed in command of the ships:

BATTLESHIP and CRUISERS

Jaime Primero	Midshipman Carlos Esteban
Cervantes	Lieutenant Commander Federico Monreal
Libertad	Commander Fernando Navarro

DESTROYER FLOTILLAS — Lt. Vicente Ramírez de Togores

Sánchez Barcáiztegui	Sub-lieutenant Alvaro Calderón
Almirante Valdés	Lt. Fernando Oliva Llamusí
Alcalá Galiano	Lt. Eugenio Calderón Martínez
José Luis Díez	Lt. Cdr. Luis González de Ubieta
Almirante Ferrándiz	Sub-lieutenant José Luis Barbastro
Almirante Miranda	Lt. Cdr. Nicolás Pinero Bonet
Churruca	Lt. Manuel Núñez Rodríguez
Alsedo	Sub-lieutenant Federico Vidal Cubas

This set of junior officers commanding destroyers and even a battleship (was the *Jaime I* so politicised that only a midshipman was acceptable to the crew?), subordinated to a middle ranking officer as fleet commander and a lieutenant as Head of Operations, reflects the problems that the Republic had in reorganising the navy.

Lieutenant Prado laboured to make Málaga into an advanced operational base. He established his headquarters in the Hotel Cataluña, where he put together a staff of warrant officers. The Sailors' Committee of the Fleet and the so-called 'Red Guard' of the *Jaime I* also had their headquarters in Málaga. To defend the city and the port, the battleship and the two cruisers remained anchored in the harbour as floating artillery.

Despite its convenient geographical position, Málaga was unsuitable as a base of naval operations, because the city was in a state of absolute anarchy. Six military commanders were dismissed and replaced one after another, but none was able to dominate the chaos.[5] The situation was made worse by the lack of decision and confidence of the officers, and the low morale of the crews of the ships, who were poorly trained and unable to defend themselves competently against the attacks of the Italian Savoia-81 bombers which Mussolini had supplied. Lieutenant Prado recommended a heavy attack on Algeciras, which was a vital port for landing insurgent troops and armaments. This, however, would have required a well-planned joint operation by air, on land and from the sea, which the chaos of the Republican command rendered impossible.

There was an acute shortage of qualified personnel. The government issued an order on 2 August 1936, according to which any competent person could be temporarily raised to an acting rank corresponding to the task required of him.[6] The second in command of the Málaga naval base was engineer warrant officer Baudilio Sanmartín. He would prove to be competent, but without a proper and established structure of command his efforts would always be in vain.

José Giral was overwhelmed by the pressures of being Prime Minister as well as Minister of the Navy. He resigned the latter post and was replaced on 22 August by the Under-Secretary. To replace the latter, the government appointed Benjamín Balboa, the radio-telegraphist who had played such an important part in warning the crews of the disloyalty of the officers or, in the opinion of pro-Franco historians, of encouraging the crews to mutiny. At the same time Commander Fernando Navarro, probably unable, after more than thirty years service, to adapt to the new and revolutionary situation, was appointed naval attaché in London and Paris and replaced as commander of the Republican fleet by Lieutenant Commander Miguel Buiza.

These changes reflect the beginnings of the effort which successive Republican governments would make to reorganise the fleet, accepting the revolutionary situation but trying to appoint commanders who would re-establish as far as possible pre-war structure and discipline. The chaos of the Republican zone had to end, and the revolutionary impulse had to be channelled. José Giral, consequently, resigned in favour of a widely-based government headed by the veteran socialist and trade union leader

Francisco Largo Caballero, who took office on 4 September 1936. The following day, the official *Diario Oficial del Ministerio de Marina*, now to be called the *Diario Oficial de Marina y Aire*, announced the appointment of the leading socialist Indalecio Prieto as Minister for the Navy and the Air Force of the Republic.

II Prieto's Reorganisation. Apppointment of Bruno Alonso. New Commands and Staff

Because of the evident unwillingness of many professional officers who had not been involved in the insurrection to serve in a navy whose traditional high level of hierarchical discipline had almost disappeared, the authorities of the Republic had no alternative but to accept and try to channel the revolutionary spirit among the crews.

The early *Instrucciones generales* of 20 July 1936 had accepted the reality of the situation. On 23 August, Lieutenant Prado, Head of Operations, issued a second set of orders. The main sailors' committee, the *Comité General*, was to ensure that all operational orders were obeyed, appoint inspectors of the various services such as engineers, artillery, radio and so forth, who could be selected from any men of suitable technical ability and unimpeachable loyalty to the Popular Front, irrespective of their rank. Prado was giving the Committee functions analogous to those of the fleet commander, who would be required to recognise the authority of a number of low-ranking men. What gave Prado the authority to issue these orders? Was he the only officer whom the Minister could trust? He held the low rank of lieutenant but seemed to be acting independently of the Minister. Indeed, on 21 August he was called to order for making arrangements for operations which the government had not planned. For the moment, he was told, he should remember that the fleet was to limit itself to blocking the Strait of Gibraltar. He was not to suggest mining the approaches to ports such as Melilla on the north coast of Morocco which, 'in present international circunstances we cannot do.'[7] This comment demonstrates to what extent the Republic was prevented from defending itself because it was not recognised, particular by Britain, as a belligerent, with rights to stop traffic making for Insurgent-ports held by Franco.

Perhaps it might have been valuable to allow Prado some latitude in operational planning, as in fact was happening in Franco's three-warship navy under Captain Moreno. But the latter was a senior officer, equivalent to a captain in the Royal Navy, and his orders would not raise anyone's hackles, whereas Prado was a mere lieutenant. Was Prado using the Committee on the *Libertad* to increase his own power? Whatever the case, Commander Navarro lost authority over the fleet and his resignation is unsurprising.

Soon after Indalecio Prieto took over the Navy Ministry, he issued a further general instruction, whose first article clarified the source of authority for the time being. The Head of Operations had to be in agreement with the Central Committee and, if they disagreed, the Committee's view should prevail [*en caso de discrepancia prevalecerá la opinion del Comité*].[8] Thus the Central Committee was given very wide authority. It ran the ships and oversaw the actions of the officers, at the same time 'without diminishing the functions (*mermar las atribuciones*) of the officers'. However, the Committee kept the codebooks, which gave it absolute power over all messages.

In the revolutionary atmosphere of the early weeks of the Spanish civil war, the Republican fleet had committees, but the new Republican army had political commissars.[9] The latter were literate and politically aware men, who were nominated to a large extent by the rapidly expanding Spanish Communist Party, in order to give the untrained militia confidence in the professional officers. In the navy, in contrast, the sailors were professionals who knew enough to be able to keep a check on the few junior officers on the ships. While the task of the thousands of commissars at all levels in the army was educational and even social, politicising the men and often teaching them basic literacy, the higher level of politicisation and skills in the navy probably made this unnecessary. Over and above these considerations, while the army commissars had been introduced to help maintain the authority of the officers, in the navy the committees were by definition suspicious of the officers and were there to watch what they did. Yet, in many ways, the committees were unhelpful. Even Benjamín Balboa, who received floods of communications from the committees in his office as Under Secretary of the navy, found it necessary to radio Prado to instruct the committees that he would not take any note of petitions and representation unless they

Cruiser *Libertad* (ex-*Príncipe Alfonso*), flagship of the Republican Navy.

were confirmed by the Central Committee. If every committee made contradictory suggestions, he said, it would lead to mere confusion.[10]

At the same time, however, the new ships' commanders were inexperienced and mostly of very low rank. Nevertheless, they did have some specialised knowledge of the technical aspects of the ships and there was a major risk that they would use their abilities to, for example, navigate the ships in such a way as to surrender them to the enemy. To this extent, therefore, the committees were valuable. Unfortunately, they were unable to keep check on a number of submarine commanders, which explains the failure and indeed sabotage of many of the Republic's twelve submarines.

The committees were set up to channel the demands of the crews, but it would seem that the committee on the *Libertad* wanted to prevent all links between the commander and the sailors. This body suggested that:

No commanding officer can discuss any official matter with a crew member without authorisation of the committee, and the fleet commander cannot speak to any crew member without permission of the Central Committee.[11]

This proposal does not seem to have been accepted, but it indicates the fear that the officers might deceive the crews, as had happened in some ships in the first couple of days of the military uprising.

It is hard to measure the level of interference by the committees in the running of the ships of the Republican navy, but on the flagship *Libertad*, for example, the Central Committee, composed of delegates from all the ships, discussed tactics heatedly. At least, this was reported by Commander Kuznetsov, the Soviet naval attaché. However, this communist and professional naval officer would quite naturally criticise such behaviour when he observed it from the bridge of the *Libertad*.[12] When Indalecio Prieto became Navy Minister on 4 September 1936 he noted the power of the committees and resolved to regulate them closely. The government then agreed on a formal decree, published in the *Gaceta de la República* on 19 November 1936. According to the decree, the ships' commanders would issue orders directly, without the mediation of the committee. Furthermore, the Minister himself would appoint a Political Delegate, who would chair the Central Committee, thus assuring ministerial control over the fleet. On 29 December 1936, this post was filled by Bruno Alonso, a socialist of Prieto's moderate wing, who knew nothing of naval matters, but his appointment was Prieto's first attempt at enforcing his authority over the committees, and it emerged against the background of the struggle of the new government, which was wide-based, including anarchists and communists, to control and channel the revolution that had taken place in anti-Franco Spain. The new administration would strive, to a large extent successfully, to restore Republican legality.

The decree of 19 November was followed by a new series of appointments of commanders, most of whom of very junior rank. On 26 December, Prieto re-established the naval staff. Lieutenant Prado was removed and appointed commander of the old and not very useful cruiser *Méndez Núñez*, while the other members of the staff were mostly officers who had been instructors at the naval college and not in command of ships.

Some of these appointments favoured officers who had been dismissed because of suspicions about their loyalty and were now readmitted to the active list. Benjamín Balboa, the Under-Secretary, protested, which led to his dismissal and replacement on 22 January 1937, after which he occupied less important posts. In his exile in Mexico, Balboa spoke at length to his biographer, who transcribes Balboa's words.[13] Balboa admitted that the committees hampered the efficient command of the ships, but at the same time he insisted that they ensured that none of the Republic's ships would pass over to the enemy. The committees lost influence, and were abolished on 11 May 1937.[14] In Balboa's view, the appointment of the Political Delegate brought politics into the running of the navy as it did into the Republican army. From then onwards, political delegates were posted in each ship, under the authority of Bruno Alonso. They could be appointed and dismissed by the Minister at will, rather than elected by the crews.

Prieto tried to appoint professional officers to command even small ships and to bureaucratic posts. There was a severe shortage, however, of suitable men for command posts. The losses had been enormous, either of officers who were known to be serving the Insurgents, or those who had been arrested in the Republican zone, murdered, or dismissed for suspicion of disloyalty. In 1936, the Spanish navy had included eighteen admirals and 676 other officers, a total of 694 in the *Cuerpo General*, that is the admirals, commanders of ships, seconds-in-command and junior officers of the ships, but not the specialised branches such as artillery, engineers, supply, and other branches. Up to 19 October 1936, 612 had been removed from the active list leaving 82, but the whereabouts and activities of many of these was not known. In the other branches of the service, of 621 men, 378 were dismissed, leaving 243.[15] About half of the petty officers and warrant officers were dismissed. The pool of competent and loyal officers to command the comparatively large number of Republican ships was thus very small. Consequently, Lieutenant-Commander Buiza, now commander of the fleet, suggested conscripting all merchant marine skippers and pilots into the naval reserve. Several merchant marine officers were already serving unofficially as navigation officers on warships. The decree admitting merchant navy officers into the naval reserve appeared tardily in March 1937.[16] 111 merchant navy officers were commissioned as sub-lieutenants or lieutenants of the naval reserve. The official new Navy List of September 1938 shows that the shortage of officers had been to some considerable extent relieved by the admission of these merchant navy captains and even more by ships' engineers who received naval ranks.[17]

Far from being revolutionary in promotions, the Republican navy was less inclined to award permanent promotions than the Insurgent one. There was only one new admiral. This was *capitán de navío* (equivalent to Captain RN) Valentín Fuentes, who, having been promoted to that rank on 16 January 1937 was later that year made up to the provisional rank of rear-admiral, the only other one in the Republican navy being Camilo Molíns, who was dismissed from command of the Cartagena base, but considered seriously responsible for the death of many of his Insurgent fellow-officers and executed by a Francoist court-martial after the war.

Despite the revolutionary images in the Madrid press of photographs of triumphant sailors after they had taken over the ships and arrested the officers, there was nothing revolutionary about the uniforms of the officers, such as there had been for the first few weeks in the army. Here, many officers had cast aside their uniforms and wore the boiler suits and overalls of the militiamen whom they tried to command, but the naval officers of the Republic remained formally uniformed.

III Reorganisation of the Insurgent Navy

Once the first few tense weeks were over, the temporary Insurgent government, known as the *Junta de Defensa Nacional*, published its first appointments. Some of the vice-admirals – the highest naval rank in Spain – were dismissed for being lukewarm in their support of the uprising. Admiral Azarola had been executed, and a number of others had lost their lives in the Republican zone. There was only one vice-admiral left. This was Juan Cervera Valderrama, who had been removed from the command of the Cartagena base a few months earlier by the Popular Front government and who was now appointed to head the new Insurgent naval staff. Likewise, only one of the twelve rear-admirals was still available for a command. This was Manuel Ruiz de Atauri who was appointed to command the Cádiz base. On 16 October 1936 Captain Francisco Bastarreche was entrusted with the new cruiser *Canarias*. Two further admirals were brought out of retirement, one to command the El Ferrol base, whose previous chief had been unwilling to sign execution warrants for officers who had refused to support the insurrection.

The Junta of officers governing Insurgent Spain had no minister for the navy, so it was not until 3 October 1936 that a form of war ministry was established, called the *Secretaría de Guerra*, which had one section for each of the three arms, land, sea and air. Its task was to establish simple and not over-bureaucratised structures for only the most essential matters.

In El Ferrol, the new cruiser *Canarias* was about to go into service. Its twin, the *Baleares*, would do so within a few months. In the meantime the new navy mobilised a large number of deep sea fishing trawlers, or *bous*, which it armed with artillery. On 22 October the commanders of the bases at El Ferrol and Cádiz were instructed to accept volunteers and recall the first reserve. Sailors and marines about to come to the end of their period of service were not released. On 27 October an order militarised the crews of the armed merchant ships which were being used to hinder the delivery of arms shipments to Republican ports. Merchant marine personnel were brought into the navy provided that their politics and personal histories were approved. Even so, Admiral Cervera wrote later that some of them showed some signs of a poor disciplinary attitude.[18]

On 18 February 1937 all Merchant Marine personnel were called up, even if they were out of the country, and threatened with prosecution if they did not report for service. On 10 April 1937 men of eighteen and over, even if married, were invited to volunteer for the navy, but they would have to offer proofs of ideological loyalty to the new regime. There was a serious shortage of personnel to man even the relatively small number of ships that the Insurgents possessed, given that a large number of sailors and petty officers had been executed for their part in the events of 19–21 July 1936 and many more were in prison or had been discharged. Petty officers were in particularly short supply and emergency promotions were soon being made.

In the Republican navy, with its sailors' committees and political delegates, politisation was evident. In contrast, in the Insurgent or Nationalist (the English translation of *Nacionales*, as they insisted on being called) navy politisation took the form of allowing access to the service only to those men who could prove their political orthodoxy: did they accept the principles of the 'Glorious National Movement'? During the first four weeks of induction and preliminary training, careful note would be taken of the conduct of new recruits.

The remedy adopted for the scarcity of junior officers was to shorten the courses of cadets and midshipmen and the time they spent in the most junior rank, the *alférez de fragata*. In November 1937 an order was issued that nine of these very junior officers would be made up to the next rank, *alférez de navío*, by an examination to be taken the following February. The even more junior cadets and the junior officers would be moved up a rank, but four years later they would have to pass the entire diet of examinations to be able to achieve the rank of lieutenant.

Thus, both navies had problems, but there was no shortage of senior officers in the Insurgent fleet. Those few who had opposed the uprising were court-martialled, and executed, imprisoned or dismissed. Sailors and petty officers who had opposed the uprising were arrested, court-martialled and removed from the ships and the base. Until October there was no naval staff, and there would not be a civilian Navy Minister or department, but a simple secretariat, a circumstance which allowed a more or less free hand to the senior officers in the bases of El Ferrol and Cadiz, and aboard the ships. This contrasts with the Republican navy, where many naval officers were unwilling to serve in the new navy or on the staff. The few professional officers who did take commands were of junior rank, often mistrusted or unable to adapt to the revolutionary system and the existence of sailors' committees. Prieto, the Navy Minister who took over in September, had to work hard to bring the navy under control, still heady as it was with revolutionary ardour following the mutinies,

The advantages to the Republic of a large fleet of modern destroyers, as well as a powerful battleship and two quite modern cruisers were thus lost. General Franco, who would become Generalissimo at the end of September 1936, would not be prevented from shipping his troops over from Morocco to Spain, and the chance to recover Majorca for the Republic was lost. Internationally, the denial of belligerent rights to the Republic, added to the aid swiftly provided by Italy and Germany and the cooperation of Portugal, would give immediate advantage to the Insurgents.

Chapter 5

Off the Northern Coast

I The Insurgents Begin Their Campaign

The Insurgents possessed few ships. Consequently they had to improvise. There was little that could be done in the Strait of Gibraltar or the Mediterranean. The cruiser *República*, the only warship of importance based at Cádiz, was not in a fit condition to go to sea. Franco's first troopships, which had brought troops from Ceuta to Algeciras on 5 August 1936, had been escorted by a mere gunboat, the *Dato*, plus a torpedo boat and a coastguard cutter. The Republican fleet was supreme in the Strait.

However, there was another front. This was the roughly 250 miles of coastline of northern Spain in Republican hands between the French frontier and the beginning of Insurgent territory, The Insurgent naval command had to devise a strategy which could be carried out along this coast by the battleship *España*, the cruiser *Almirante Cervera* and the destroyer *Velasco* while waiting for the modern cruisers *Canarias* and *Baleares* to go to sea.

The repression on the ships and at the El Ferrol base had been very severe.[1] Besides those executed, many other men were imprisoned or dismissed from the navy. Discipline was very rigorous. No delay could be tolerated in finishing the necessary repairs to the cruiser *Almirante Cervera*, the first ship to sail out into the Cantabrian Sea. On 23 July, the *Almirante Cervera* raised anchor under the orders of Commander Salvador Moreno Fernández, whose brother Francisco was fleet commander. In contrast with the reconstructed Republican navy, the Insurgent line of command and the administrative structure were simple. Without a Navy Minister or chief of staff, Francisco Moreno, who would be promoted to acting rear-admiral in November, had to plan and animate the activities of this embryonic but potentially powerful force, but he had the enormous advantage of beginning at zero and not to having to concern himself with any of the revolutionary and politically correct practices of the enemy. Moreno could also count on a relative abundance of enthusiastic and capable officers. His words describe the situation as he saw it:

> El Ferrol went its own way. We had no news of the rest of Spain. The National Defence Junta did not tell us anything of importance. We did not know who was at the head of the uprising. Only now and then did General Mola [commanding insurrectionary forces in northern Spain] issue orders which in most cases we could not carry out for lack of men and ships.[2]

Moreno thus acted without higher authority. Improvisation was of course facilitated by the savage repression which had taken place at El Ferrol, but it says much for Francisco Moreno's ability that he swiftly managed to complete crewing the battleship *España* and the cruiser *Almirante Cervera*, organising the auxiliary flotillas and speeding up the completion of the new cruisers.

While the *Canarias* and the *Baleares* were approaching completion, the Insurgent naval officers energetically saw to the arming of a large number of requisitioned deep water trawlers, whose role would be to patrol the waters of the Cantabrian Sea and to watch out for and stop merchant

Cruiser *Almirante Cervera*, of the Insurgent Navy.

traffic making for the Republican ports along the northern coast. Each armed trawler was commanded by an officer. By the autumn, there would be nineteen armed trawlers based at El Ferrol, Ribadeo and Pasajes. On one of them, the *Virgen del Carmen*, there was a mutiny when the crew overcame the commander and sailed the trawler into Bilbao. In the brutal atmosphere of the civil war the officers were shot and the trawler's name was changed to the *Donostia*, the Basque name for the city of San Sebastián.

The first mission of the cruiser *Almirante Cervera*, once the brief training period of its volunteer sailors was finished, was to support the military garrison of the Simancas barracks at Gijón, at the extreme western end of the fringe of Republican territory in the north of Spain. The garrison, having declared itself in favour of the military insurrection, was desperately resisting militia and other forces loyal to the government. The departure of the *Almirante Cervera* for Gijón was known to the Republican authorities, but no ships were sent to attack it. The cruiser bombarded the coast, but with little effect.

The *Almirante Cervera* returned to harbour to replace its depleted stock of shells, and sailed out again, this time accompanied by the battleship *España*, under Commander Luis de Vierna, and the destroyer *Velasco*, under Lieutenant Francisco Núñez Rodríguez.

Now began a period of intense activity and improvisation. The three ships returned to port only to refuel and take on ammunition, food and water. They divided their efforts between shelling Gijón and the forts at San Sebastián, and obstructing fishing boats. The *Velasco* set fire to the oil tanks at Santurce, at the mouth of the Bilbao estuary. On the night of 18 August, the *Almirante Cervera* received orders to return to its position off Gijón, but despite its shelling, the garrison was overwhelmed. The *Almirante Cervera* now devoted itself to stopping cargo boats. In a month of intense activity, it left and returned to port ten times, covering altogether 2,152 miles in almost continuous service. The crew had not even disembarked.[3] It had fired 1,200 shells. This long physical closeness of men and officers had perhaps established the esprit de corps and the sense of common purpose which had been absent in the pre-war navy where mutual distrust had often been the norm. Admiral Peter Gretton, from his vantage point as a senior officer in the Royal Navy, underlines this view:

The close-quarters life aboard warships [...], demands conscious and determined effort by the officers to avoid a 'them and us' situation developing. The Insurgent navy soon learned this lesson and the atmosphere on board was soon excellent.[4]

Other countries, except of course Germany and Italy which were already supporting Franco's Nationalist Insurgents, could not tolerate his navy's interference with merchant ships. Nevertheless, when the Republican government officially proclaimed the *Almirante Cervera* a 'pirate', because it was serving the cause of an armed rebellion against a legitimate government, there was no reaction by foreign navies. During the early weeks of the war in Spain, foreign warships limited themselves to evacuating their nationals and Spanish refugees. German aggressiveness, however, became evident when the new pocket-battleship *Deutschland* dropped anchor in the harbour of San Sebastián, still in Republican hands, on 26 July 1936. The commander of the British destroyer *Veteran*, despite his lower rank, managed to overcome Admiral Rolf Carls's intention to land an armed patrol, which might have had serious international consequences.[5]

Lacking ships, the Insurgent campaign of obstructing foreign merchant shipping in the Cantabrian began slowly. Furthermore, care had to be taken, given that most of the merchant vessels which usually traded with the ports of northern Spain were British, and interference with them might cause grave consequences. However, there was an international incident when on 23 August 1936, the Insurgent trawler *Tritonia* fired at the Estonian merchant ship *Lenna* to try to stop and search it. The *Lenna* managed to escape and take shelter in Bilbao, protected by an aircraft and by Basque trawlers.

The first incident with a British ship occurred on the 16 and 17 September when an Insurgent trawler tried to stop the cargo ship *MacGregor*, which it suspected of carrying arms to the enemy. A British destroyer approached and escorted the *MacGregor* to the beginning of Spanish territorial waters (recognised as three miles from the coast) whence a Republican submarine accompanied it into Santander, its destination.[6] Previously, on 9 August, there had been a tragic accident when the *Almirante Cervera* shelled a private British yacht, the *Blue Shadow*, whose captain, Rupert Saville, was killed and his wife and two crew members injured. The British ambassador to Spain, who had been evacuated to Hendaye, protested and the captain of the *Almirante Cervera* apologised. However, doing what was thought necessary in the circumstances and apologising afterwards would be characteristic of the interference with foreign merchant shipping which was the major function of the Insurgent navy.

The Soviet Union had no warships in the area, so when two Russian freighters, the *Vtoraya Pyatiletka* and the *Potrovski*, were off the northern coast nothing could be done to defend them when they were stopped and obliged to sail into Corunna and El Ferrol.[7]

II Republican Submarines in Northern Spanish Waters

Despite the relative weakness of the Insurgent blockade off the northern coast, the Republican government decided to send some of its twelve submarines to that area. A submarine would not seem to be the ideal warship for protecting commercial traffic. It does not have enough speed to respond with sufficient urgency to protect a vessel which is being obstructed. On the surface a submarine is only lightly armed. Perhaps it was thought that the mere presence of submarines would force the Insurgent ships to sail with a level of caution which would dissuade them from trying to stop merchant ships. However, the independence and disloyalty of the submarine commanders had serious consequences.

On 15 August 1936, submarine *C-6*, commanded by Lieutenant-Commander Mariano Romero, sailed for the Cantabrian Sea. During the mutinies, Romero had avoided a confrontation with his crew. In later investigations into Romero's activities it emerged that he had simulated a malfunction in the navigation system to avoid a situation where he might be ordered to attack an Insurgent ship.[8] He was arrested, together with his second-in-command, Sub-lieutenant Ferrando, but was fortunate not to be murdered like so many other captive naval officers, because the crew stood up for him. His crew's support made him appear suitable for command of the *C-6* as it sailed north. It was accompanied by the *C-3*, under Sub-lieutenant Arbona, who was highly respected by the crew. However, they were unaware that Arbona had sympathies with the Spanish Fascist movement, the *Falange*.[9] When the *C3* was off the Portuguese coast, Arbona reported a malfunction and turned back to Cartagena.[10] Whether this was faked or not, it might be considered a relatively minor matter. Perhaps Arbona was unwilling to be ordered, for instance, to torpedo an Insurgent warship. On the other hand, the crew might have been reluctant to proceed and the commander was unable to prevail over them. Meanwhile, Romero and the *C-6* continued to Gijón.

Some time later, Romero had the *Almirante Cervera*, and later the *España*, in a position where he could have launched torpedoes, but decided not to do so.[11] The crew of his submarine arrested him and decided to return to Cartagena, where he was fortunate enough to be sent to a post in the Navy Ministry in Madrid.[12] A month later he disappeared and probably made his way to the Insurgent Zone. When his conduct was examined after the war, it was approved by the Francoist victors. He remained in the navy and reached admiral's rank. The *C-6* returned to the Cantabrian Sea under the command of a warrant officer. It was followed by the *C-2* and the *B-6*. Meanwhile, the *España* escaped once more when a torpedo fired from the *C-5* failed to explode.

Those five Republican submarines, under loyal and resolute commanders, could have represented a grave danger for the three Insurgent warships in the Cantabrian. As it was, the only submarine which served the Republican cause was the *C-5* under Lieutenant Commander Remigio Verdiá, but its effectiveness was reduced by the low standard of training and faulty torpedoes.

On 19 September the destroyer *Velasco* spotted and sank the *B-6*. Its commander, Sub-Lieutenant Scharfhausen, whose brother had lost his life in the Republican zone, was commanding the boat. He survived and was interrogated by the Insurgents. He claimed to have tried to sabotage the *B-6* and to have exposed his submarine to the guns of the *Velasco*. He insisted that he had tried not to hit an armed trawler against which his submarine had fired. However, the enquiry, conducted at El Ferrol, had its doubts and Scharfhausen was obliged to demonstrate his loyalty to the cause of the uprising against the Republic by undertaking a series of secret and dangerous missions until, after the fall of Bilbao to Franco in June 1937, he rejoined the Insurgent navy. Three members of his crew, rescued by the *Velasco*, were executed.

Meanwhile, the submarine flotilla had been entrusted to the loyal Remigio Verdiá, who was ordered to share out the few torpedoes available, and to carry out a check of men and equipment so that the flotilla could join the rest of the fleet, most of which would be in the Cantabrian Sea by 22 September 1936.

III The Cruise to the North

The submarines which had been sent to the north were not much of a threat to the Insurgents because of their poor operative condition and the disloyalty of their captains. Yet it was important not to neglect the fringe of Republican territory along the northern coast. Thus the Republican command had to tackle the three Insurgent warships which had contributed to the loss of San Sebastián and of Irún. There was no longer any possibility of arms coming to the Republic through the French frontier. It was thought that the presence of a large fleet would encourage resistance and would also support the authority of the Madrid government against the emerging separatist tendencies, not only in the Basque Country, which had been given its autonomy and taken defence into its own hands, but also in the two provinces to its west, Santander and Asturias. Additionally, because the Insurgents had not yet been able seriously to contest the Republican naval blockade of the Strait of Gibraltar, it was thought safe enough to transfer a substantial part of the fleet from the Strait to the Cantabrian coast. Deficient Republican information suggested that the *Canarias* would not be completed in the near future. The cruiser was thought, mistakenly, to have been damaged by a bomb from one of the long-distance Potez aircraft which had flown to the North from Madrid on 22 August.[13]

The Republican battleship *Jaime I*, the two cruisers, *Miguel de Cervantes* and *Libertad*, together with six of the destroyers, sailed north, leaving the destroyers *Churruca*, *Ferrándiz*, *Gravina*, *Alcalá Galiano*, and *Sánchez Barcáiztegui* in the Strait of Gibraltar.

The Soviet naval attaché and senior adviser, Commander Nikolai Kuznetsov, who sailed on the *Libertad*, wrote the following account of the voyage north:

On the evening of 21 September 1936, the battleship and the cruisers formed up in a column and, protected by the destroyers, sailed out of Cartagena. In first position was the cruiser *Libertad*, followed by the battleship *Jaime I*, and then the cruiser *Miguel de Cervantes*. During the day, the destroyers protected the big ships from the front. As the fleet approached the Strait of Gibraltar and night fell, the destroyers took their places in the column. From the moment the voyage began, the ships were on high alert and their engines ready to develop maximum speed. Thick smoke poured from the funnels. The ships could not fail to be seen.

The news that there were large calibre batteries at Ceuta and Algeciras worried the command. A German cruiser appeared soon [...].

A profound silence fell on the bridge of the *Libertad* as, in the depths of night, the ships began to pass through the narrowest part of the Strait – between Ceuta and Algeciras – and the beams of the searchlights of the coastal batteries played over our vessels. We expected them to fire a broadside when the beam lit up one of our ships, but there were no signs of life from the batteries. Either our fleet was sailing out of their range or they had not fixed its position. Buiza [the fleet commander] walked up and down nervously on the bridge, more concerned for the other ships than for the *Libertad*.

Before long, Gibraltar with its lights was left behind [...] Ceuta was behind us and the batteries of Algeciras were distant enough not to be worrying. The nervous tension gradually eased.[14]

The reports that went to Moscow were more critical. Kuznetsov's assistant, Commander Annin, who sailed on the destroyer *Lepanto*, reported that the ships were commanded inefficiently and took several hours to get into formation. They were not darkened and no guards were set. A German cruiser followed the Republican ships.[15] Throughout 22 September, the Republican fleet avoided the usual routes. That night, off El Ferrol, an aircraft flew over the ships. As night fell, the fleet turned east to enter the Cantabrian Sea. On the following day, the ships of the Republican fleet reached Gijón. Three of the destroyers continued to Santander.

What were the effects of the presence of the Republican navy in the Cantabrian? Firstly, the Insurgent trawlers were no longer able to blockade the coast. Secondly, the operation against Bilbao planned by General Mola was paralysed.[16] Thirdly, troops had to be detached in case government reinforcements were landed.[17] But that was all. The Insurgent warships remained safe in El Ferrol, and the Republican fleet, while it freed its own commerce from interference, did nothing to secure command of the sea, because it did not establish a blockade to prevent cargo ships coming from Germany to unload war material at Vigo or to sail south along the Portuguese coast and up the river Guadalquivir to Seville, the other destination for imported war material.[18] Nor did the Republic use its temporary control of the Cantabrian Sea to land troops along the coast. However, the major result of the absence of clear and decisive strategic decision was the breakout of the *Canarias* and the *Almirante Cervera* and their unexpected appearance in the Strait of Gibraltar.

IV Insurgent Incursion into the Mediterranean; Return of the Republican Fleet and the Battle of Cape Spartel; Loss of Submarines

During the weeks when the Republican blockade of the Strait of Gibraltar had been tightest, Captain Francisco Moreno, newly appointed to command the small Insurgent fleet, had suggested that the cruiser *Almirante Cervera* should sail south to the Strait of Gibraltar and challenge the enemy fleet. This bold but foolhardy offer might have lost the only ship the Insurgents possessed which combined fire power with reasonable operative modernity, and it was quite properly rejected.[19] The completion of the cruiser *Canarias*, however, changed the situation. Two cruisers not only doubled the firepower, but also required double the number of Republican destroyers to shadow them.

In El Ferrol, raw recruits, many of them eager young *Falangistas* who had been enrolled to replace the sailors who had been shot or imprisoned, underwent crash training courses.[20] They were joined by apprentices from the artillery firing range at Marín and twenty-four cadets who had been on a voyage in the training ship *Galatea*. Officers scoured ports for trained seamen. However, some important posts on the *Canarias* were occupied by ex-civilians. The commanders of two of the artillery turrets were reported to be a doctor and an architect, and the British Admiralty learned that the senior gun aimer on the *Cervera* was an eighteen-year old.[21] Hard work, a competent commander and rigid discipline made the *Canarias* ready for action. On 18 September 1936 she put to sea for a four-day shakedown cruise. Except for heavy seas which incapacitated her seasick crew, all went well. She returned minimally ready for battle, or as ready as Captain Moreno, the fleet commander, and Captain Francisco Bastarreche, commander of the cruiser, could make her.

As for artillery, the old battleship *España* lent four 101.6mm surface guns from her battery, now effective to up to only three miles, and two even more ancient Nordenfelt 57mm pieces, which were mounted on the *Canarias* where anti-aircraft guns should have been. Vickers had refused to deliver the fire-control apparatus that had been ordered because Britain had agreed to observe the pan-European agreement of August not to supply arms to either side. An officer solved the fire control problem by ingeniously removing a Vickers system from a 152.4mm coastal battery and modifying it for use at sea. A Henderson gyroscopic apparatus came from the Portuguese Navy at the last moment, even though Portugal was also a signatory to the Non-Intervention agreement, On the night of 15–16 September 1936, prisoners at El Ferrol cleaned the hull and the bottom of the *Canarias*. The cruiser did not yet have its 20 mm and 40 mm. anti-aircraft guns, nor its twelve torpedo tubes nor the small catapulted aircraft which it was designed to carry.

On paper, the *Canarias* was much more powerful than the Republican cruisers *Cervantes* and *Libertad*, for its 203 mm guns had a range of twenty thousand metres in contrast with the eighteen thousand of the 152 mm Republican weapons, and because the *Canarias*'s artillery could hurl a shell weighing 120kg, more than double the weight of a shell from the Republican ships. The new Insurgent cruiser had also much greater fuel storage capacity, which gave her more range, her horsepower was greater, and her armour protection was no less and in certain parts thicker than that of the Republican cruisers. Ideal for commerce raiding, with a wide range at economical speed, but with a top speed of thirty-three knots, the *Canarias* was nearly as fast as a destroyer. With skilled leadership and discipline it represented a major threat to the Republican navy.

Once intelligence reported that a fleet of Republican ships had left the Strait, General Mola, commander of Insurgent forces in the north of Spain, suggested to Captain Moreno that the *Canarias* and the *Almirante Cervera* should make for the Strait, break the blockade, obstruct traffic and shell the coast. As most of the Republican fleet was now cruising towards the Cantabrian, the *Canarias* and the *Almirante Cervera* prepared to sail south, reaching the Strait in the early hours of 29 September. The *Canarias* continued into the Mediterranean and at 0530 hours spotted a destroyer at 30,000 metres. Uncertain whether the warship was Spanish or British, Captain Bastarreche fired a warning salvo. The destroyer was the Republican *Ferrándiz*, under the command of Sub-lieutenant José Luis Barbastro, who had been elected captain by the crew. Clearly outgunned, he began to turn away, relying on the destroyer's high maximum speed. The cruiser opened fire at 21,000 metres. A salvo fired at 0650 hours at a distance of 16,000 metres hit the *Ferrándiz*, setting its fuel tanks alight. The destroyer sank quickly, eighteen miles south of Marbella. The *Canarias* rescued thirty-one men, and a French liner, the *Koutoubia*, another twenty-five, including the commander. Despite the inexperience of its gunners, the *Canarias*'s artillery had managed to score six hits out of eighty-one shots.[22] José Luis Barbastro, commanding the *Ferrándiz*, was later sentenced to twelve years' imprisonment and expulsion from the navy.[23] He was fortunate to save his life.

A hideous consequence of the loss of this Republican destroyer was that the violent and undisciplined sailors aboard the battleship *Jaime I*, anchored at Bilbao, assassinated about fifty captives held on a prison ship moored alongside.[24]

Meanwhile, off Tangiers, the *Almirante Cervera* had attacked the Republican destroyer *Gravina*. It fired almost 300 shells from its 152mm guns, but only three hit the Republican destroyer. Among other reasons, many of the fuses were found to be defective. The *Gravina*, under the command of Sub-lieutenant Alberto del Caso Montaner, sought refuge in Casablanca, after having defended itself without losses. The consequence of this success, known as the battle of Cape Spartel, was soon evident. That same afternoon, 29 November, the *Canarias* escorted a troopship from Ceuta to Algeciras. Thousands of troops crossed the Strait without incident in the next few days, and from then onwards passage was unopposed. It would be impossible now to re-establish blockade of all the ports in the area without the presence of the entire Republican fleet.

After escorting troopships, the *Canarias* and the *Almirante Cervera* sailed into the Mediterranean and shelled the oil tanks at Almería. The sinking of the *Ferrándiz* and the putting to flight of the *Gravina* were followed by the sinking of two coastguard cutters (the *Uad-Muluya* and the *Uad-Lucus*) by the *Almirante Cervera* as it shelled the Málaga coast.

The psychological impact of the loss of three ships and the flight of a fourth, together with the evident lack of will or incapacity of the Republican command to use its submarines and aircraft aggressively, was the result of a set of unavoidable circumstances and errors. Its ships were commanded by inexperienced and politically unreliable officers. The Republican leadership lacked a clear vision of the strategic imperatives. The absence of real and determined organs of command paralysed the Republican side, while the Insurgents gave entire liberty of action to Captain Francisco Moreno who improvised furiously with his inexperienced crew and his incomplete equipment.

The Republican government had neglected the North in the early weeks of the war, just at the moment when they ought to have been trying to block the arrival of war material from Germany. When at last, two months after the war had begun, they decided to send a fleet to the Cantabrian Sea, they did so more because the political leaders in northern Spain appealed to them than for any strategic imperative. Sending the submarines to the Cantabrian would have been wise perhaps, if the commanders had been loyal. The fact that some submarines were not efficiently operative and that the crews trusted only some of the commanders and that these were unwilling to wage warfare against Insurgent warships meant that the submarines could not prevent the movements of the two Insurgent cruisers.

It seems incredible that Prieto, the Navy Minister, and Buiza, the Republican fleet commander, even without a competent naval staff, thought it advisable to abandon the blockade of the Strait of Gibraltar. They committed the classical error of dividing the Republican fleet when their enemy concentrated their two powerful cruisers and launched them against weaker Republican vessels in the Strait and the Mediterranean.

The importance of Insurgent control of the Strait cannot be overstated. They were now in control of a narrow and vital strip of water, as well as the hinterland where they had their bases, the ports of Cádiz, Seville and Algeciras, and Ceuta on the Moroccan coast, as well as the air base at Tablada close to Seville. They would now be able to establish another naval base at Palma on Majorca. The lack of adequate support for the attempt to recapture that island from the Insurgents in August would now be seen as a disastrous mistake.

It took four days for the Republican leaders to learn that the *Canarias* was in the Mediterranean, and only then from information provided by a British destroyer visiting Málaga.[25] The sinking of the destroyer *Ferrándiz* put into relief the failure to scout the area with aircraft, expressed in the following message sent by Buiza to the Minister:

> On learning of the sinking of *Ferrándiz* I protest in name of entire Fleet about the neglect and the seriousness of abandoning the heroic crew. We have insistently asked for and been promised aerial exploration, which would have avoided such a pointless sacrifice of life.

Prieto rejected the implied criticism of the air command, of which he was also the Minister, because

> With a scarcity of aircraft which puts them in gross inferiority the air force has been displaying a marvellous spirit of self sacrifice.[26]

In reality, the shortage was more that of pilots than aircraft, and of a clear strategic vision. The aircraft that the Republic had at its disposal ought to have been concentrated in the Strait and to have kept the *Canarias* under continuous watch.[27] There was, however, no air-sea cooperation, although the Republic had retained the naval air base at San Javier on the Mediterranean coast, but with few reliable pilots.

The lack of liaison continued, nevertheless, and as late as 17 December 1936 the fleet commander again complained that he was receiving no information from scouting aircraft about the presence of the second new Francoist cruiser, the *Baleares*, which was almost ready to sail from El Ferrol.[28] How could the naval staff function without discovering the location of enemy ships? The same criticism was made a year later by the Soviet rear-admiral N. A. Piterski in a memorandum which he wrote after succeeding Kuznetsov as naval attaché and adviser.[29]

The immediate consequence of the irruption of the two Insurgent cruisers into the Mediterranean was an order from Madrid on 2 October, requiring Lieutenant-Commander Remigio Verdiá, an submarine officer of unquestioned loyalty, to return to the Strait with the *C-6*, the *C-3* and the *C-4*.[30] The *C-2* and the *C-5* remained in the north.

Meanwhile the destroyer *Gravina* was under repair in Casablanca. Spanish Insurgent agents in the city reported to General Orgaz, High Commissioner in Insurgent Spanish Morocco, that the captain, Sublieutenant Alberto del Caso Montaner, was pro-Insurgent. He had indicated that naval officers who were commanding Republican ships were intent on maintaining a passive attitude and not attacking Insurgent ships. Of course he could not have consulted every officer in question, but probably a significant number of those to whom he had spoken were indeed hesitant about engaging in active combat against their erstwhile comrades. According to the agents, the crew of the *Gravina* had accepted an offer of one million pesetas, evacuation and asylum in Portugal and amnesty afterwards, in exchange for surrendering the *Gravina*. The money was certainly offered, as the crew later told the Republican Navy newspaper *La Armada* of 10 December 1938, when they were back in their base at Cartagena.[31] Most of the crew refused to accept the bribe but perhaps some of them wanted to. The press took up the matter. It was suggested that the commander aimed to delay the repairs, which alarmed the French authorities in Casablanca, who wanted to have the essential repairs carried out quickly and for the ship to leave.[32] Probably for this reason the Spanish government sent Lieutenant-Commander Luis González de Ubieta to Casablanca to restore order on the *Gravina* and to take it back to Cartagena. Del Caso Montaner made arrangements to go to the Spanish Zone of Morocco and join the Insurgents. He was later acquitted of rebellion, that is opposing the Francoist insurrection, by a court-martial. Nevertheless, because he had consented to command a Republican ship, after the war he was removed from the Spanish Navy List and pensioned off with the rank of lieutenant.[33]

Prieto and Buiza now decided that the fleet should return to the Mediterranean, leaving in northern waters only two C class submarines, a torpedo boat and the destroyer *José Luis Díez*. The plan was that the fleet should meet the *Gravina* on its way back from Casablanca, and that other ships should come out from Cartagena to assure its safety. On 18 October the Insurgent naval command learned that the Republican fleet had passed through the dangerous part of their route, the narrow

Strait of Gibraltar. It was probably too risky to endanger the *Canarias* and the *Almirante Cervera*, the only two Insurgent cruisers, against the twenty or so Republican warships.

Nevertheless, the presence of almost the entire Republican fleet in the Mediterranean did not inhibit the *Canarias*. It found other targets, as it sailed up and down the coast, shelling Barcelona and the ports of Rosas and Palamós halfway between Barcelona and the French frontier, and capturing the steamship *Ciudadela* as it crossed from Port Mahon to Barcelona.

Despite its size, the Republican navy seemed impotent. The *Gravina* had been repaired but the submarine *B-5* was lost. It was attacked off Estepona, near Málaga by a seaplane, whose pilot thought he had sunk it. But many years after the civil war, it was learnt that it had been sabotaged by its commander, Lieutenant Commander Carlos Barreda Terry, who died with it.[34]

Thus two submarines, the *B-5* and the *B-6*, had been lost, probably by the actions of their own commanders, who had been forced to take command but had succeeded in deceiving the crews. This put Captain Remigio Verdiá, who was submarine flotilla commander, in a most difficult position. He had not reported that the commanders were suspected, although he probably had sufficient proof of their unwillingness to command the boats and their determination not to sink Insurgent warships. But Verdiá was efficient and determined and while he was in command the enemy did not venture to attack the submarines at anchor in Málaga. The Soviet adviser Kuznetsov, usually quite critical of the Republican officers, describes Verdiá as 'a model of heroism and loyalty to the Republic'.[35] Verdiá's death on 2 January 1937 during an air raid put an end to any possibility of reorganising the Republican submarines, which sank no ships throughout the civil war.

Many of the twelve Republican submarines had already been lost. On 12 December, 1936, the *C-3* was lost off Málaga. The report on the loss concluded that there has been an internal explosion. Suspicion fell on the commander, Sub-lieutenant Arbona, who had received a radio message from the enemy on 18 August accusing him of cowardice, since he had been heard to express sympathy for the *Falange* in the past.[36] Another author suggested that the submarine had been attacked by an Italian submarine.[37] In fact, it was sunk by a German U-boat (see below). To complete the list of disasters, on 30 December 1936 the *C-5* disappeared during a mission off Bilbao. The boat was almost certainly sabotaged by its commander, Lieutenant Commander José Lara y Dorda.[38] Consequently, out of twelve submarines, by the end of 1936, the Republic had lost the *B-5*, the *B-6*, the *C-3* and the *C-5*.

Chapter 6

War Material Comes from Abroad.
The Insurgents Try to Block Merchant Traffic

I The Importance of Foreign Merchant Shipping

Spain's exports and imports travelled overwhelmingly by sea. Its own productive capacity would not have supported more than a few weeks of war. Imports of raw materials and armaments and exports of products which could earn foreign currency were essential. Hence control of merchant shipping was the most important aspect of the Spanish civil war at sea and appears frequently in the naval and diplomatic history of the conflict.

The majority of the Spanish merchant fleet was small and not suitable for international traffic. When war broke out the larger vessels were at sea, in foreign ports or in the harbours where the insurrection failed, such as Barcelona, Valencia and Alicante in the Mediterranean, and Bilbao, Santander and Gijón on Spain's northern coast. Not all, however, were available to be used. Often there was doubt about the loyalty of the officers. Some merchant ships sailed to Insurgent ports or remained in foreign harbours as instructed by the ship owners. Others were rendered unusable.[1] In some cases the Republican authorities requisitioned ships and in others the crew took them over. The atmosphere was tense, because the merchant shipping industry had recently emerged from a strike which had led to the establishment of sailors' committees to manage working practices. The continuation of private ownership meant that the committees remained active, hindering to some extent the most efficient running of the ships. This problem was regularly underlined by the seamen's union newspaper, *CNT Marítima. Organo del Sindicato Nacional del Transporte*.[2] This publication launched continual attacks against the mixture of neglect, idleness, sabotage, and indiscipline which its reporters observed, in particular when the ships were in foreign ports, where the crews were exposed to bribery by Francoist agents, who tempted seamen to change sides. In the view of the newspaper, the government ought to have requisitioned the entire Spanish merchant fleet. This insufficient, inefficient and badly disciplined merchant fleet made it even more essential for the Republic in particular to rely on foreign ships.

At the outset of the Spanish war the Republican navy attempted to blockade merchant traffic making for the Moroccan ports and for Algeciras, Cádiz, and the deep river port of Seville, which had fallen at once into Insurgent hands. Although the substantial Republican fleet could have stopped merchant vessels making for Insurgent ports, the navy was ordered not to risk losing the support of the international world, particularly Britain, by assuming the rights of a belligerent. These rights, which would have permitted Republican warships to stop and seize the cargoes of ships while they were on the high seas (that is, outside the limit of Spanish or territorial waters) were never granted to the Republic. Once, however, from late September 1936, the Insurgent cruisers *Canarias* and *Almirante Cervera* reached the Mediterranean from their base at El Ferrol, the Republican fleet grew more concerned about its own security and the merchant ships it was called upon to escort than about interfering with enemy traffic. Yet even during its brief period off the Cantabrian coast in September 1936, where it was in the overwhelming majority, Republican warships had not tried to obstruct merchant shipping bringing war material from Germany into the Insurgent-held ports of El Ferrol and Vigo. The inefficiency, lack of clear strategy and possible treachery of the Republican fleet was becoming evident, although it soon became clear also that trying to prevent German ships entering Spanish Insurgent ports would evoke a fierce response.

The Insurgents recognised how important it was not only to stop merchant ships making for Republican ports, but also to capture as many vessels as possible for their own needs and to convert some of them into armed merchant ships which to some extent could compensate for the scarcity of Insurgent warships in the struggle to block Republican traffic. Before the end of 1936, the Insurgents had captured fifteen Spanish merchant ships of over one thousand tons and nine smaller vessels, thus hugely increasing their import capacity, and had sunk five enemy merchant ships of over one thousand tons each.[3]

The Insurgents disguised their own merchant shipping to give the appearance of being Italian or German-registered. None was ever accosted by a Republican warship.[4] However, it was not until the end of the year that the Insurgents were able to begin a sustained campaign to prevent war and other material reaching the Republic.

The situation changed because Germany and Italy, which had been supplying the Insurgents with war material since the end of July 1936, were now going themselves to protect their ships, freeing the Insurgent navy to continue the war against Republican shipping.

The two dictatorships were supplying Franco with war material in frank contravention of their agreement not to do so. At the beginning of August 1936 the French government had proposed the pan-European Non-Intervention agreement. The assumption was that only the most rigid prohibition against supplying arms to both sides in Spain would avoid the risk of an international clash which might and, in the view of many, probably would, provoke a major European war only eighteen years after the end of the 1914–1918 conflict. Hitler's Nazi Germany and Mussolini's Fascist Italy had consented to Non-Intervention, as the policy became known, although they doubted its viability and intended to continue sending aid to Franco. Their justification was that there was no guarantee that Léon Blum's French Popular Front government, not to speak of the Soviet Union or USSR, would not supply the Republic.[5] The Russians, also signatories to the Non-Intervention pact (which was not a formal treaty but merely an exchange of letters stating the intention of all the signatories to introduce legislation forbidding their own nationals to supply arms to either Spanish side), noted very soon that Germany and Italy were not adhering to the agreement.[6]

II German Traffic

During the dictatorship (1923–1930) of General Primo de Rivera, Germany had cooperated to some extent with Spain in arms development in order to avoid the limitations imposed on German rearmament by the Treaty of Versailles which had ended the 1914–1918 war. Admiral Wilhelm Canaris, striving to combat the powerful British influence on Spanish warship-building, introduced German business into Spain and created new companies. The German attempt to supplant British influence was not however successful. More important, perhaps, were the preparations for a German Intelligence system which would cause problems for the Allies in the Second World War. Nevertheless, there is no indication that the Nazi state had knowledge of the military uprising which was being planned in 1936.

Rarely has rapidity in taking a decision, and energy and efficiency in carrying it out, been more evident than in the three hours in which General Franco's emissaries spoke to the German leader on the night of 25–26 July 1936 when the Fuehrer decided to aid Franco's Insurgents. His decision was surrounded by profound secrecy, which reflected the delicacy of the matter and required the camouflaging of the dispatch of German war material to Spain. The agreement to send aircraft to Franco to carry his men from the Spanish zone of Morocco over the Strait of Gibraltar to the Peninsula was taken late that night. By 9 the next morning an aircraft had already fetched Admiral Lindau from Hamburg to Bayreuth, where Hitler was attending the Wagner festival, to receive orders to prepare the port for the secret embarkation of men and the dispatch of aircraft by ship in sections. General Milch, Under-Secretary for Air, had received his orders and was back in Berlin with instructions to create a special Staff – *Sonderstab W* – to oversee the sending of aid to the Spanish general, 1,500 miles away in Morocco. Within *Sonderstab W* Milch set up the department for sea voyages or *Schiffahrtsabteilung*, which would direct the sailings of cargo ships to Spain.[7]

This department was established to camouflage German merchant ships as they sailed to Spain after two voyages of German vessels in the first weeks of the war had been publicised. One of them, the *Usaramo*, reached Cádiz on 6 August without being stopped by patrolling Republican warships, probably because its voyage was organised in minute detail. The ship, which carried the men of *Unternehmen Feuerzauber* or Operation 'Magic Fire' to Spain to fly the German aircraft, possessed advanced communication systems and an *ad hoc* code provided by the Germany navy.

Despite the secrecy in which the project to send aircraft and men to Spain was wrapped, rumours that Hitler was aiding Franco were circulating. On 27 July, a journalist noted 'Party circles are beginning to talk of help for the Rebels'.[8] Some evidence suggests that surviving anti-Nazi organisations among the Hamburg dockworkers got a message out to the Spanish socialist *UGT* organisation.[9] The Republican fleet would be on the watch. On 18 August the German ships *Kamerun* and *Wigbert*, wary of being stopped, unloaded their cargoes in Lisbon whence they were sent into Insurgent Spain by the sympathetic Portuguese government. However, despite fierce German threats to protect the freedom of their ships to enter ports controlled by the Insurgents, the fleet of German warships which had been sent to the Straits and the south-western Mediterranean – the battleship *Graf Spee*, the cruisers *Nürnberg* and *Leipzig*, and the destroyers *Jaguar, Wolf, Greif,* and *Falke* – received orders to avoid incidents, for the time being, with the Republican fleet.

The solution to the problem would consist in preparing the voyages of merchant ships with extreme thoroughness, camouflaging departures, changing the names of the ships, and imposing very strict radio discipline. At first Germany chartered ships for the arms traffic from Mathias Rohde & Co. of Hamburg, a firm which could be relied upon to maintain confidentiality. Loading would take place at night in an inconspicuous part of the port of Hamburg. German airmen and ground crew going to Spain, all in civilian clothes and with false papers, gathered at terminals under the banner of a travel agency. Buses would take them to the ship after dark, and they would all disappear below deck until the ship was out of sight of land. Artillery arrived at the dockside in furniture removal vans. The radio call signals were those of ships known to be in distant waters.

When in September 1936 larger contingents of men and material were dispatched to Spain, the port of Stettin was used, since military units and equipment were regularly leaving that port for East Prussia, and additional contingents could leave without causing any unusual notice. Ships' papers showed all cargoes consigned to Genoa, although Cádiz and Seville were the actual destinations. Ships were to leave and enter port only at night. Frequently these ships would load bulk Spanish copper or iron ore for the return journey.[10]

Germany chartered thirty-five merchant ships, which made 180 trips altogether to Spain. In the first months of the war, between August and December 1936, Germany merchant ships made fifty-nine voyages with 217,997 tons of war material for Franco's forces.[11] Only between 10 January and 27 March 1937, before the Sea Control Scheme of the Non-Intervention Committee came into operation, the *Schiffahrtsabteilung* dispatched sixteen *Sonderschiffe* or 'Special Ships' with a total of 18,774 tons. Once the naval patrol of the Non-Intervention Committee was functioning, the Germans organised a mock Panamanian shipping line, with cargo ships named *Acme*, *Balboa*, *Colón*, *Golfo de Darién*, and *Golfo de Panamá*. A ship would leave Hamburg or Stettin under its real name. Once on the high seas it would adopt the name of a Panamanian-registered cargo boat which was known to be in some distant ocean, but would revert to its real name as it entered German territorial waters on its return. The departure of the vessel could not be linked with its presence in the English Channel, in the Bay of Biscay or in an Insurgent harbour. Thus Germany got around the Non-Intervention control scheme. Even if it were suspected that the ships were carrying war material, Panama was not a signatory to the Non-Intervention agreement and its ships could not be legally stopped and searched. The extraordinary level of planning and secrecy, the ships equipped with the most up-to-date radio apparatus, the special codes, the imposition of complete radio silence except with German headquarters and the naval attaché stationed in Burgos, the Insurgent capital, explain the success of the covert supply of war material to Franco without the need to protect the cargo ships with warships. Admiral Raeder, Head of the *Kriegsmarine*, told Hitler on 22 August 1936, that there was no alternative to the procedures adopted.[12]

III The *Palos*

Not all ships which sailed from Germany to Spain were 'special' ships. Normal trade continued and many manufactured products were not war contraband as specified by the Non-Intervention Agreement. The *Palos*, a German cargo ship, was captured on 23 December 1936 by the armed Basque fishing trawler *Bizkaia* off Lequetio, a fishing port about fifty miles east of Bilbao. It was making for Pasajes, near San Sebastián, which was in Insurgent hands. The *Bizkaia* had captured the *Pluto*, another German cargo ship, on 20 December but had released it on the grounds that it was on the high seas. The captain of the *Palos* refused to allow his ship to be searched, insisting that the Basque trawler was not a naval vessel. The *Bizkaia* forced it to make for the Basque capital, Bilbao, where the *Palos* was searched and found to be carrying portable telephone equipment, celluloid in sheets ready to be used for preparing artillery shells, as well as some items of machinery intended for an Insurgent armed trawler. The *Palos* had been stopped five miles offshore, which was within the limit of territorial waters as claimed by Spain. The German navy reacted vigorously. The cruiser *Königsberg* sailed into Bilbao, demanding the release of the *Palos*, which it obtained on 29 December, though without the cargo, which Germany insisted was not directly or indirectly war material, and one of the passengers.[13] The German response to the Basque action was immediate. On 1 January 1937, off Almería on the south-east coast of Spain, the battleship *Graf Spee* seized the Spanish passenger ship *Aragón*, belonging to the *Compañía Transmediterránea* and en route to Málaga. On the same day the *Königsberg* pursued the steamship *Soton* until it ran aground at the entrance to the northern port of Santander. On 3 January, the *Königsberg* seized another ship, the *Marta Junquera*, with six hundred tons of cargo. The German naval command announced that it intended to take more of these severe measures until the cargo of the *Palos* was released, together with the Spanish passenger it was carrying. The German Foreign Ministry, the Wilhemstrasse, was told that even stronger measures might be taken, including attacks on Republican naval forces and shelling a coastal town. [14] The Wilhelmstrasse commented that it had doubts about shelling a town, because if doing this did not produce the required result, how much further could Germany go? Seizures of shipping, on the other hand, could be approved because the ships could be held as bargaining counters. The German High Command agreed to this and prepared an order in those terms with an ultimatum.[15] Time ran out on 8 January, 1937. The crews of the captured ships were released but the vessels themselves were handed over to the Spanish Insurgents. In the meantime the Spanish government had offered to submit the cargo of the *Palos* to international inspection. However, the Non-Intervention Committee was unwilling to risk proof of German supply of arms to the Insurgents, for it would contradict a major purpose of the Committee: to keep Germany, as well as Italy, which was also supplying Franco with arms, attending the meetings and, at least in theory, respecting the agreement not to supply arms to Spain. Fortunately, the matter had not gone too far. No Spanish Republican naval warship had been attacked and no town shelled by the German navy.

The *Palos* question is important. The questions of where the limits of territorial waters were to be drawn, of the rights of belligerency, the transport of war material and the right to stop, search and seize neutral ships were to influence the war on sea traffic throughout the Spanish conflict. Major questions were involved.[16]

Without belligerent rights, the navy of one side in a civil war may interfere with neutral traffic only within territorial waters (and in Spain the limits of these were disputed). Belligerency (implying the right to stop and search neutral ships on the high seas) should be granted to the constituted authority. In the Spanish war, this was the Republic, but absolute neutrality in the Spanish war required the same concession to be given to the Insurgents. To recognise the belligerent status of both sides, however, would have the effect of destroying the entire edifice of the Non-Intervention policy. Thus, during the entire Spanish Civil War, neither side was granted belligerent rights because, for the larger part of the conflict, such a concession would have benefited Franco principally, since the Republican navy did not dare to attack the ships of Germany and Italy, countries which did not recognise the legality of the Republican government. Consequently, both sides felt a strong sense of injustice: the Republic, internationally recognised, was trying to repress an internal rebellion by its own armed forces, while the Insurgents claimed that the Republican government was illegal and that the armed forces were obliged, by the *Ley Constitutiva del Ejército* of 29 November 1878, to defend Spain against 'internal' as well as external enemies. According to this argument, the Spanish Republic had been threatened by revolution and had not taken adequate steps, such as declaring martial law; therefore the armed forces had been obliged to do so, and this was the basis of the Insurgents' legal status. The Insurgents bitterly resented the British refusal to grant them belligerent rights and thus justify their interference with neutral traffic on the high seas.

The *Palos* case reinforced the German and indeed the British view that the Republican navy had no right to stop merchant ships on the high seas. Evidently, Germany was determined to run risks as it protected the 'special' ships, the euphemism for vessels carrying arms to Franco's Insurgents. At the same time, Germany would mask her own intervention by gathering and reporting to the Non-Intervention Committee information on everything to do with the naval movements of the Republic and ships carrying war material to Republican ports from other countries but principally from the Soviet Union from October 1936 onwards.

Consequently, German warships regularly informed the Franco side about Republican ships' movements.[17] *The Times* of 25 January 1937 reported this. On 4 June 1937, as Republican warships shelled Ceuta, the Spanish enclave on the Moroccan coast opposite Gibraltar, a German cruiser followed them, signalling to Insurgent ships. The Republicans complained to a British destroyer in the vicinity 'Please note the incessant harassment to which we are being subjected by a German cruiser.'[18]

More active aggression had became evident from late 1936 when, as part of the Condor Legion, the expeditionary air force which Germany kept in Spain until the Franco victory in 1939, squadron *AS/88* (*AufklärungsgruppeSee* or Sea Reconnaissance Group with the numerical value of "HH' or 'Heil Hitler!') arrived with Heinkel 59 sea-planes. These carried out long-range reconnaissance missions from Cádiz and were later transferred to the Moroccan coast to watch out for ships arriving from the Soviet Union and about to make the final dash from the north African coast to Cartagena. There were frequent complaints from shipping companies that the Heinkels were attacking them, in one case driving a merchant vessel aground.[19] They also attacked warships, achieving a hit with a 250 kg bomb on the Republican battleship *Jaime I* on the night of 23–24 May 1937.[20] A British supervisor working at the dockyard in the Insurgent naval base of El Ferrol for the mostly British-owned Sociedad Española de Construcción Naval, told the commander of the British destroyer HMS *Esk* on 3 October 1936 that the merchant ship *Nyassa* had brought anti aircraft guns and skilled German personnel.[21] On 17 October 1936 the captain of HMS *Electra* reported:

I am convinced that war material from Germany is being regularly landed on the coast of Galicia, with the help and connivance of German warships in these waters.

Nevertheless, added the captain of the British destroyer, 'Little can be done without prejudice to our own position, which depends entirely on the relations between our consuls and the local authorities.'[22] It was later confirmed that groups of German sailors had paraded through Spanish ports and that anti-aircraft batteries were being set up.[23] This reflects a strange contrast with the high level of secrecy maintained by the *Sonderschiffe*.

Germany contributed significantly to the Insurgent fleet. 121 requests for Franco's navy were sent to the organisation known as the HISMA (*Hispano-Marroquí de Transportes*), set up as a company in Tetuán on 31 July 1936 to conceal official German help. German aid for the Insurgent navy was calculated to total, from 3 March 1937 until 13 March 1939, 6,672,732.32 Reichmarks, equivalent to £572, 766 sterling. The naval material included steel plating, electrical cable, tubing, telemeters, spare parts for diesel engines, valves, artillery, platinum wire, shells, electric motors, voltamperimeters, radio-telegraph systems, searchlights, binoculars, chronographs and fire control systems.[24] The source for this information does not include details for the first few months of the war. Nevertheless, since the total value of material sent by Germany to Spain up to May 1937 was about 150 million Reichmarks, and since the navy's share of this was about four per cent, it suggests that about six million Reichmarks' worth was imported in the first six months of the war. In any case, German Foreign Office documents show that HISMA was not the only company involved.[25] On 29 October 1936 four 105 mm anti-aircraft guns and two 20 mm weapons arrived for the battleship *España*, four 20 mm anti-aircraft guns, three telemeters, a Telefunken radio receiver and twelve pairs of binoculars for the new cruiser *Canarias*, a radio goniometer for the base at Cádiz, ammunition and Telefunken radio equipment for the second new cruiser *Baleares*, the destroyer *Almirante Cervera* and the El Ferrol naval base as well as machine guns and depth charges for the armed trawlers and merchant ships. Heavy 150 mm guns were sent for the coastal batteries at the mouth of the river Gualdalquivir in the extreme south.[26] All this material came on the 'Special Ships', efficiently organised for this purpose by the *Sonderschiffeabteilung*. German aid was to some extent concealed, but given the presence of Royal Navy ships often inside the ports where the material was landed, Britain could hardly have been unaware of it.

In Insurgent Spain there was a German Naval Mission, composed of ten officers and seventy specialists, under the command of Lieutenant Commander Kurt Meyer-Döhner. They were stationed in Corunna and Vigo, supervising the unloading of war material and its installation on Insurgent ships. It was also tasked with instructing Spanish naval personnel in communications, coastal defence, mines and torpedoes. Specialised German personnel were to be found aboard the minelayers and minesweepers under construction and in the training centres for naval gunners. A small number of German petty officers were based in the naval college at San Fernando near Cádiz. Admiral Cervera writes, perhaps sincerely but also perhaps diplomatically in view of complaints about German brusqueness which often appear in accounts of the Germans in the Spanish civil war, that the Germans carried out their mission with absolute courtesy and good manners.[27]

IV Operation Ursula

How far was the German navy going to go in the direction of actively participating in the war on Franco's side? The diary of Rear-Admiral Rolf Carls, who commanded German warships in Spanish waters in 1936, is quite explicit. In October he wrote, using the term 'Whites' for the Francoist Insurgents:

> The protection of German lives and property is complete. Now we are going to begin the hidden but active participation of German naval forces in favour of the White cause [...] the Red fleet would be unable to act if the *Cervantes*, the *Libertad*, and the *Jaime I* were rendered unable to fight, but the Whites cannot do this.[28]

As Admiral Carls wrote, the German fleet was not authorised to attack Spanish Republican warships. However, if the minute Insurgent navy was unable to prevent war material reaching the Republic, something would have to be done. Were U-boats the answer?

Although submarines had been forbidden to Germany by the Treaty of Versailles, the German navy had kept its submarine designers together after 1918, developing plans for submarines for Spain among other countries. Once Hitler took power in January 1933, plans for building U-boats were reactivated.[29]

Lieutenant-Commander Arturo Génova, a submarine officer who had resigned from his post as naval attaché in the Paris embassy and returned to Spain to offer his services to the Insurgents, suggested appealing to Germany and Italy for submarines which could be used to attack the Republican fleet. He was sent to Berlin and Rome but in neither case were his missions fruitful. In Germany, in particular, Admiral Raeder, who was in overall command of the fleet, considered involving U-boats to be politically unwise and in any case did not want to risk losing a submarine at that early stage of German naval rearmament.

However, by late November Soviet arms supplies, including aircraft, were reaching Spain. Madrid had not fallen. Germany had sent its expeditionary air force, the Condor Legion.[30] The German High Command now changed its view and decided to send two U-boats to Spanish waters. The mission would be called Operation Ursula, the name of the daughter of Admiral Doenitz, overall U-boat commander. It was argued that operations off the Spanish coast would be valuable training for submarine crews. It may also have been thought politically advisable not to abandon submarine patrols completely to the Italian navy, which had already been active off Spain in that role.

Rear-Admiral Hermann Boehm would coordinate the activities of the *U-33* and *U-34*, commanded by Lieutenant-Commanders Kurt Freiwald and Harald Grosse. Leaving Wilhemshaven on the night of 20/21 November 1936, they slipped through the English Channel and past Gibraltar at night a week later. All visible markings had been removed. Their mission was to attack Republican warships and merchant shipping but always with great care and without coming to the surface. Even the Insurgents would not be notified. The German crews were threatened with the death penalty if any information about the U-boats emerged. They were to remain submerged all day, coming to the surface at night to recharge their batteries and communicate, in a special one-off code, with Rear Admiral Boehm. For emergencies they could make for the Italian port of La Maddalena on Sardinia.

The Italian submarines which had been operating in Spanish waters were relieved by the two U-boats on 29 November 1936. These began to patrol between Cartagena and Alicante. They attempted to torpedo a number of Republican warships. At 1902 hours on 1 December the *U-34* fired a torpedo at a Republican destroyer. On 5 December another torpedo missed the *Almirante Antequera*. 8 December saw another failed attack. Grosse reported that some of the torpedoes probably malfunctioned. It was also difficult to manoeuvre a U-boat into position to fire a torpedo at a fast-moving destroyer. On 8 December one of the U-boats identified the older Republican cruiser *Méndez Núñez* but was prevented from attacking it by a screen of destroyers.

On 10 December the German War Minister, Field Marshal von Blomberg, ordered the end of Operation Ursula. It had achieved little if anything and the risks of it being identified were too great. On 11 December 1936 the submarines left their patrol areas.

However, the following day, 12 December, at 1400 hours the *U-34* was on its way to the Strait of Gibraltar when, about four miles off the Málaga lighthouse, Lieutenant Commander Grosse raised his periscope and spotted the Republican submarine *C3* on the surface. At 1419 hours he fired a torpedo which hit the Spanish submarine amidships. The *C3* sank at once in seventy metres of water. Only three crew members were saved, probably because they had been in the conning tower and were hurled into the water when the submarine was hit. One was the second in command, a merchant navy officer with no submarine experience. Probably no watch was being kept.

The *U-34*, following orders, moved off at top speed. The Republican authorities issued a communiqué saying that their submarine had been torpedoed by an unknown foreign submarine, a euphemism for the Italian boat which they suspected had sunk the *C3*. Later reports, based on statements by fishermen and a coastguard cutter which was in the vicinity, said that there had been no explosion, but a sudden blaze and a puff of white smoke. The loss of the *C3* was attributed to an accidental internal explosion, either of the batteries or of a compressed air cylinder. Presumably the torpedo did not explode. This was the official view for many years after the war, although it was also suggested that the commander, Sub lieutenant Antonio Arbona, had sabotaged the *C3*.[31] However, oil bubbles were often noticed coming to the surface. In 1997, an amateur diver discovered the remains of a ship and in the following year professional Spanish navy divers confirmed that it was the *C3*.

Lieutenant Commander Grosse had taken a chance. There were other vessels in the vicinity which could have identified his submarine. He had to raise and lower his periscope very quickly to position himself. He reported that he did not raise his periscope to observe the result of the attack but that his hydrophone reported sounds of sinking. When he surfaced that night he radioed that he had sunk a Republican submarine of the C series.[32]

Germany was unwilling to suffer the international opprobrium of being accused of sinking merchant shipping, and so left the responsibility of conducting a submarine campaign to the Italian navy. Thereafter Germany would continue to provide Franco with war material but its role in Spain would be largely to contribute an air force, the Condor Legion, to be flown by Luftwaffe pilots.

V Italian Help for Franco's Insurgents

Mussolini's policy during the Spanish Civil War was aggressive, ignoring accepted standards of diplomatic behaviour. Fascist Italy could not allow Franco to lose. Victory for the Republic would be a triumph over Fascism for the Popular Front policy of the USSR. It would affect Italian prestige and strategic interests, such as control of the Western Mediterranean, the neutralization of the Balearic Islands and the constant fear that a left-wing Spanish regime would permit French colonial forces to cross from Africa to France in the case of a conflict between France and Italy.[33] Consequently, Mussolini reacted quickly to Franco's appeal for help, sending twelve Savoia-Marchetti SM-81 bombers, nine of which arrived safely on 30 July 1936. In later weeks a substantial number of other aircraft arrived.[34]

The first Italian arrival by sea with aid for the Insurgents was the *Emilio Morandi*, which brought the high-octane fuel that the bombers required. Up to the end of 1936 thirty Italian voyages brought war material. On 14 August Fiat fighters came on the *Nereide*. On 27 August arms came to Majorca on the *Emilio Morandi*. On 29 September more material arrived at Vigo in the *Città di Bengasi*. Other merchant ships arrived at Seville with war material from October onwards.[35] British consular records show that arrivals of Italian merchant ships in southern Spanish ports under Insurgent control more than doubled in number between 1935 and 1937:

	1935	1936	1937
Seville	13	19	111
Cádiz	19	10	37
Huelva	41	34	35
Totals	73	63	183[36]

Italian cargo ships would pick up a Spanish escort at Palma (Majorca). This island had been secured in August 1936, to a great extent by Italian aircraft which dispersed the Republican warships and thus deprived the expeditionary force of Republican militias, led by Captain Alberto Bayo, later an adviser to Cuba's revolutionary leader Fidel Castro, of support as they tried to overcome the Insurgent garrison. The Italian cruiser *Fiume* remained in Palma harbour until November, under the command of Captain Carlo Margottini, who, together with the brutal Fascist Arconovaldo Bonaccorsi, (nicknamed 'Conde Rossi'), galvanised the Spanish Insurgent command.

On 4 August, less than three weeks after the military uprising had begun in Morocco, an attempt was made to rationalise Nazi and Fascist aid to Franco. Admiral Canaris, head of the *Abwehr* or German Military Intelligence, travelled to Italy to coordinate the two countries' activities with his opposite number General Mario Roatta. Nothing concrete was established but an echo of the talks can be heard in a comment made by the pro-German Italian Foreign Minister, Galeazzo Ciano, son-in-law of Mussolini, to the German ambassador in Rome and repeated by the latter to Berlin:

> In any case [said Ciano] it would be convenient for officers of both our countries to come to an agreement [...] and fortunately it looks as if this is going to happen.[37]

Italy adhered to the Non-Intervention Agreement on 21 August, probably because she feared that without it the Soviet Union and Popular Front France would escalate their so far very little concrete aid to the Republic. Italian opinion was that Non-Intervention would be unlikely to place any physical barrier to supporting the Insurgents. In any case, as the German chargé d'affaires wrote frankly from Rome, Italy had no intention of respecting Non-Intervention.[38] In Rome a special body, the *Ufficio Spagna*, was set up to coordinate Italian military, air and naval activities in Spain.

Admiral Domenico Cavagnari, chief of staff of the Italian navy, was strongly opposed to any major participation in Spain.[39] Nevertheless, he was overruled by Mussolini and Ciano. On 28 August, Canaris met Roatta once more to plan the details of each country's military aid to Insurgent Spain. So far, the quantity of support from both countries had been relatively small, consisting of eighty aircraft, five small tanks, thirty-two anti-aircraft guns, ninety machine guns and eight thousand rifles.[40] From now on there would be many more voyages to Spain. The Italian naval mission to Insurgent Spain reached Cádiz in September, led by Captain Giovanni Remedio Ferreti. The Fascist navy was about to take a much higher profile.

On 21 October 1936, by which time the Insurgents were becoming alarmed at the quantity of armaments being shipped from the Soviet Union to Republican ports, Italian fast motor torpedo boats or MAS were dispatched to the Sicilian Channel between Sicily and Tunisia in order to keep watch over shipping making for Spain. At the same time Italian warships were patrolling Spanish waters. Unlike the wary Germans, the Italians did not conceal their activities, ignoring their agreement not to intervene in the Spanish war. The captain of a British destroyer sent an alarming message to the Admiralty reporting that an Italian naval officer had warned him that Italian warships were about to shell a Mexican ship anchored in Alicante and which was suspected of having brought a cargo of arms.[41]

While this threat was not carried out, Italy did agree to supply submarines. By their very nature, submarines cannot comply with international law as it applies to the sinking of cargo ships, because they cannot rescue passengers or crew. Captain Ferretti and Admiral Cervera, chief of staff of the Insurgent navy, held talks. The Italians were unwilling to send submarines openly to take part in the war, so on 4 November four Spanish officers arrived at La Maddalena, the Italian naval base on the island of Sardinia, to take over formal though not actual command of the submarines which were to be sent. In this way, it was hoped that Italian participation could be hidden.[42]

Italy would send a total of thirty-eight submarines, in several groups, to the Spanish Mediterranean coast. On 8 November 1936 the submarine *Naiade* left harbour under Italian Lieutenant Vocaturo, but with Spanish Lieutenant Commander Arturo Génova in nominal command. The orders of the *Naiade* were to destroy merchant ships flying the flag of the Spanish Republic or of the Soviet Union making for Cartagena. To this were added instructions that the submarines could attack Republican warships wherever they were. Merchant ships could not be attacked outside of territorial waters and the submarine captains had to be sure that they making for Cartagena. The presence of the submarines had to be kept secret. They had to submerge if there was a risk of being seen. If a submarine was wrecked or captured the Spanish officer aboard it was to claim to be the captain. The submarines would leave La Maddalena at night. They would spend ten days in Spanish waters, surfacing at night to charge their batteries.

On 9 November the *Topazio* left La Maddalena, followed on 15 November by the *Antonio Scesa* and on 17 by the *Torricelli*, all with a Spanish officer as notional commander. On 22 November, at 0950 hours, the *Torricelli*, commanded by Captain Zarpellon and with Commander Génova and at least one other Spanish officer on board, achieved a significant victory, seriously damaging the cruiser *Miguel de Cervantes*, at anchor in the outer part of Cartagena harbour without anti-submarine protection, which was not thought necessary because all the Spanish submarines were in Republican hands. Periscope visibility was good. At the last moment the battleship *Jaime I*, which was the main target, began to turn away, so two torpedoes were fired at the *Miguel de Cervantes* at 1,000 and 750 metres range after the *Torricelli* waited for a British destroyer, the *Glow Worm*, to move out of the way. The *Miguel de Cervantes* was sideways on and an excellent target. Both torpedoes hit the cruiser, creating a large hole on the starboard side and filling the engine room with water. The *Miguel de Cervantes* was too large for the Cartagena dry dock and would not be fit for sea duties for over a year.

To avoid risk of identification the Italian submarine moved away as swiftly and as silently as possible, without raising its periscope to check the result of its attack. The report of the attack underlines the poor response of the other Republican ships in the area. No depth charges were dropped.[43] The commander of HMS *Glow Worm* reported that the Republican cruiser *Méndez Núñez* and three destroyers criss-crossed the area trying to locate the submarine, but the low-ranking commanders of Republican warships did not seem to have been trained to corral a submarine after a torpedoing.[44]

The Insurgents possessed no submarines. Unwilling to admit that the submarine which had holed the *Miguel de Cervantes* was Italian, they muddied the waters by claiming that the submarine was the Spanish Republican *B-5*. This had been sabotaged by its captain but the Insurgents claimed that they had recovered and repaired it.[45] The commander of the Republican submarine flotilla, Remigio Verdiá,

reported on 7 December that the torpedo which was recovered was a
Whitehead 533, like those used by the Spanish navy but with steel screws
to fix the warhead to the compressed air chamber, proving it to be of
Italian manufacture.[46] Furthermore, the size of the torpedo showed that
it could not have been fired from the *B-5*. The captain of HMS *Glow
Worm*, which had passed briefly between the submarine and its target,
stated in his report that the torpedoes were certainly not Spanish.[47] The
Republican government insisted that a foreign submarine had attacked
the cruiser and accused the German navy, whose aggressive behaviour
in favour of the Insurgents was notorious.[48] The Republican authorities
asked the Captain of the *Glow Worm* to certify that the submarine was
German and that it had been informed of the presence of the *Miguel de
Cervantes* by the German warship *Leopard*, which had dropped anchor
in Cartagena on 20 November. However, since German submarines
were not known to be in the area, the Republican government failed
to convince the Non-Intervention Committee, which was in any case
generally unwilling to provoke the German or the Italian representative
because Britain and France wanted to keep Germany and Italy on the
committee and try to lessen their intervention in Spain. So, despite the
efforts of the Opposition in the House of Commons, the First Lord of
the Admiralty, Sir Samuel Hoare, well-known as a Franco supporter,
refused to open an investigation. If Germany or Italy were proved to have
attacked the *Miguel de Cervantes* in territorial waters, the entire edifice of
Non-Intervention would collapse and it was feared that this would lead to
a severe international crisis and perhaps war. Yet it seemed obvious that
the submarine which had attacked the *Miguel de Cervantes* was Italian. If
the submarine had been forced to surface, the presence of Spanish officers
would have demonstrated that Italy was supplying the boat and the crew
to the Insurgents.

On 10 December 1936 Mussolini went further and ordered Italian
participation in the land war in Spain. Three thousand Fascist militia
were to fight for Franco.[49] As for cargo vessels, the Insurgent naval staff
under Admiral Cervera instructed its ships and the Italian warships that
they might stop and search ships flying the Mexican and Soviet flag
(neither country had warships in the vicinity to escort their merchant
shipping), but that they should be prudent and not fire in the case of
ships of other nationalities. In the case of British vessels, Insurgent naval

commanders were to advise Gibraltar or a British warship, and fire a shot over the bows to stop the merchant ship if it refused to stop, but no further action was to be undertaken.

Nevertheless, Insurgent progress in stopping foreign merchant shipping reaching Republican ports was not thought satisfactory. Apart from the successful attack on the *Miguel de Cervantes*, the thirty-eight Italian submarines which patrolled the Spanish coast in groups between 8 November 1936 and 14 February 1937 sank only two merchant ships with innocuous cargoes. The Italian submarines had indeed a very difficult task. Their results, leaving aside the torpedoing of the *Miguel de Cervantes*, were poor, although probably they had inhibited Soviet-registered ships from approaching Republican Spain. Because they had orders not to surface, submarine captains complained that even in daylight it was hard to identify the flag or the name of a freighter. The torpedoes frequently misfired. One interesting phenomenon was that the Spanish officer on board in one case, reported by the captain of the *Naiade* on 12 November 1936, was clearly unwilling to give a positive identification of a Spanish warship. The Italian captain suggested that 'this must be due to a premeditated and intentional sense of loyalty ('*Doveva essere una omertà voluta e premeditata*') to the Spanish fleet, even though the latter was under the flag of the Republic.[50]

A greater contribution was made by the thirteen Italian cruisers and twenty-two destroyers which escorted sixty-two ships carrying the *Corpo di Truppe Volontarie* or *CTV*, the 42,500 troops that Mussolini sent to Spain. The Republic fleet did not try to stop them, although the cruiser *Méndez Núñez* spotted merchant ships on the 12, 14, 16, 21 and 21 of January 1937 and its commander, Lieutenant Prado, suggested:

It might be wise to check to see if any of these ships are carrying Italian war material or troops

The somewhat diffident tone of the message, which did not receive a reply, contrasts with the very clear orders received by the Insurgents, who recognised the most urgent tasks that had to be accomplished.

Yet another conference was held on 30 December between the now Rear Admiral Moreno, the senior German commander, Rear Admiral Hermann von Fishchel, the Italian vice admiral Angelo Jachino, the naval attachés, and the Italian naval mission. There was a certain amount of tension. The Germans were critical of what they judged the 'inactivity' of the Insurgents, who had two cruisers in the Western Mediterranean, one of which was the ultra-modern *Canarias*, apart from the minor naval forces which they had in the Balearics. The Germans thought that the Insurgents should be much more aggressive against all merchant ships, although this might have risked British intervention. The Germans insisted that the two Insurgent cruisers should attack Republican warships which were escorting convoys bringing war material into Alicante and Cartagena. The Spaniards thought that the Germans did not realise how exiguous the Insurgent forces were and how short even the *Canarias* was of essential equipment.[51] This probably represents differences in national traditions and psychology. The Germans, aware of even small chances of success, told Moreno that his ships should cruise at nightfall around seventy miles from Cape Palos at a point where the merchant ships picked up their escorts. His views were contested and voices were raised when the German admiral suggested a joint command. What the Insurgents wanted were foreign warships who would obey Spanish orders, an unlikely outcome. When the Spaniards declared that they wanted 'to make things clear', the German commander, according to the account of the meeting, beat a retreat and said he was thinking of liaison officers only.[52]

It would appear from this important document that the Insurgent Spaniards were exaggerating their weakness. They put forward in their arguments that the 'Reds' had 200 naval officers and 500 other Russians, and there were rumours of 20,000 troops. The truth was that the Republican navy had barely fifty-five officers of the *Cuerpo General*, many of them junior and untrusted; there was a handful of Soviet advisers and the 'twenty thousand men' referred to scarcely-trained volunteers, none of whom were Soviet, for the International Brigades. The Italians and the Germans, whose information seemed of high quality, doubted the capacity and will to fight of the Republican submarines, and this inclined them to urge the Insurgents to be more aggressive.

Clearly Germany wished to reduce its overt collaboration with the Insurgent navy. The U-boats of Operation Ursula returned home. The German Foreign Ministry had told the German ambassador in Rome, Count Ulrich von Hassell, that Italy had more urgent interests in Spain than Germany and that German participation in the Spanish war should be lessened. Von Hassell analysed the situation in a letter to Berlin of 18 December 1936. He was becoming unsure of whether the German intervention in Spain was wise. It would be better to allow Italy to take the lead in helping Franco. Germany had no diplomatic interests in Spain, other than to prevent a communist takeover.[53] Nevertheless, Germany kept two flotillas off Spain, with the pocket battleships *Deutschland* and *Admiral Scheer*, cruisers and six destroyers, probably for reasons of prestige and rivalry with the Royal Navy, which maintained two flotillas of destroyers patrolling between Gibraltar, Alicante and Barcelona.

On 17 November 1936 Franco had warned the British government that he intended to shell Barcelona and that British ships should not anchor in the port.[54] The British response referred to an Act which Parliament was about to pass (it would be the Merchant Shipping (Carriage of Munitions to Spain) Act of 3 December 1936), which would prohibit ships flying the Red Ensign from carrying war material to Spain, even if the cargo originated in countries which had not agreed to participate in the Non-Intervention Agreement.[55] Sir Henry Chilton, British ambassador to the Republic, who now resided in Hendaye, just over the French frontier, and communicated messages from London to Insurgent Spain, explained that Royal Navy ships would be able to stop and oblige British-registered merchant ships to go to Gibraltar or Malta, where they could be searched. Thus there was no need for Insurgent warships to interfere with British freighters. The Insurgents in general respected British insistence on this point, although it was always possible that no British warship was available to oblige the merchant to stop. Nevertheless, the Insurgents told the commanders of their ships that British merchant ships would respect the rules and that they should treat them with kid gloves.[56]

There was soon a case of interference with an innocent cargo ship. This was the Norwegian *Lisken* – with no warship to defend it – carrying potatoes from Dundee to Valencia. Armed Insurgent fishing trawlers stopped the *Lisken* off Finisterre in north-west Spain and forced it to sail into the Galician port of Vigo, where the potatoes were removed from the hold. The *Lisken* had sailed with a British cargo from a Scottish port and so Opposition members of Parliament besieged Anthony Eden, the Foreign Secretary, with questions. Was this not a case of bare-faced piracy? The *Lisken* was a neutral and its cargo could not be described as armaments, unless virtually anything could be. Labour members pressed the government to take some action, such as sequestering an Insurgent ship or blockading the port from which the armed trawlers had emerged to force the *Lisken* to follow them. The government refused, as it would throughout the Spanish conflict, to take the aggressive action that Labour MPs demanded. It contrasted strongly with the German response to the Basque capture of the *Palos*.

This would be the general pattern. Franco's Insurgent navy wanted to avoid clashes with Britain, but its habit was often to act first and then make excuses. The British government never undertook action against the Insurgent fleet and certainly not against German or Italian ships, even when, as happened more and more often, British merchant ships were attacked.

Nevertheless, even though the Insurgents set up a network of Intelligence with agents in Marseilles, Bucharest, the Dardanelles, Oran, Algiers, Bordeaux, St Nazaire, Le Havre and other ports, they were often slow to react, and the information was often incorrect. Ships bringing war material to the Republic were usually able to take refuge under the protection of Republican warships before the Insurgents took action. Even when British vessels were stopped, and taken to Gibraltar or Malta by a Royal Navy warship, they were found to be carrying non-military cargoes.

Chapter 7

The War Against Traffic Continues as the Russians Send War Material to the Republic

I The Insurgents Become More Active

In the first five months of the Spanish Civil War Franco's Insurgent navy had enjoyed little success in blocking shipments of weapons to the Republicans. However, now that the Italian navy was obstructing the movements of the not very active or efficient Republican fleet, the Insurgents, with their armed trawlers and their disciplined and politically purged crews, began to act more aggressively.

On 31 December 1936, the British freighter *Etrib*, sailing from Haifa to Liverpool, was stopped off Europa Point, at the tip of Gibraltar.[1] At the same time, the likewise British *Bluebell* was fired on as it entered a port on the northern coast of Spain to take on iron ore.[2] Another British cargo ship, the *Bramhill*, steaming between Barcelona and Bilbao, was stopped on the high seas west of Gibraltar, on 13 January. The cruiser HMS *Sussex* forced the Insurgent ship to desist.[3]

The Insurgents had no right in international law to stop foreign cargo ships. However, they judged that British traffic was significant, particularly back and forth to ports in northern Spain, even if the ships were not bringing war material, because to supply Basque heavy industry with British coal, to ship Basque iron ore to British iron and steel factories, thus earning foreign currency, and to take in foodstuffs, were activities which supported the war effort of the Republican zone of northern Spain. Furthermore, it was British ships in large part which carried the coastal traffic from the Mediterranean ports to the Cantabrian coast, which was the only way that the main part of Republican Spain could communicate with its northern zone.

Therefore the Insurgents decided to remove even non-military material from ships which they stopped.[4] A diplomatic protest was the worst they could expect, but they seemed willing to risk more aggressive reaction given that some British-registered ships were suspected of bringing in arms. Such suspicions were aroused perhaps because towards the end of 1936 and the early part of 1937, Admiralty reports concluded that some six British-registered cargo boats were carrying war materials from non-British ports to both Spanish sides.[5] The masters were concerned only with selling the war material to one party or the other. When, for example, the skipper of the *Stanmore* found that the Insurgents were refusing to accept the aircraft he carried because they did not come equipped with suitable bombs, he sold the machines to the Republican authorities in Alicante.[6]

The *Stanmore* belonged to the Stanhope Company, controlled by the British shipowner Jack Billmeir. Beginning in 1934 with only two ships, this enterprise expanded enormously during the Spanish war, taking advantage of the great volume of freightage which was on offer. On 30 October 1936, Billmeir was questioned by Board of Trade officials. He admitted that his ships carried coal and foodstuffs to Spain. He also said that his ships had been chartered to carry aircraft and spare parts from Rotterdam, but this was not illegal until the Merchant Shipping (Carriage of Munitions to Spain) Act of 3 December 1936 came into force. Billmeir insisted that he did not know the nature of the cargo until it came on board the ship. In any case, he said, temporary charters were too risky and he was not going to accept any more. Some days later, the British consul at Marseilles cabled urgently to tell London that the *Stanmore* was loading packing cases that had arrived from Antwerp in sealed railway wagons. This was probably a piece of information from a spy. Nevertheless, the consul was instructed to visit the *Stanmore*. He concluded that the cases were probably empty. The Foreign Office accepted this and for the time being no further questions arose about the Stanhope Shipping Company.

Another shipper attracted Board of Trade attention. This was Angel, Sons and Co. of Cardiff. Their ship, the *Hillfern*, was observed on 28 October at Gdansk preparing to take on a cargo destined for Spain. Mr Angel was called in for interview. He said that his ship had been chartered. He hoped he could expect the protection of the Royal Navy, as was his right, if the Insurgents tried to stop the *Hillfern*. He was doing nothing illegal and other British shipping companies were doing the same. This was right, but arms traffic coming from neutral countries in British ships was embarrassing for the British government which was playing such an important part in advocating Non-Intervention. This time the officials of the Board of Trade, who could perhaps exercise means of pressure which they did not minute in the accounts of their meetings with the shipowners, persuaded Mr Angel to cancel his chartering agreement, though it was too late to stop the *Hillfern*, which arrived safely at Bilbao. He did not, however, repeat the arrangement.

Another of the Board of Trade interviews with shipowners was somewhat more dramatic. Maclay and MacIntyre of Glasgow were offered the chance by the Soviet Union to carry freight to Spain. Its nature was not revealed. When the Board of Trade discovered this, or perhaps Maclay and MacIntyre consulted the officials, they warned the shippers that the voyage would be dangerous and that the Royal Navy could not offer adequate protection. Mr Maclay replied that his captains received general cargo and could not be sure that no war material was included. The Admiralty was consulted, and replied in somewhat informal language that 'The Russians are not doing this to send Christmas crackers to Spain.' This was a biased comment. The Russians might well be sending military material but they were certainly sending non-military goods as well.

The Russian effort to help the Spanish Republic, conducted by a country with no naval presence in the Mediterranean, was important and *sui generis*. It came as a result of several weeks of almost unconcealed German and especially Italian aid to Franco in the form of aircraft and all sorts of military hardware, as well as air force personnel. Although no Soviet warships took part, the Russians sent naval officers and other experts to Republican Spain. Another Soviet contribution was accepting, storing, smelting and selling, on the international market, the Spanish gold reserve. Four Russian ships, the *Kuban*, the *Neva*, the *KEM* and the *Vongoles*, reached Odessa on 2 November 1936 carrying 7,800 cases containing 510 tons of Spanish gold bars and coins.[7]

II The Russians Enter the Scene[8]

Commander Nikolai Kuznetsov was commanding a cruiser on manoeuvres in the Black Sea when he was ordered to go to Republican Spain as naval attaché of the embassy which had arrived on 27 August 1936 and, for the first time since the Russian revolution, had established diplomatic relations between Spain and the Soviet Union. In a set of essays about

Nikolai Kuznetsov, senior Russian naval adviser to the Spanish Republican fleet, taken probably when he was Soviet Minister of the Navy. (*Source: Ministry of Defence of the Russian Federation, Mil.ru*)

Soviet officers in Spain, Kuznetsov describes his long and complicated journey to Madrid.[9]

On 23 August 1936 the USSR had agreed to the Non-Intervention proposal made originally by the French Foreign Ministry. Aware of the support that Portugal was giving to the Insurgents, the USSR had made its participation in the scheme conditional on Portuguese cooperation because the landing of German war material in Lisbon to avoid the Republican navy blockade and its transport into Insurgent Spain was well-known. The USSR, however, had no naval interests and no presence in the Mediterranean. Its motives for aiding Republican Spain were ideological and political. In this it contrasted sharply with Italy and to a lesser extent Germany. The former had major naval and political interests in the zone, while the latter maintained a large naval presence there. Both dictatorships were interested in hindering the British and French dominion of the western Mediterranean. The Soviet dilemma was that, as the world leader of the interests of the working-class, it could not look on indifferently while the Insurgents won the conflict against a progressive Republic with the help of Fascist Italy and Nazi Germany, but at the same time it could not allow itself the luxury of intervening openly as an ally of the Republic. To do so would prejudice the other major plank of Soviet policy: to persuade Britain and France that Germany and Italy, and not the USSR, were the real expansionist powers. Thus, at the outset of the war, Soviet help to the Republic was limited to the mobilization of the extensive propaganda resources of the communist world, massive collections to send food and medical aid, and to the organisation by world communist parties of volunteers who would man the International Brigades of the Popular Army of the Republic.[10]

Like most of the Russians who went to Spain during the civil war, Kuznetsov did not speak Spanish.[11] In contrast, Germans who were to liaise with Spaniards were in many cases chosen precisely because they had lived in Spanish-speaking America, while others learned to speak the language. Italians, one supposes, were to a considerable extent able to make themselves understood in Spanish. In the Russian case, the deficiency was serious. If a Russian adviser did not speak Spanish or even French, especially if he was unfamiliar with specialised terms for aircraft, artillery or naval equipment and terminology, there was a risk of serious misunderstanding. In any case, conversation would be limited to simple phrases. Interpreters were, therefore, essential for the Russians. There is evidence of about 150 interpreters serving in Spain, most of whom have Russian names, though some were Latin Americans who had lived in the USSR.[12]

Among the interpreters were Anatoli Gurevich, Mikhail Ivanov and Pyotr Naimushin, who were students at the Leningrad School of Foreign Tourism. They crossed the frontier into Republican Spain on 30 December 1937. After an intensive but short course in Spanish, Gurevich, alias 'Antonio González', Semyon Pankin alias 'Simón Rubio', and Mikhail Ivanov alias 'Miguel Viñas' were sent to Cartagena to interpret for the navy. Gurevich later served on the Republican submarine *C4* under Lieutenant Commander Burmistrov. This submarine was used to send Lev Vasilevsky as a guerrilla leader to Majorca in summer 1938.[13] However, the mostly female interpreters in the navy were not permitted to sail, with the exception of Maria Skavronskaya, who interpreted on board the cruiser *Libertad* for Captain Nikolai Basistiy, the Russian adviser.[14]

Like many of the Russian advisers who arrived in Spain, Kuznetsov stresses, perhaps overmuch, that no particular mission was reserved for him. His rather innocent tone ('as for what I was to do, for the moment nobody was able to give me specific instructions') could not be quite genuine.[15] His rank was the equivalent of a Royal Navy commander and he must have been entrusted with preparing the arrival and unloading of Soviet war material and been given orders regarding his relations with Spanish naval officers. In Madrid, he met Lieutenant Prado, at the time Head of Operations of the Republican navy, who accompanied the Russian to the naval base of Cartagena. Here he met Lieutenant Antonio Ruiz, commander of the base. According to Kuznetsov, Ruiz 'was not fond of hard work and observed rather than directed daily business at Cartagena'.[16]

For the moment, Kuznetsov did not have authority to go to sea on a warship. At the beginning, he spent several days, he writes, wandering around in the summer heat, trying to gather information. Nobody gave him any but eventually Kuznetsov received permission to visit all the naval installations in Cartagena. In his book he criticises the Spanish Republican officers. He thinks that their professional competence was poor, their capacity to organise and their discipline insufficient, and that it was poor organization and leadership, together with a grave lack of Intelligence which led to their loss of control over the Strait of Gibraltar and their failure to prevent the Insurgents using Algeciras as their major port for disembarking reinforcements from Morocco.[17]

In time Kuznetsov was able to gather information which informed Moscow in detail of the deficiencies of the Republican fleet, its shortage of torpedoes and anti-aircraft ammunition. Later he concluded that there were only forty experienced Republican naval officers, which was probably an over-estimate. He writes that most of the officers were low-ranking. There was not one officer with staff qualifications. Operatively and tactically, he adds, the Republican navy was not even minimally ready for a naval war. Officers had had only insufficient and out-of-date training. The secret communication codes had not been changed and could be read by the enemy. What is more, the Spanish officers were obstinately inclined to refuse to accept advice, and none of the Russian advisers could speak Spanish.

However, what most appalled Kuznetsov were the on-board sailors' committees. This for him was infantile revolutionarism, which the Soviet navy itself had had to crush at Kronstadt. For Kuznetsov, the lack of organisation, leadership and firm direction, added to anarchistic indiscipline, rendered ineffective the efforts of petty officers and officers.[18] When he was officially received by the Central Committee of the fleet he surprised them by telling them that they had made the same mistake as the Bolsheviks in 1917: they had got rid of the officers rather than using them.[19]

In October 1936 the Soviet ambassador summoned Kuznetsov to Madrid and informed him that the USSR considered that Non-Intervention had failed and that Moscow was going to send arms to the Republic. His responsibility would be to supervise the unloading of the war material at Cartagena, the base of the Republican navy.

The first Soviet freighter to arrive was the *Neva*. This ship left Odessa on 18 September 1936, dropping anchor at Alicante on the 25. It was not carrying war material but butter, margarine, sugar and other foodstuffs, the result of the collections of funds made in the Soviet Union and described by the German chargé d'affaires in Moscow, von Tippelskirch, in a message to Berlin.[20] Von Tippelskirsch concluded his analysis of Soviet actions by doubting the rumours which were circulating about Soviet arms shipments, although he noted the fierce Soviet criticism of the Non-Intervention policy. In a further letter von Tippelskirch added that a further cargo of foodstuffs was being prepared and would arrive in the *Kuban*. However, the size and type of packing cases being used and the restrictions on access to Black Sea ports, were suspicious. He wondered whether the *Neva* had landed rifles and ammunition as well as foodstuffs.[21]

It would have been strange if the Russians had not taken the opportunity to include small amounts of war material amid the sugar and the margarine. On the other hand, if the secrecy of the shipments was as rigorous as the German diplomat described, there was no sure way of knowing that arms were indeed included. German agents in Black Sea ports and in the Dardanelles probably reported what they thought their readers wanted to know and would reward.

The importance of the voyage of the *Neva* was that it allowed the Soviets to plan later ones. The NKVD or Soviet secret service approved the captains and the crews of ships which sailed to Spain. It had already sent Captain Kornievski, of the Long Distance Sea Service, to Spain in August and September.[22]

At the meeting on 4 November 1936 of the ambassadors in London who constituted the Non-Intervention Committee, German, Italian and Portuguese complaints against the USSR were discussed. Twelve air force pilots were alleged to have arrived on the *Neva*, while the *Kuban* was said to have brought ammunition.[23] There may have been some leak of information when a Spanish vessel, the *Campeche*, had sailed from Feodosia, arriving on 4 October with twenty thousand old rifles and 750 machine-guns.[24] Nevertheless, this was much less than what had already been brought to Franco's Insurgents by the German 'Special Ships' and Italian escorted freighters, not to mention the activities of the fleets of both Italy and Germany off the Spanish coast.

12 October 1936 marks the first arrival of substantial military aid from the Soviet Union to the Spanish Republic. On that day the *Komsomol*, the first of what were designated *Igrek* or 'Y' vessels, dropped anchor in Cartagena with a cargo of Soviet tanks and a group of tank drivers under the command of Colonel Semyon Krivoshein.[25] In contrast with the extraordinary measures of security taken when the ship left, its arrival was widely observed by foreign ships, including the German destroyer *Luchs*, whose commander immediately communicated the news of the arrival of tanks and crews, as did the British destroyer *Grafton*.[26] In fact, several ships on their way to Spain were observed by the spies working for the Italian naval attaché in Istanbul, who reported the passage through the Dardanelles of, among others, the *Komsomol*, the *Kursk*, and the *Blagoev*.[27]

Twelve days before the *Komsomol* arrived, the Russian representative on the Non-Intervention Committee announced '[...] my Government is obliged to state that if these (German and Italian) violations do not cease immediately it will consider itself free from its obligations under the Non-Intervention agreement'.[28] Possibly the USSR hoped that the publicity of the arrival of the *Komsomol* would call attention to the activities of the Committee of Enquiry into Alleged Breaches of the Non-Intervention Agreement in Spain, a body which had been set up by the British Independent MP Eleanor Rathbone, and by the motion before the British Labour Party conference on 5 October which criticised the Non-Intervention Committee.

The *Komsomol* was followed by the *Stari Bolshevik*, the *KIM*, the *Volgoles*, the *Lepin*, the *Andreev* (from Leningrad to Bilbao), the *Kursk*,

Soviet cargo ship *Kursk*, unloading at Alicante.

the *Blagoev*, the British *Hillfern*, several Spanish freighters, the *Chicherin* and the *Turksib*. The latter arrived with Soviet personnel on 16 February 1937. Thereafter the ships which brought material from the USSR up to August 1938 were either Spanish or belonged to a new line specifically created by the Spanish Republican government helped by the French Communist Party and called France-Navégation (see below).[29]

Several other Soviet ships were reported by agents to be sailing to Spain with war material. However, it is likely that either these vessels were not bound for Spain or, if they were, they were not carrying war material.[30]

Russian archival evidence underlines the relative difficulties of assembling war material to send to the Republic, compared with German and Italian deliveries to Franco. There were great difficulties in bringing aircraft, heavy artillery and tanks from far-flung places in the Soviet Union to a Black Sea port. Kuznetsov mentions problems in finding shipping space, because the total tonnage of the Soviet Merchant Marine was a fraction of that of the other great merchant navies of the world. To ship the Soviet Tupolev SB bomber, for example, required vessels with large hatches. In contrast, German bombers flew to Spain via Italy, while Italian machines flew from Sardinia to Palma and then the mainland.

Soviet warships did not enter the Mediterranean. The Soviet navy was hampered by an unimaginative defensive tradition, an aged fleet, poor training and little operational experience. It was not ready to face a challenge from a modern fleet. Kuznetsov, a future People's Commissar or Minister for the Navy, himself admits that:

> During the events in Spain, we [the USSR] could not develop our role [...] because we lacked adequate ships. It was then that we realised how important the sea was for us and how much we needed a strong navy.[31]

Consequently, escorting the freighters which brought arms from the USSR was the most important mission allotted to the Republican navy, which, as a result, failed to develop an aggressive mentality as had been characteristic of the Insurgents since the beginning of the war.

III Soviet Personnel in the Republican Fleet

According to the official Soviet account of the international contribution to the Spanish Republican war effort, seventy-seven Soviet naval personnel were in Spain at some time during the civil war, acting as advisers and occasionally taking active roles in the Republican navy.[32]

Strangely, the Navy Minister, Indalecio Prieto, could not identify foreign personnel serving as advisers in the Republican navy. On 13 September 1937 he ordered the Central Committee of the fleet to provide a list of absolutely all foreign personnel, as well as their ranks and salaries. The reply listed fifteen names with ranks ranging from *Capitán de Corbeta* (Lieutenant Commander) down through the ranks to an interpreter, adding that there were others on the destroyers who had not been included.[33] The Spanish Navy Historical Service added a few names to this list in 1963.[34] Most of these were Russians, although 'T. Hadivin' was named on the 1963 list. He was identified later as the British Tommy Hadwin.[35] This was the extent of information available until Soviet archives were opened.[36]

Kuznetsov and Nikolai Annin were the first of seventy-seven Russian personnel to arrive for service in the Republican navy. They were followed in November by Valentin Petrovich Drozd (alias 'Ramón Hernández').

Returning to the USSR he reached the rank of Vice-Admiral and was killed on 29 January 1943. Drozhd was accompanied by Semyon Ramashvili (alias 'Juan García'), who later rose to the rank of rear admiral. Ramashvili, who soon learnt to speak good Spanish, became adviser to the commander of the Cartagena base, and Drozhd adviser to the commander of the destroyer flotilla.

At first the Soviet naval officers encountered opposition. Kuznetsov tried to explain this to his superiors. When he had suggested more systematic training for the Republican fleet, the Sailors' Committee objected that they knew how to fight. Considerable tact was needed to persuade the Spanish commanders to undertake the naval exercises that the Soviets thought essential.[37] In time, however, things changed and the Soviet officers began to organise specialised courses. With great effort the Republican warships began to act like professional navy vessels although the lack of equipment and properly trained naval personnel would always be a drawback.

Many more Soviet officers arrived on the *Chicherin* on 26 November 1936. Among them were Lieutenant Commander Ivan Bykov, who was attached to the artillery command of the cruiser *Méndez Núñez*, and Labudin (alias 'Juan Sánchez'), artillery adviser on the battleship *Jaime I*, together with others. Later Ivan Burmistrov (alias 'Luis Martínez'), a submarine officer, commanded Spanish submarines (see below). Thirty-two more Soviet advisers arrived in mid-1937, among them Commander Vladimir Alafuzov, who succeeded Kuznetsov as senior counsellor, and Captain Aleksandr Alexandrov, who acted as adviser to the Republican navy commander in the Cantabrian Sea.[38]

Given the relatively small number of warships in the Republican navy, there would have been at least one Russian adviser on each ship. Nevertheless, because of problems of language and the fact that the Russians were no more than advisers, they could not compensate for the lack of senior Spanish naval officers. No Soviet naval officers remained in Spain for more than a year and some stayed only a few months. Kuznetsov's advice on this was ignored.

III The Insurgent Blockade and Soviet Freighters

The Insurgents strove to establish a blockade of the coasts of Republican Spain. They did so with the help of information received from wherever in

Europe the Republican government was negotiating to buy war material, together with the Intelligence received from German and Italian sources.

The Insurgents' achievement was to use their scarce resources in the most energetic and efficient way possible. They possessed abundant and competent officers and were impeded neither by ideological or political considerations or badly-disciplined crews.

On 10 November 1936 the first and second Insurgent flotillas of armed deep-sea trawlers were restyled the Flotilla of Patrol Boats. The coasts at Tarifa, Punta Carnero (close to Algeciras) and el Hacho (Ceuta) had been supplied with powerful and often new guns, together with searchlights. An article in the London *Daily Telegraph* of 11 January 1937 began a long period of parliamentary questions and investigation by British agencies about the extent and the nature of the coastal artillery installed around the Strait of Gibraltar. The Admiralty was extremely perturbed. The Insurgents appeared to be in control of the entire western Mediterranean, as well as the northern coast of Morocco. Their gunboats and patrol boats were on constant alert, ready to detain and examine cargo ships suspected of carrying war material to the Republic. All the Insurgent ships were equipped with radio communication.[39] The Strait of Gibraltar was now effectively closed to enemy traffic.

Nevertheless, the large Republican fleet constituted a potential threat, so it was essential to put its only base, Cartagena, out of action. It was the German Condor Legion which set about this with heavy bombing on the night of 25–26 November 1936. From then on, the Republican fleet would have to leave the base at night and anchor at sea. In addition, the Italian submarine campaign began at this time, and torpedoed the cruiser *Miguel de Cervantes* on 22 November. On the 18th the Insurgents announced that they were going to blockade Barcelona, but without a sufficiently large blockading fleet, Insurgent declarations of blockade were not necessarily a serious threat. The Insurgents informed the governments of other countries of the danger facing their merchant shipping. They were acting like belligerents, although they did not enjoy that status. Even though through diplomatic channels and especially from London, the Franco government was warned that it was acting illegally in international law, the British government had to recognise the reality of the situation and accept a limited area of the port of Barcelona where vessels could anchor without being bombed. This concession was humiliating for Britain, coming as it did from a party lacking the status of a belligerent and imposing an illegal blockade.

The Republican fleet was heavily engaged in escorting Russian and Spanish freighters which were arriving with war material, food and other goods. It did not risk an encounter with the enemy after the loss in September 1936 of the destroyer *Ferrándiz* and the damage done to the destroyer *Gravina*. The Republican navy was weak, given that the cruiser *Miguel de Cervantes* was in dock undergoing lengthy repairs and its submarines had been seen to be no threat. Thus the new Insurgent cruiser *Canarias* sailed up and down the coast unchallenged.

In general, however, merchant shipping was competently protected by the Republican navy, but this role inclined the fleet to act defensively. This was even more so when the cruiser *Baleares*, sister ship to the *Canarias*, entered service on 28 December 1936. The Insurgents now had two very modern cruisers and one slightly older one, the *Almirante Cervera*, in the Mediterranean. The Republicans had only the cruiser *Libertad*, much inferior in firepower to the two new Insurgent warships. The *Miguel de Cervantes* was under repair, while the *Méndez Núñez* was old, poorly armed, and no match for the *Canarias* or the *Baleares*. Three Insurgent torpedo boats, the *Cánovas*, the *Dato*, and the *Canalejas*, together with the armed trawlers and coastguard vessels, completed a small but efficient force. Off the northern coast, Insurgent torpedo boats and the destroyer *Velasco* maintained a threatening presence, although that front was less active over the autumn and winter of 1936–1937 while Franco was still trying to take Madrid. German aggressiveness, as in the case of the *Palos*, kept German traffic safe for the regular voyages of the 'Special Ships' between Hamburg and north west Spain, while Italian ships were escorted by their own warships.

Insurgent 'Instructions for the war on merchant traffic', issued by the naval staff on 5 November 1936, had laid down that Russian ships were 'fair game' (*presa permitida*), while ships flying other flags had to be treated with prudence. The Russian response was to load and sail for Spain as secretly as was possible. Once in a Spanish port, they unloaded war material mostly at night and 'innocent' cargo by day. Russian ships carried documents indicating that the consignee was based in a country other than Spain. Another trick was to accompany the Russian arms-carrying ships with other Soviet vessels carrying non-military cargoes. In the last days of

1936, for example, as well as Russian ships unloading in ports in Belgium, England, Italy, Greece, Turkey and elsewhere, there were many more at sea. One of the responsibilities of the freighters accompanying the 'Y' ships was precisely to deceive hostile patrols and allow war material to reach harbour in a Republican port such as Cartagena or Alicante.

These circumstances explain the growing frustration of the Insurgent naval chiefs and their frequent arrest of Soviet ships which turned out to be carrying innocent cargoes. For example, the tanker *Soyuz Vodnikov* was stopped in the Strait of Gibraltar by the *Almirante Cervera* when on its way to Belgium. It was taken into Ceuta and freed two days later. The *Kharkov* was detained on 30 November, as were several other Soviet ships, among them the *Krasny Profintern*, the *Komiles,* and the *Vtoraya Pyatiletka*.[40] The *Stepan Khalturin* underwent the same experience on 4 December. In the new year, Maxim Litvinov, Soviet Minister for Foreign Affairs, complained to his opposite British number, Anthony Eden, that almost all Soviet freighters passing through the Strait of Gibraltar had been stopped and taken into Ceuta or Melilla.[41] Although the Russian ships were set free within a short time, the Soviet representative on the Non-Intervention Committee later claimed that 84 Russian vessels had been stopped by the Insurgents between 30 October 1936 and 10 April 1937, but only one of them had been making for a Spanish Republican port.[42]

The Insurgents did not usually claim that they had discovered armaments in these ships' holds. The complicated methods of deception and the efficient escort system organised by Kuznetsov and the Spanish naval officers, assured the safe arrival of the armaments ships. Nevertheless, in comparison with what Franco was receiving from Germany and Italy, the figure of 'more than twenty large freighters' which Kuznetsov mentions, even if it is underestimated and does not include arms shipped in Spanish vessels, explains the statement of Willard C. Frank, who describes Soviet supplies as 'mediocre caricatures of the super-efficient activity of Germany and Italy'.[43]

V The *Komsomol*

The very different fate of the *Komsomol*, which had already been identified twice by British and German warships while it was unloading tanks and lorries, was one exception to the rule that the Insurgents were not normally successful in stopping arms-carrying ships. On its third voyage to Republican Spain, on 14 December 1936, this freighter was sunk.

The official Soviet newspaper *Pravda* printed a statement on 20 December, six days after the sinking.[44] The *Komsomol* had sailed from Poti bound for Belgium with 6,909 tons of manganese ore. The crew was highly selected. Captain Mezentsev was in possession of the Order of Lenin and many of the young crew possessed Soviet decorations. Unexpectedly, the *Komsomol* was spotted and stopped by the Insurgent cruiser *Canarias*. The cruiser sent a boarding party, looked at the documents but did not inspect the cargo. This would not have been feasible at sea, so the *Komsomol* would have had to be taken into Palma or Melilla. Admiral Moreno later wrote that he feared an attack by escorting Soviet submarines (though there was never any justified suspicion that Soviet submarines were in the Mediterranean), so the *Canarias* limited itself to taking off the crew of thirty-four men and two women.[45]

For some reason, the true details of the sinking of the *Komsomol* were kept secret in the Soviet Union. Perhaps the news might have shown that the USSR was unable to defend its own cargo ships. Probably it would have proved that the Russians were engaged in the arms traffic, hidden beneath the manganese ore. The crew, released by the Spanish Insurgents in groups, returned to the USSR, and began to spread true accounts of what had happened which contradicted the brief official statement. According to these rumours, war material was concealed under the mineral ore. The ship was low in the water. As it approached the Spanish coast, the *Komsomol* had to stop and change course a number of times to avoid the Insurgent blockade. By accident, the *Komsomol* steered into the course of the *Canarias*, the Insurgent cruiser which had not been detected by the accompanying Russian ships which were meant to guide the *Komsomol* into Alicante. The *Canarias* stopped the *Komsomol*. Captain Mezentsev urgently radioed the Black Sea Navigation Board. He was ordered to open the hatches, scuttle the ship, and refuse any aid except from the *Canarias*, so that all the crew should be interned. The purpose of this order was, presumably, to demonstrate that the innocent crew of a neutral ship was in a Fascist prison. An alternative explanation is that the reason for refusing the help of a nearby Belgian ship was the fear that some of the crew would seize the opportunity to remain outside the Soviet Union and at the same time reveal the true nature of the cargo of the *Komsomol*.

Consequently the crew, according to the very full information revealed by the anonymous author of *Soviet Shipping in the Spanish Civil War*, set fire to the *Komsomol* and scuttled the ship, thus concealing the fact that the ship was carrying arms.

The Soviet reaction was slow in coming. A veil was drawn over the affair. Even the major Spanish Republican newspaper *ABC* did not publish news of the sinking until 21 December, and then merely repeated the Soviet press communiqué. Even more interesting is that Kuznetsov does not mention the event. The British Admiralty knew of the incident at once, because it had broken the Insurgent naval code.[46] The Foreign Office decided not to reveal this to the Soviet authorities.

The Soviet ambassador in London insisted that Britain consider some form of international defence against what he called 'piracy'. The Foreign Office decided that no scheme would work. If one were agreed, the Royal Navy would have to take the greatest responsibility. In the end, it was decided to continue the present arrangement where each country protected its own ships, a decision which was unhelpful to the USSR, which had no warships in the Mediterranean.[47]

The decision taken to sink the *Komsomol* made it impossible to verify the contents of its hold, a mystery which awaits the findings of undersea archaeology. According to his sons, Admiral Moreno ordered the *Canarias* to fire at the Soviet ship and sink it, rather than leave the cruiser's assigned position in order to escort the *Komsomol* to a harbour to be searched.[48] Whether the *Komsomol* was indeed carrying war material has never been discovered.[49] The young ages and descriptions of the highly-disciplined and reliable crew, nevertheless, suggest that the voyage was not a mere run of the mill voyage carrying ore to Belgium.[50] The result was, however, that the USSR would henceforth dispatch its arms supplies in Spanish Republican freighters.

That the Insurgents thought they had the right to treat Russian vessels as if the USSR had no ability to defend its traffic and as if it did not dare to protest for fear of increasing suspicion that it was supplying the Spanish Republic with arms, was again demonstrated on 9 January 1937, when the Insurgent destroyer *Velasco* captured the *Smidovich*, at the end of its voyage to Bilbao. The *Smidovich* was carrying lentils, wheat and barley, badly needed in northern Spain which was cut off from its agricultural hinterland. This was the first of seven ships declared 'fair game' by the Insurgents and renamed for Spanish castles. The *Smidovich* became the *Castillo Peñafiel*.

Chapter 8

Winter and Spring 1937 in the Mediterranean

1 Málaga, January–February 1937

The Republic controlled a wedge of territory on Spain's south coast which began a few miles west of Estepona and continued to a point almost due south of Granada. Along that coast were fishing villages and small towns, among them Marbella, Fuengirola and Torremolinos, which are now built over with the hotels, resorts, golf courses and motorways of today's Costa del Sol. For the Insurgents, this wedge was both a threat to the territory which they had already occupied and required them to guard an overlong front.

Consequently, the Francoist command resolved to use the Italian infantry and armour sent by Mussolini in December 1936 to reduce the pocket, whose most important port and city was Málaga.

From the naval aspect, Málaga had been declared a secondary base from which the Republican fleet could, at least in theory, threaten Insurgent activities in the Strait of Gibraltar and the northern coast of Spanish Morocco. However, in Insurgent hands Málaga could menace Cartagena, the main Republican base. It would also shorten lines of communication with Morocco and the new base at Palma and perhaps corral the Republican fleet.

While the secondary naval base at Málaga was well-commanded by the engineer warrant officer (*segundo maquinista*) Baudilio Sanmartín, and the submarine base by the loyal and efficient lieutenant commander Remigio Verdiá, the situation in and around the city was chaotic. A series of Republican army officers had tried hard and failed to impose discipline on the unruly Spanish militias, largely anarchist in ideology, to militarise them, create properly organised units, and to build fortifications. The result was that Francisco Largo Caballero, Prime Minister and Minister of War of the Republic, had declared 'For Málaga, not one rifle or cartridge'.[1]

Málaga was defenceless. It had no anti-aircraft guns and only a few out-of-date aircraft.[2] Lieutenant Commander Verdiá was loyal to the Republic, and his personality might have gone some way to compensate for material deficiencies, but he was killed in an air raid on 2 January 1937. On 11 January, when Insurgent naval operations began which would lead to the loss of Málaga, the only ships present were a coastguard vessel, a floating naval hospital and a survey ship. No plan for cooperation between the fleet and land forces had been devised. No useful intelligence was gathered about the enemy's movements in the days which preceded the attack.

On 11 January 1937, the Insurgent cruisers *Canarias* and *Almirante Cervera*, temporarily abandoning their campaign against freighters bringing war material into Republican ports, arrived off Málaga. The cruiser *Baleares*, sister-ship to the *Canarias*, spent a month at Cádiz finishing the installation of its artillery and other equipment, before joining the other cruisers in early February. There was a marked contrast between the urgency with which the workers toiled in the Insurgent dockyard at Cádiz, admittedly under severe discipline, and the tardiness at the same time in repairing the Republican cruiser *Miguel de Cervantes* in Cartagena.

On 14 January, General Gonzalo Queipo de Llano, who had overrun western Andalusia for the Insurgents and was commanding the operation against Málaga, embarked on the *Canarias*. He would stay on the ship for one day only, but the very fact that he did so, and the publicity given to it, and the general's request for two naval officers to be posted to his headquarters in Seville, together with the constant radio contact maintained between the Insurgent warships and their advancing troops, indicates that the Insurgents were aware that land-sea cooperation was important. There was no equivalent awareness among the Republicans.[3]

As the Insurgents began to advance along the road towards Marbella, the Insurgent cruisers *Canarias* and *Almirante Cervera*, the gunboats *Cánovas del Castillo* and *Canalejas*, and three coastguard cutters, as well as some deep-sea trawlers, and two fast German motor torpedo boats renamed *Falange* and *Requeté*, kept up a continuous bombardment against Republican roads, trenches and strongpoints, preventing the arrival of reinforcements. Success was complete and the Insurgents occupied Marbella on 17 January 1937. Insurgent forces were reorganised and, on 4 February, the attack against Málaga was launched, this time reinforced by the *Baleares*, and by Insurgent and German seaplanes which patrolled the area searching for possible Republican submarines. In case the Republican fleet appeared, Italian submarines were asked to set up a barrier between Marbella and Málaga. General Martínez Monje, the commander of the Republican Army of the South, which was no more than an accumulation of recently-formed brigades and divisions, telegraphed the chief of staff, General Martínez Cabrera:

> The large [Francoist] ships shell our positions from close in, while the smaller ones approach even nearer and machine-gun the roads so that we cannot send reinforcements.[4]

During this time, Republican aircraft attempted, unsuccessfully, to bomb Insurgent warships. But where was the Republican fleet? On 14 January and subsequent days, the two available cruisers, the *Méndez Núñez* and the more modern *Libertad*, were ordered to seek and attack the Insurgent warships, but they could not find them. On 20 January, the two Republican cruisers and four destroyers left Cartagena with the mission to 'attack the enemy if you find him', but fear of Italian submarines limited the search. There seems to have been little enthusiasm to endanger the Republican fleet, now reduced, by the delay in repairing the *Miguel de Cervantes*, to one older cruiser and one modern and fast cruiser, but whose firepower was much less than either of the two ultra-modern Insurgent cruisers, together with some unreliable submarines. Lieutenant Commander Luis Junquera, chief of staff of the Republican Navy, gave his view on the situation to Lieutenant Commander Miguel Buiza, commanding the fleet:

> I think that there is little that we can do with the *Libertad* and the *Méndez Núñez*, and we risk a great deal.[5]

He was probably right, but with capable, sufficient and trusted officers, and disciplined and determined crews, the destroyers and the submarines could have been a major threat to the Insurgent cruisers.

Junquera advised Buiza to have three or four destroyers ready every night, and to try to attack during the hours of darkness. Buiza replied that was indeed what the destroyers were trying to do, but they had to find the cruisers and get themselves into a position from which torpedoes could be launched.

On 24 January, the Republican naval staff gave Buiza an operational order. The cruiser *Libertad*, the battleship *Jaime I*, eight destroyers and those submarines which were still functional should attack the Insurgent fleet in a coordinated action with the air force. However, most of the Republican fleet did not proceed to the Málaga coast where the Insurgents were shelling and machine-gunning the roads and defensive positions. Why was this? Were the sailors' committees so powerful that they could prevent the commanders from undertaking what was indeed a very risky mission, given the speed, armour and particularly the firepower of the *Canarias* and the *Baleares*? Or was the order disobeyed because of pressure from the Soviet advisers, whose main concern was not to risk the Republican fleet which was the only force protecting freighters bringing arms from the Soviet Union? Or, as was later suggested, was Buiza unwilling to attack? In a civil war, especially when so many of his fellow-officers had been murdered, how could he balance his conscience between loyalty to the Republic and to his erstwhile naval comrades.[6]

Between the approach of Insurgent forces to Málaga and the final assault which began on February 4, an Italian submarine, the *Ciro Menotti*, sank the *Delfín*, a Spanish cargo ship sailing to Málaga with flour. This event not only made it difficult to provide bread for the forces defending Málaga, but also reinforced the doubts in the Republican naval command about risking their ships in those waters. Nevertheless, orders were issued on the 4, 5, 6, and 7 February to the destroyers and the cruisers to look out for Insurgent ships, but not until 7 February were two destroyers ordered to attack the enemy, while four were instructed to cut off an enemy retreat westwards to the Strait of Gibraltar. Nothing, however, came of these orders. The destroyers did not find the enemy. Is this possible? Perhaps they were unable, given the high speed of the new Insurgent cruisers, to place themselves in a position to launch their torpedoes without being blown out of the water by the more heavily armed *Canarias* and *Baleares*.

On the other hand, few cargo vessels making for Republican ports were stopped by the Insurgents. One exception was the *Nuria*, whose captain and radio operator had notified Insurgent agents in Oran that they wanted to hand the ship over, although the crew were hostile, armed and likely to resist. A German Heinkel 59 seaplane, used for long-distance reconnaissance, spotted the *Nuria* when it was about to enter Cartagena harbour, and harassed it, obliging it to turn about and sail for Melilla on the Insurgent-controlled Moroccan coast.

The senior Russian adviser, Commander Kuznetsov, who does not spare his excoriation of anarchist disorder and indiscipline, thinks that the fleet learnt of the Insurgent offensive too late. This is in itself a criticism of the poor Intelligence service of the Republican fleet.

II The Republican Fleet Fails to Defend Málaga

The inability of the Republican fleet to defend Málaga shows up its deficiencies. While the Insurgents adhered to the principle of concentration of forces, and had at one moment three cruisers bombarding the coast, taking the necessary precautions against enemy air or submarine attack, the Republicans did not use their advantages. Even if they had not been able to sink an Insurgent cruiser, a determined action, gathering the submarines that were available to them and spreading a rumour that there were more, might have reduced the confidence of the Insurgents. With careful preparation a night attack might have been possible. The reasons for the passivity of the Republican fleet have already been suggested. However, the hierarchical structure of the navy command may perhaps also be responsible for the apparent paralysis. For example, a telegram from the chief of staff in Valencia – to where the government had been transferred from Madrid in November 1936 – to the fleet commander in Cartagena on the final day before Málaga was occupied by the Insurgents, read 'Enemy warships are shelling *a placer*'.[7]

This means that the Insurgents were taking no precautions and that they were not receiving any armed response to their shelling. The Republican fleet commander, Lieutenant Commander Buiza, could not act without an order from the staff, and the staff was, apparently, required to follow orders from the Navy Ministry. Yet the relative speed of the Republican destroyers would have made an immediate response feasible. This is an example of how bureaucratic and 'unrevolutionary' the forces of the Spanish Republic were, in contrast with the wide level of independence and the initiative enjoyed by the Insurgent command in the actual area of battle. So, although the whereabouts of the Insurgent ships was known, the

Republican fleet did not attack. Buiza said that he could not because he had no air cover. Finally, a message from Málaga reached the fleet commander on 7 February 1937 asking at least for a reply to previous messages sent by warrant officer Baudilio Sanmartín, and requesting the fleet to act.

Sanmartín's later report sheds much light on the last hours of Republican Málaga.[8] On 7 February Buiza had replied to Sanmartín's message, and promised that the fleet would act 'if conditions were favourable', but as the day wore on and the army commander in Málaga and the provincial and city officials fled, Sanmartín asked for orders, for there was no sign of the fleet. As he waited he burned the code books and any documents which might be useful to the Insurgents. Then he received an order from the Navy Minister, Indalecio Prieto, in Valencia. He was to set fire to all the fuel in the tanks of the Spanish oil company CAMPSA. Unable to discover how to do this, and in the absence of the staff of CAMPSA, who had departed, Sanmartín did not obey the order. That night, he was the only person of authority left in the city. He did all he could, sinking the coaster cutter *Xauen*, two launches and the hospital ship *Artabro*. At 4 am on 8 February he collected some technical machines and left Málaga with some junior personnel.[9]

To return to the intriguing question of the passivity of the Republican fleet, the Insurgents commented after listening to messages between the Republican ships and the naval staff:

> Although the destroyers are ready, they are talking about a mission which is more interesting (important?) than Málaga. They do not seem willing to go to Málaga even though since 14 January they have known that the *Canarias*, the *Almirante Cervera*, the *Cánovas*, and ten seaplanes are there. The Minister and the commander in Málaga insist that the fleet sail there.[10]

A cable from the fleet commander, Buiza, this time to the chief of staff, is more enlightening:

> It is pointless, because it would be useless and dangerous, given the strategic position of the enemy, apart from other reasons which you know well, to think of some action by the fleet.[11]

This text would seem to reflect a division of views between the fleet commander and the chief of staff. Nevertheless, after the loss of Málaga and the panic in the next city along the coast, Almería, which the Insurgents might attack, Buiza held a teleprinter conversation with the chief of staff. He asked 'What has the Minister decided?' When told that Prieto had not yet arrived, Buiza replied

> Before noon when the ships will be ready to leave I want to know clearly if I should hoist anchor and search for the enemy, whatever the cost, or if I should limit action to night attacks by the destroyers.

He ended in a sarcastic tone:

> Since I assume that the Minister rises before noon I think I could be given a clear answer.

On 9 February, the chief of staff told Buiza:

> You must not do any crazy thing with irreparable consequences because of what people may say ('por el que dirán').

This last phrase seems to have meant that the Minister and the chief of staff knew that people were saying that the fleet ought to at least try to succour Málaga. But what were the mysterious 'other reasons' in the earlier message? Were the Soviet advisers counselling prudence to avoid losing ships in combat with the powerful new cruisers of the Insurgents, or was the indecision caused by the parlous state of discipline in the fleet where the newly arrived political commissar, Bruno Alonso, was struggling to dominate the sailors' committees, who themselves had difficulty in maintaining their authority over some of the crews? As for the 'strategic position', did this refer to the decision to abandon Málaga to its fate, which would have the advantage of shortening the front? Whatever the strange, strangulated phraseology of these messages meant, the real problems appear to have been the indecision which had gripped the Minister and the staff of the Republican navy. What sort of role did the chaos of the fleet allow it to play? Was it only a defensive strategy? To lose a cruiser and perhaps two or three destroyers, or even suffer damage to ships when Cartagena did not have the same level of repair facilities as the Insurgent El Ferrol, would have been a disaster just at the moment when transports were arriving from the Black Sea and requiring escort as they made the final dash from the North African coast. Success against the new and powerful Insurgent cruisers was very chancy. Even if one of them were sunk it would leave the Insurgents in a better position than the Republicans because the *Miguel de Cervantes* was still under repair. Even without Russian pressure and the problems of the inexperienced junior Republican commanders, the situation recommended prudence. The apparent confusion along the line of command only reflected the dilemma. The result was that the apparent lack of decisiveness increased the confidence of the Insurgents and confirmed the sense of inferiority of the Republicans.

III The State of Affairs as Seen by the Navy Staff

What was the real condition of each of the Spanish fleets? Could they be compared? The Republic appointed its new naval staff on 26 December 1936. It wasted no time in presenting the Minister, on 2 January 1937, with a long and important document. This gave not only details of the two navies but also reveals how the Republican staff, composed mostly of relatively junior lieutenants and lieutenant commanders, saw its own situation.

The report indicated that the Republican battleship *Jaime I* was not in a fit state to operate because of the condition of its boiler tubes. It considered that the equivalent Insurgent battleship, the *España*, was in like condition. Yet the *España* had been playing an active and useful role as a floating artillery platform. Its 305 mm guns had pounded the enemy's positions. It had also blockaded the Cantabrian coast. The Republican battleship *Jaime I* had also been used as floating artillery at the beginning of the war, but since then it had been kept in the port of Almería as protection. It had not been used actively at sea at all.

Passing to the cruisers, the Republican naval staff reported that the *Miguel de Cervantes* was waiting for the dry dock at Cartagena to be enlarged so that the cruiser, torpedoed by an Italian submarine in November 1936, could be repaired. The third Republican cruiser, the *Méndez Núñez*, slower and with less firepower, was considered a hindrance. Evidently, nobody had considered whether some role could be found for this older cruiser. When it came to the new Insurgent cruisers *Canarias* and *Baleares*, the report emphasised the superior power of these ships over the Republican cruisers. Interestingly, the report totally ignored the useful part played by the older Insurgent destroyer *Velasco*, but if the *Velasco* could be useful in shelling the coast and interfering with commercial traffic, so could its sister-ships, the Republican destroyers *Alsedo* and *Lazaga*. As for the submarines, the report complained that the Republic had insufficient undersea boats to cover the Spanish coast and repairs took a long time. In any case, Republican Intelligence did not know exactly what was available to the Insurgents. Indeed, continued the report, it might be possible to find and destroy the Insurgent cruisers. The report, however, did not admit that the real problem was the operative condition of the submarines and the loyalty of the commanders.

No consideration was given to how to use the warships which were available. The lack of strategic foresight and information was grave. Control over the Strait of Gibraltar had been lost once the Insurgent cruisers had appeared there in September 1936, and after the *Ferrándiz* had been sunk and the *Gravina* damaged and put to flight. By now, to seek to establish a naval base at Málaga, as the report recommended, would have been a waste of time and resources. It would have been more important to calculate how to neutralise Palma which was becoming the main Mediterranean base for the Insurgents.

Passing to the northern coast, the report concluded that Bilbao should become a support base. This was evident. The Insurgents had the benefit of two bases, Cádiz in the south and El Ferrol in the north, but the distance between them was only half that between Bilbao and Cartagena. El Ferrol on the Northern coast, Cádiz on the Atlantic and Palma in the Mediterranean were three equidistant points under Franco's control, in comparison with the Republic's one base in Cartagena. The report concluded that the Republic's problem was more one of bases than of ships. The staff evidently thought that its fleet equalled that of the Insurgents, despite its lesser firepower and its unreliable submarines. However, a base without adequate protection against air attack had little value. This was the problem with ports such as Alicante and Valencia. Cartagena had powerful coastal artillery, but its harbour was small. Stationary ships offered an easy target, which obliged the Republican fleet to anchor outside the harbour at night. The torpedoing of the *Miguel de Cervantes* had been a disaster, but had the lessons about anti-submarine protection been learned?

Nevertheless, material factors are not all. The delay in repairing damaged vessels led to rumours of sabotage in Cartagena reaching the British Foreign Office.[12] In Insurgent-controlled El Ferrol warships were speedily repaired, probably owing to greater efficiency and undoubted fear of repression. To be fair, the Insurgents were able to acquire spare parts and special machinery more easily from Germany than the Republic could from other signatories to the Non-Intervention agreement. Moreover, in July and August 1938 repeated orders went from El Ferrol on behalf of the partially British-owned *Sociedad Española de Constructores Navales* or SECN to British firms such as Vickers, the Anglo-Overseas Engineers and Merchants Ltd, Morgan Crucible, Wild-Barfield Electrical Furnaces, British Ebonite, Everstead and Vignoles, British Insulated Cables and others. If the material supplied did not contravene the Non-Intervention agreement, why could the SECN in Cartagena not have done the same?[13]

As for the strategic vision of the new staff of the Republican navy, its priority was to achieve control in the Mediterranean and the Strait of Gibraltar. How was this to be done? The answer was by developing Port Mahon on Minorca in order to block Palma, and by making the bay of Gibraltar and Algeciras unusable by the Insurgents by developing Málaga as a base. The emphasis on the development of bases underlines the deficiencies of the strategic vision of the staff. At that moment the *Canarias* and the *Almirante Cervera* were at large in the Mediterranean. The priority ought to have been to curtail the freedom of these two Insurgent cruisers by a coordinated attack by all the Republican forces, reinforced from the air. The fact that the other modern Insurgent cruiser, the *Baleares*, would be sunk, although more by accident than by design, by Republican destroyers in 1938 shows that a more pro-active stance would have inhibited the movements of the Insurgents.

As for Algeciras, the opportune moment had passed. In the early weeks of the war a concerted attack by all the air and naval forces of the Republic might have made that port useless for the Insurgents, but the powerful coastal artillery now installed on either side of the Strait negated the possibility.

When the report came to immediate requirements, it was right to underline the need for aircraft for watching enemy movements at sea. However, what could be done once the position of enemy ships was discovered? Quite unrealistically, the report asked for more submarines, even though its authors must have known that loyal commanders were scarce even if the Republic could find a way of purchasing or borrowing undersea boats. The report spoke about acquiring fast motor launches and arming deep-sea fishing trawlers, but said nothing about how such small vessels might be used. The Insurgents used armed trawlers widely for stopping merchant shipping but international diplomatic considerations made this impossible for the Republic.

There was an obvious defensive air about this report, but it was also true that the shortages of armament in the Republican destroyers made it difficult to recommend that they be more pro-active. There were only eighty instead of the two hundred torpedoes that were thought necessary, but how were even the available missiles to be used?

To sum up, this report analysed the two opposing fleets, described an essentially defensive strategy and listed a number of essentials, many of which were impossible to achieve. While it would be unfair to describe it as defeatist, it lacked the energetic sense of improvisation characteristic of the Insurgent naval leaders. That was to be expected because in the Republican navy a cumbersome structure continued to exist when on the other side the Francoist uprising itself had at least partially destroyed the bureaucratic infrastructure. The defensive stance possibly imposed by the Soviet advisers does not deserve all the blame.[14] Kuznetsov, the senior Russian adviser, remarks on the absence of clear strategic direction and of coordinated action on air, land and sea.[15]

IV Comparison of Behaviour

In the Insurgent fleet maximum demands were made on the three cruisers, the brand-new *Canarias* and *Baleares*, and the older *Almirante Cervera*. War material had to be prevented from reaching the Republican ports of Cartagena, Alicante and Barcelona. Insurgent troop movements from Morocco had to be escorted as did convoys to and from Palma. With Italian help the latter port was being rapidly made ready so that cruisers based there could harass freighters approaching the Republican coast. In

Cádiz and El Ferrol repairs and the frequent replacement of boiler-tubes rarely took long, reflecting the Insurgents' well-developed organization and sense of urgency. This high level of activity made great demands on the crews, who had sometimes to spend entire days in the artillery turrets, the engine-room and boilers, to emerge pale for lack of air and sleep.[16] One sailor on the *Canarias* recalled that in a month he spent only three days ashore. Since only half the crew could disembark, a sailor could hope to sleep ashore only one or two nights a month.[17] In contrast, the slowness of activity in the Cartagena dockyard was proverbial. The British destroyer *Glow Worm* reported that the battleship *Jaime I* and the Republican cruisers delayed leaving the harbour on the pretext of work which had to be done. Some of the management was sympathetic to the Insurgents. They hindered productivity, tolerated idleness and were slow to issue spare parts. It is unclear whether the commander of the *Glow Worm* was repeating what the management told him, or if the British specialists in the dockyard were accusing their Spanish colleagues.[18] The chief engineer officer of the Republican destroyer *Jorge Juan* complained about the Cartagena work force to the fleet commander: 'All they do is hinder progress'. The *Jorge Juan* was new, but it lacked all manner of equipment and there were problems with its boilers.[19] Inefficiency, or perhaps sabotage, was often the subject of comment. In a teletype to the chief of staff, the fleet commander commented that breakdowns in the motors of the submarine *CI* were 'incomprehensible after eight months work'.[20] The Sailors' Committee, on board the cruiser *Libertad*, accepted that the problem was serious, and blamed it on 'reactionary elements among the workers'.[21] The situation may explain the report sent from the Insurgent cruiser *Canarias*, for the week of 13–20 December 1936. After underlining the 'lack of combativity of the Red ships', especially the submarines, the *Canarias* noted a major change:

> In recent days, as if due to a change in command, everything points to uncharacteristic activity among the destroyers.[22]

The commander of the *Canarias* put the increased activity down to the arrival of the Russians and the supposed presence of Soviet submarines. The change was indeed probably the result of the arrival of Commander Kuznetsov and of his organization of escorts for the Soviet freighters. It is doubtful, however, if anything had changed on board the batttleship *Jaime I*, which on 13 November 1936 had spent two weeks just taking on coal. According to the commander of the British destroyer *Gallant*, little work was being done on the *Jaime I*. Sailors were enjoying leave in Cartagena. The committees were seeking pretexts not to go to sea and there was 'indescribable dilapidation, dirt and confusion'.[23] Nothing had changed since 29 October 1936 when the commander of HMS *Gipsy* had reported in similar terms.

It was at this point that Bruno Alonso was appointed Political Delegate to the fleet on 29 December 1936.[24] There was a huge amount to be done. In the destroyer flotillas the Sailors' Committee was writing letters to the fleet commander, proposing candidates for command. On the destroyer *Almirante Antequera*, the Committee proposed dismissing the deputy commander, since 'his character is not in tone with the current circumstances, which require special tact' (!). The deputy commander was not an officer, but a minor petty officer who had been proposed for the post on 16 November and who obviously though mistakenly thought that his post required him to give orders as needed.

To appoint men to positions of authority who were not of the appropriate naval rank and who probably did not enjoy the respect of the crews could easily lead to such a situation. The cruiser *Libertad* reported that a particular seaman, who returned late from leave

> [...] was reproved and punished by being forbidden his next two shore leaves. He took up an arrogant (*chulesca*) attitude to the Committee. On another day, the same seaman boarded a shore-leave boat. When he returned he said that he did so because the President of the Committee also did what he felt like.[25]

These pieces of evidence reveal petty resentments where sailors protested:

> We are longing to overturn once and for all the personal benefits and privileges of class, but not so that a few ex-seamen [...] should prescribe tyranny for some and favours for others.[26]

The examples may perhaps not represent the state of the Republican fleet in general. Yet there can be no doubt that the mutinies of July 1936 had led to a general relaxation of shipboard discipline. It would take a great effort to restore it. A warship functions or does not. The committees themselves strove to remove men whom they saw as troublemakers. For example, the Committee of the *Libertad* got rid of a petty officer and a stoker on 20 November 1936 'for incompatibility with this Committee'.[27]

The task would, nevertheless, take a long time. Even on the submarines, with specialised crews, as the flotilla commander, Remigio Verdiá, wrote to the fleet commander:

> The shortage of officers has led to a crisis. It has created the poor state of the equipment despite the efforts of the Committees on the submarines.[28]

The roots of these conflicts were obvious. Sailors were concerned more with their rights than fighting the war. Without a commander with authority, a navy cannot fight aggressively. Bruno Alonso, the Political Delegate appointed by Indalecio Prieto, Minister for Air and the Navy, spent much time justifying his actions. He claims to have treated everyone equally, but not the 'perturbadores' or disruptors. He did not attack a particular faction, suggesting that, though he was a socialist, he did not act against the supporters of the anarchist CNT who were probably in their majority in the fleet. In any case, he claims that he handed over his salary to the Central Fund for Victims of Fascism.[29] This would suggest that he felt the need to defend himself.

Behind everything lay a deep lack of trust in the professional officers. A postcard, with spelling mistakes, probably held back by the censor and kept in the archives, reads:

> Comrades, we are being betrayed. The fall of Málaga was the fault of our commanders. If we don't recover Málaga they will be shot.[30]

V Insurgent Succcesses in Spring 1937

Once again, the Republican chain of command and authority seems to have been weak and uncertain. Who decided the strategy to follow? Was it the Minister, Prieto, properly advised by a chief of staff and obeyed by the fleet commander? Obscure Soviet manipulations may not always have been responsible, but nevertheless the essential task of protecting transports coming from the USSR was paramount.

Sometimes the Insurgents also made errors. Their level of information was not always equal to their skill and determination. A Republican freighter, the *Marqués de Comillas*, was being watched at Odessa and as it sailed through the Bosphorus, agents alleged that it was carrying sixty artillery pieces, thirty-five tanks, fifty lorries, fifteen hundred tons of other items and one thousand tons of foodstuffs. The Insurgent fleet set up a barrier along the Spanish coast with the cruisers and a number of armed merchant vessels.The *Marqués de Comillas* was stopped on 28 January fifteen miles off the coast.[31] When it was searched, its sole cargo was cotton. Probably, the Russians had set up a skilful deceit in order to draw the Insurgent warships away from a vessel carrying military items.

However, a few weeks later the Insurgents triumphed when they captured the *Mar Cantábrico*. This vessel carried aircraft and other war material worth US $2,775,000 which had been bought from the Vimalert corporation of New Jersey, whose president, Robert Cuse, acted as an agent for the Soviet trading entity Amtorg. The aircraft were part of a major deal in the United States, which had maintained a 'moral embargo' since 11 August 1936 against selling arms to either side in the Spanish war. Unscrupulous dealers could ignore it. As the aircraft were being dismantled to be stowed in the hold of the ship, President Roosevelt asked Congress to extend the Neutrality Act of 1935 to civil wars. On 6 January 1937 two senators presented bills which would make sales of arms to Spain illegal. The ban would begin on January 8. The stevedores managed to load eleven aircraft on the *Mar Cantábrico*, according to the information reported by *The Times* on 6 January. The ship would not, however, complete its journey to Republican Spain.[32] Having called at Vera Cruz to pick up some more war material, the *Mar Cantábrico* sailed at 0600 hours on 19 February. Its course and the date and port of arrival ought to have been kept rigorously secret. Nevertheless, Prieto told Aguirre, the Basque President, that arrival was expected at Santander on 5 or 6 March, and revealed the signal codes and details of the cargo.[33]

The Insurgents were alerted first by the publicity given to the loading and departure of the *Mar Cantábrico* from New York. They would have been aware of the official messages, sent with little concern for security, and possibly by information from the Republican destroyer *José Luis*

Díez, whose officers deserted in Bordeaux where it had anchored in flight from the *Canarias*.[34] On 8 March, the *Canarias* stopped a merchant ship which it suspected was the *Mar Cantábrico*, although it claimed to be the *Adda*, a freighter belonging to the British Elder-Dempster line. The two words 'New Castle' (in error for 'Newcastle') had been painted under the false name. Coincidentally, a ship of the same line, called the *Aba*, picked up the emergency call of the so-called *Adda* and retransmitted it, with the result that a group of British destroyers – the *Echo*, the *Eclipse*, the *Encounter* and the *Escapade* – hastened to protect the ship that they thought was a British merchant ship asking for aid. Captain Salvador Moreno of the *Canarias* heard the SOS and later quoted it in his report:

We are in danger stoped (*sic*) by unknown battleship. In danger we neeks halp(*sic*).[35]

The second urgent message was

PSE [probably please] advise English authorities we are in danger being bombed we proceed to save passengers lifes.

The deficient English (an English speaker would say 'shelled' and not 'bombed') would not have deceived Captain Salvador Moreno. Nevertheless, the *Mar Cantábrico* refused to surrender, transmitting 'please wait until English warship comes', although an English-speaking captain or radio-operator would have said 'British'.

The first British destroyer which appeared assured Captain Moreno that the cargo ship was not the *Adda*. The *Mar Cantábrico* then surrendered and was sailed to El Ferrol by a scratch crew, where the Spaniards nationals were executed.[36]

In Parliament fifteen Conservative MPs protested at the attempt of the *Mar Cantábrico*'s captain to claim that his ship was the *Adda*. However, the Foreign Office claimed that the deceit was an acceptable *ruse de guerre*. Pretending to be another ship was known to be a subterfuge which ships sailing to Insurgent ports also used frequently.

The most striking aspect of the case was the neglect of security. How could Prieto, a minister of the Republican government, have communicated so openly with the Basque President? What was the point of a *ruse de guerre* when obviously a message radioed to London would show it to be false? If it were not possible – though why not is not easily understandable – to provide a naval escort for the *Mar Cantábrico*, the best way to bring it safely to Santander would have been to use a roundabout course, to disguise the ship, to keep radio silence, or imitate the Russians and try to deceive the *Canarias* with false signals from another ship, and then wait for a suitable moment and make speed for the Republican zone of northern Spain. The loss of the *Mar Cantábrico* displayed gross carelessness.

The trio of victories for the Insurgent navy ended on 29 March 1937 when two armed Insurgent deep-sea fishing trawlers forced the Spanish *Mar Caspio* aground in French territorial waters off Cape Breton.[37] The ship was on its way from Newcastle to Bayonne with two thousand tons of coal. Thus even in terms of the illegality of interference with neutral shipping in the Spanish war the action was an outrage because the ship was not even bound for Spain.

In their struggle to block arms traffic to the Republic the Insurgents planted agents in European ports to bribe the captains of merchant ships to allow their ships to be captured. Among the successes achieved by the Insurgents in this way was the capture of two merchant ships, the *Sylvia* and the *Rona*.

The case of the *Sylvia* illustrates the murky depths of the arms trade to which the Non-Intervention Agreement forced the Republic to have recourse. The *Sylvia* was carrying a cargo of out of date war material sent by the Polish semi-official company SEPEWE. Poland's military government was hostile to the ideals of the Spanish Republic but not averse to earning money by selling leftover military material. The *Sylvia* was taken over by the Insurgents in the Strait of Gibraltar, and the Swedish *Rona* in the Bay of Biscay.[38] On 11 July 1937 the Insurgents captured the Greek tanker *Ionia* with nearly 9,000 tons of fuel. This was a result of negotiations between the owners, the captain and Insurgent agents, who agreed to pay the owners and the captain a percentage of the value of the cargo. On 30 August the Greek *Nausika* was captured with 7,000 tons of fuel.[39] On 1 September the *Mar Negro*, returning from the Soviet Union loaded with lorries, was surrendered in Algiers to the *Canarias*.[40]

VI The Two Fleets Clash: 23 and 24 April 1937

The Insurgents noted that the Republican navy was pulling itself together and showing signs of a more aggressive stance. On 25 April, the Republican fleet raised anchor and sailed out of its base at Cartagena with the mission to search for and attack the enemy cruisers, especially the *Baleares*. The fleet carried out coordinated searches with the aid of aircraft, but when the Insurgent air force appeared, the Republican ships, untrained to reply to air attack and insufficiently equipped with anti-aircraft guns, dispersed.

At this time, shelling ports was the major activity of the Republican fleet. According to the Soviet chief adviser, Commander Kuznetsov, shelling hostile ports was recommended because it quietened the press about the '*inmovilidad*' of the fleet, and hid what the Russians saw as the navy's primordial mission: escorting ships into port.[41]

Nevertheless, on 23 April 1937 the battleship *Jaime I* left Almería, where it had been idle, joining the cruisers *Libertad* and the older *Méndez Núñez*, and some destroyers, in search of the Insurgent cruisers, which always seemed, perhaps because of better information, difficult to find. Kuznetsov sailed on the destroyer *Almirante Antequera*, together with Lieutenant Vicente Ramírez, the flotilla commander, and the latter's adviser, Valentin Petrovich Drozhd.[42] The Republican warships shelled the coast and the cities of Málaga and Motril. Each ship shelled in turn but apparently without properly identifying objectives, certainly not any major ones.

Now, however, two new elements came into play. Five fast German motor-torpedo boats or *Schnellboote*, now named *Falange*, *Requeté*, *Oviedo*, *Badajoz* and *Toledo*, had been sold to the Spanish Insurgents. They were lightly armed with a 20 mm. machine gun, and carried two 533 mm. torpedoes.[43] A hit from a destroyer would destroy one of these light vessels, whose prime task was to penetrate a harbour, launch a torpedo and get out quickly. Two of these motor torpedo boats, the *Oviedo* and the *Badajoz*, launched torpedoes against the Republican destroyers from 2,800 and 2,000 metres respectively. Republican destroyers bracketed them with gunfire and the torpedo boats retired rapidly. Two others emerged from Málaga but heavy seas and a breakdown forced their retreat to a sheltered position.[44] On the way back to Cartagena Kuznetsov noted the improvement in morale of the Republican crews, who seemed to lose heart again when the *Jaime I* went aground while entering Almería, an indication of the inexperience of the commander or the crew. When the *Libertad*, with the fleet commander aboard, heard the news, they discussed whether to make for Almería to protect the *Jaime I* or to sail to their safe haven at Cartagena. Finally they decided to sail to Cartagena. Fortunately, the *Jaime I* had gone aground on sand and, with some difficulty, was towed off and made harbour safely at Almería.

At this moment the second element came in play. The German cruiser *Leipzig* appeared on the horizon in its role as part of the international patrol to prevent arms reaching either side, which had recently begun operations. The *Leipzig*, as the Republican commanders knew, was communicating information to the Insurgents about the movements of their enemy.

On the morning of 25 April the *Canarias* found the Republican fleet, but lost it in thick fog. The *Baleares* opened fire against a destroyer which responded with a salvo of torpedoes. Then the Insurgent cruisers attacked the destroyer *Sánchez Barcáiztegui*, which, under its young and skilful commander Sub Lieutenant Alvaro Calderón, manoeuvred under a smokescreen. Finally, the *Baleares* and the *Canarias* found themselves within the range of the powerful coastal batteries at Cartagena, and abandoned the chase. Two Republican cruisers, now emboldened as Commander Kuznetsov describes, sailed out of Cartagena in unsuccessful pursuit of the Insurgent cruisers.[45]

The risk for the Insurgents had been great. One of the new cruisers might have been torpedoed, and hit decisively by a shell in the fog or by the coastal artillery. Nor could the Republicans risk losing another destroyer as they had the *Ferrándiz* in September 1936. Neither side was eager for a battle.

Thus by spring 1937 the tone of the naval war off the Spanish coast had been established. The Insurgents would strive even more to prevent merchant ships bringing arms to Republican Spain, and the Republicans would continue to escort vessels on their way to Republican ports. Neither fleet would show much enthusiasm for an encounter which might endanger their navies 'in being'. Meanwhile, Franco's attempts to take Madrid having failed, he would turn his attention to the northern front.

Chapter 9

The Naval Campaign in the Cantabrian Sea

I The Basques Create a Navy

Within a few weeks of the onset of war the three warships which the Insurgents retained, the battleship *España*, the cruiser *Almirante Cervera* and the destroyer *Velasco*, as well as numerous armed trawlers, had established control over the sea adjacent to the narrow Republican shore and hinterland of northern Spain

The Republican fleet in the Cantabrian consisted of the destroyer *José Luis Díez*, the torpedo boat *T-3* and the submarines *C2* and *C5*. Sublieutenant Carlos Moya, who had survived the massacre of imprisoned officers, was in command of the *José Luis Díez*. This ship experienced frequent breakdowns, which its officers, after deserting to the Insurgents,

(Left to right) Basque police escort, Señora de Aldasoro (wife of Basque Minister of Commerce), Thomas MacEwen (owner of the *Seven Seas Spray*), Captain Roberts, Florence 'Fifi' Roberts, Señora de Monzón (wife of Basque Minister of the Interior), Ramón Aldasoro, Basque police escort. (*Copyright Sabino Arana Fundazioa*)

would claim to have been caused intentionally.[1] The *C2* was commanded by Lieutenant Eugenio Calderón, from a Republican and liberal family, but its deficiencies allowed it to remain submerged for only two hours. The other submarine, the *C5*, was commanded by the pro-Insurgent Lieutenant Commander Lara.[2] It was in poor condition and spent most of the time moored close to a railway tunnel to which the demoralised crew retreated during air raids. So bad was the situation that an armed Basque patrol took over the *C5* when the crew was in the tunnel, possibly with the connivance of the guard who told the story to a later Insurgent investigation. The submarine disappeared without known cause on 30 December 1936. However, after the war, evidence was produced that Lara had probably sunk his submarine intentionally.[3]

Since October 1936 the Basque region had been autonomous and known as Euzkadi. The Basque authorities, unimpressed by the discipline and the capacities of the Republican warships, organised their own naval forces with six armed deep-sea trawlers. Four of these, which normally fished on the cod banks of Newfoundland, were named *Bizkaia*, *Araba*, *Nabara* and *Gipuzkoa* and crewed by tough Basque fishermen organised as the Volunteers of the Sea or *Voluntariado del mar*. In addition, twenty-four fishing boats were equipped as minesweepers to keep the approaches to Bilbao free of mines.

II Reorganisation

On 15 November 1936 *Capitán de Navío* (equivalent to Captain RN) Valentín Fuentes was appointed commander of Republican naval forces in the Cantabrian Sea. Post-war reports, written by officers who were justifying having remained in what the Insurgents called the 'Red-Separatist Zone', recalled that the staff was disloyal and that most deserted to the Insurgents after the fall of Bilbao. Despite this, most merchant ships arrived safely in northern Spanish ports in January and February 1937. But soon the Basque fishing-boats would be called on to demonstrate their valour against the modern cruiser *Canarias*, in an epic clash.

III 5 March 1937: the Battle of Cape Machichaco

On 4 March, 1937, while the *Canarias* was tensely awaiting news of the freighter *Mar Cantábrico*, it was ordered to intercept the merchant ship *Galdames*, which was escorted by the Basque armed deep-sea trawlers *Gizpuzkoa*, *Bizkaia*, *Nabara* and the smaller *Donostia*. However, storms in the Bay of Biscay had dispersed the escort. On 5 March the *Canarias* found itself only seven thousand metres from the *Gipuzkoa*. This armed trawler defended itself valiantly, scoring a hit on the cruiser, but shells from the *Canarias*'s 203 mm guns sent the Basque trawler, wreathed in flames, to the coast, where it went aground, but was finally towed into Bilbao. Meanwhile, the *Bizkaia* freed the *Yorkbrook*, a cargo ship flying the Estonian flag which the *Canarias* had captured the day before and ordered to sail into the Insurgent port of Pasajes with its 460 tons of war material. This turned out to be next to useless when unloaded.[4] Next, the *Canarias* fired at the *Galdames*. This ship surrendered while the *Nabara* and the *Donostia* escaped, radioing fruitless calls for help to the destroyer *José Luis Díez*. The *Canarias* opened fire on the *Nabara*, which defended itself valiantly until the cruiser's shells destroyed it. There were only fourteen survivors, most of whom were wounded.[5] The courage of the crew would be celebrated in a poem by C.Day Lewis.[6] The *Donostia* scored a number of hits with its 101 mm guns before it escaped to a French port where it was interned until the end of the war.

IV Inactivity and Desertion of the Republican Warships

In the meantime, however, where was the Republican destroyer *José Luis Díez*? In Bilbao, the destroyer was sneeringly called 'Joe from the port' (*Pepe, el del puerto*), because it rarely left harbour. Its captain, Carlos Moya, claimed later that his ship could not maintain speed. He sailed to Bordeaux for repairs. He and the other officers then evaded the sailors' committee and slipped over the frontier into the Insurgent zone. They were absolved of responsibility and served in the Insurgent navy. The result of their desertion was that the *José Luis Díez* was left for repair in Bordeaux without officers. Despite large sums of money offered to the crew, they remained loyal to the Republic.

On 31 March 1937 Insurgent forces had begun their assault on the Basque Country. President Aguirre sent urgent telegrams to Valencia, now the temporary capital of the Republic, demanding reinforcements. The destroyer *Císcar*, commanded by Sub Lieutenant José María García Presno, was sent to Bilbao, together with the submarine *C4*. Aguirre, the Basque president described García Presno, in a letter to Prieto, as addicted to cocaine, and a frequenter of night clubs in the company of a subordinate.

Understandably, discipline was poor. The *Císcar* was due to sail to Britain and represent Spain at the coronation of George VI on 12 May. On the 10, Aguirre cabled Prieto, warning him that Insurgent agents in Britain could bribe the crew to change sides.[7] Prieto agreed and the *Císcar* remained in Bilbao. Aguirre, growing ever more desperate, suggested that more ships should be sent to Bilbao and that their crews should be replaced by Basque seamen.

On the night of 1/2 June, on orders from the Basque president, police boarded the destroyers and arrested the crews. Basque volunteers would now man the ships. José Antonio Castro, a midshipman, took over the *Císcar*.

By mid-June 1937, as Franco's forces neared Bilbao, refugees were crowding on to any seaworthy vessel. Aguirre cabled Prieto, now Minister of National Defence in the recently appointed government of Juan Negrin:

> [...] submarines and destroyers facing very difficult situation here have left [Bilbao] for Santander trying to avoid enemy ships and armed trawlers [...]

However, who had ordered this? Enrique Navarro, appointed commander of the Republican fleet in the Cantabrian Sea on 27 March, now aboard the destroyer *Císcar*, was instructed to:

> [...]clarify the origin and basis for the order that the *José Luis Díez* should leave Bilbao.[8]

And Prieto radioed the *José Luis Díez*:

> I am surprised by your radio message because I have not given the order [presumably to leave Bilbao] to which you refer. I repeat what the Chief of Staff has just transmitted to you.

From the *José Luis Díez*, Captain Evaristo López replied that the staff had ordered him to evacuate civilians. The other destroyer, the *Císcar*, had taken on the commander of the fleet as well as the chief of staff and other important people who would be in danger when Bilbao fell. However, the crew were aware that the departure was not authorised and sent a message – a fact which shows how little authority the senior Republican officers had – to Prieto saying 'Tell us what to do with these people'.

The messages went back and forth, almost certainly read by the Insurgent ships. Prieto radioed several times, 'Despite any orders you may have received, return to a loyal port.'

Prieto's words seem to imply that he suspected that the destroyers were deserting, rather than making for Santander, which was still in Republican hands. He was right; the destroyers sailed to France, where the senior officers abandoned the ships with some help from the French destroyer *L'Audacieux*, which calmed the very angry crew, and eventually made their way to the Insurgent side.[9] The *Císcar*, under the very junior Juan Antonio Castro, and the *José Luis Díez*, returned to Santander on 21 June.

V A Soviet Officer Commands a Spanish Submarine

In the meantime, the submarines *C4* and *C6* had been sent to the Cantabrian coast to replace the inoperative *C2*. The *C4* sailed under the command of Lieutenant Lasheras, yet another officer who had saved his life by agreeing to captain a Republican submarine but who avoided aggressive action. The *C6*, however, had a Soviet commander. This was Ivan Alexeevich Burmistrov, alias 'Luis Martínez'. His second in command was 'Victor Nicolas', another Soviet submarine officer. Earlier, the *C6* had been attacked and damaged. It put into harbour for the usual extremely slow repairs. An Insurgent officer was kept prisoner on board and, after managing to give his captors the slip, provided the Insurgents with some interesting information about the submarine.[10] He reported that the Soviet commander's tactics were to remain submerged all day and to come almost to the surface and use the periscope once each hour. The crew were very apprehensive of any contact with the enemy. According to this report, the

Russians were also unwilling to take any risks. At the slightest problem they returned to harbour. Decisions were taken by vote of the crew.

The *C6* began operations in the Cantabrian and soon reported sighting the *Almirante Cervera*, but on 12 May it returned to Bilbao to repair its compass. Burmistrov complained about the disruptive behaviour of some of the crew. In one case he claimed that he had been eating when a seaman passed by and removed and ate some of his food.[11] At sea once more, on 20 June, the day that Bilbao fell to Franco, and manned with replacements from the Basque volunteer force, the *C6* launched two torpedoes at the *Almirante Cervera*. The latter spotted their track and turned away rapidly.[12]

Franco's navy on the Cantabrian coast was unified and disciplined, but small. If the two Republican destroyers and the submarines had functioned properly, Bilbao might have been able to withstand the blockade which Franco had imposed during his campaign to take the Basque capital and which involved Britain in a crisis.

VI The Royal Navy and the Blockade of Bilbao

In general the Royal Navy had enjoyed good relations with Franco's naval commanders. Despite Franco's declarations of blockade, Insurgent warships had been told not to interfere with British freighters, probably because the Merchant Shipping (Carriage of Munitions to Spain) Act of December 1936, had reassured the Insurgents that the Royal Navy would stop and search British merchant ships to verify that they were not carrying arms. Thus regular traffic continued smoothly. Coal, iron ore and other goods flowed between Spain's northern ports, in particular Bilbao, and ports in South Wales and other parts of the United Kingdom.

However, by now the Insurgents were aggrieved that many cargo ships had been put on the British register when there was nothing British about them except their ownership. British law allowed officers and crews to be aliens if the ship in question habitually traded abroad. Compelling merchant ships to employ British crews had been considered, but it was more important to keep the ships under the British flag in order that they should be available in wartime. However, being on the British register entitled them to Royal Navy protection.

The British government, supported by most public opinion, refused to recognise the Insurgent blockade. Nevertheless, the First Lord of the Admiralty, Sir Samuel Hoare, was much more pro-Franco than the Foreign Secretary, Anthony Eden, and wanted rights of blockade to be granted to the Spanish Insurgents, Eden, in contrast, was growingly alarmed at German and particularly Italian military support of the Spanish Insurgents. He wrote in his diary on 21 November 1936:

> My own feeling is at present against the granting of belligerent rights to Franco for international rather than Spanish reasons. I do not want even to appear to follow Hitler and Mussolini at the moment...[13]

Eden was anxious about the growing international complications of the Spanish war. Until he resigned on 20 February 1938 he would continue to insist that the scarcely-concealed participation of Fascist Italy on the Insurgent side had to end before there could be any question of recognising Franco as a belligerent with the right to stop neutral shipping outside territorial waters. However, Franco would always consider that giving up valuable Italian help was too high a price for belligerent rights, and thus his growing aggression towards neutral shipping on the high seas would continue to maintain the Spanish crisis at a high level of intensity.

Eden thought that Franco should be satisfied that British-registered ships were not carrying arms and that, if the Insurgents received contrary information, they should notify British warships in the area and leave them to stop the freighters in question. Hoare, in contrast, shared the views of the Royal Navy, which would have preferred not to intervene to protect British merchantmen, because the mutiny in the Spanish navy, followed by the murders of so many officers, had outraged British officers. For the latter, the contrast between the Republican and Insurgent navies was evident.

> [...] on the one hand a murderous rabble of mutineers incapable of keeping their ships at sea or fighting the enemy; on the other, officers of some ability, whose conception of good manners – punctilious, elaborate, a trifle arrogant – was remarkably similar to that of the pre-war British naval officer.[14]

The Bay of Biscay now presented particular problems for Britain. Ever since the mid-nineteenth century, ships had been sailing from British ports loaded with coal destined for the blast furnaces of the Basque Country. They returned with their holds filled with iron ore. There were less tangible reasons for the special relationship between Britain and the Basques. The latter were a conservative people, but one which was enterprising and open to the world. The autonomous government of the region was conducted by the conservative, though not reactionary, Basque Nationalist Party. Anthony Eden reflected British views when he told the House of Commons on 20 April 1937, in the midst of the crisis in which the Royal Navy was protecting British merchant shipping against Franco's blockade,

> [...] if I had to choose in Spain, I believe that the Basque government would more closely conform to our own system than that of Franco or the Republic.[15]

In the first eight months of the Spanish war, fifty-five British-registered ships had left Bilbao loaded with iron ore without interference from the Insurgent navy. However, on 29 March 1937, as Franco's troops neared Bilbao, he announced that henceforth even British-registered ships would be expected to stop on the order of Insurgent vessels. This was because, claimed the Insurgents, ships flying the Red Ensign without entitlement were bringing arms into Bilbao. From London the reply was unchanged. British merchantmen outside the three-mile limit of territorial waters would not permit themselves to be searched. This reply followed a number of incidents in the Strait of Gibraltar where British ships had been stopped, often at Franco's request, but were found not to be carrying arms.[16] On 23 March 1937, Sir Henry Chilton, British ambassador to Spain but resident in Hendaye on the French-Spanish border, cabled Eden that the situation was becoming critical. In his view, the Insurgents were determined to force Britain to recognise them as belligerents and thus entitled to stop and search neutral ships.[17]

Furthermore, Admiral Moreno, Franco's senior naval commander, had told the captain of the British battleship *Ramillies* that the Insurgents were going to lay mines along the coast inside territorial waters. The captain of the battleship had not reported this because the information had been given to him in confidence. The result was the severe damage caused to the *Llandovery Castle,* a freighter which struck a mine off Cape Creus while making for Marseilles.[18] Replying to a protest from London, the Insurgents claimed that they were entitled to mine the entire Mediterranean coast, which was in 'Red hands', even though they did not try to deny that by, by mining, they were ignoring their responsibility to ensure the safety of neutral shipping.[19]

Bombing ships was also becoming an issue. When Republican aircraft attacked British ships, it was in error and the Spanish government apologised. In contrast, on 13 February 1937, the destroyers *Havock* and *Gipsy* had been bombed from 6,000 feet by an Italian bomber in Franco's service. The Insurgent command excused itself on the grounds that British and Spanish Republican destroyers were identical and that Italian pilots were not well-trained to identify ships.[20] The Admiralty recognised that mistakes were likely to occur and ordered red, white and blue bands to be painted around the artillery mountings.[21] When bombs fell near HMS *Gallant* while sailing from Valencia to Alicante on 6 April, the senior British officer in the area, Captain Tait of the cruiser *Shropshire,* protested to Colonel Ramón Franco, brother of the general and commanding the Insurgent air force on Majorca. Franco apologised. Tait hinted that he knew that the aircraft were Italian and that the Insurgents might not have complete authority over them. The Admiralty accepted that it was difficult to identify ships from heights of over 8,000 feet. Franco promised to order pilots to note the number on British ships' bows.[22]

On his visit of protest, Tait was accompanied by the British vice-consul on Majorca, Lieutenant Commander (retired) Alan Hillgarth, who was on good terms with the Insurgent naval authorities and a major source of information for London. He would later rejoin the navy and become naval attaché in Madrid, where during the Second World War he handled British clandestine intelligence operations.[23]

VII Running the Blockade

Concentrated bombing by the German Condor Legion was causing angry reactions in Britain. Prime Minister Stanley Baldwin's grim statement of 1932, that 'the bomber will always get through', was creating great alarm, as was the H.G. Wells film 'Things to Come' of 1936, which prophesied the destruction of entire cities from the air. *The Times*, the newspaper read by people of influence, published images of the destruction by bombing on 31 March of the town of Durango.[24] The British consul in Bilbao, Ralph Stevenson, suggested to the Foreign Office that the Royal Navy might escort refugee ships from Bilbao to France.

Food was running short in Bilbao. Women were standing in long queues exposed to bombing in order to buy small rations of rice, sugar, dried peas and cabbage.[25] The Basque government chartered ships to bring provisions from Spanish Mediterranean ports and elsewhere. Even so, wheat, potatoes, flour, maize, barley and sugar remained scarce.[26] Pro-Franco Spanish historians assert that some food ships smuggled arms into northern Spain, but rarely identify the ships involved. Some ships may have carried arms although in the case of British vessels there is no record that any such cargoes were found under the potatoes and flour. It would have been foolish to carry weapons to Spain, which was already prohibited to British ships by the Act of December 1936. Far from flying the British flag and demanding the protection of the Royal Navy, real arms smugglers left the British register precisely because they risked being stopped, searched and probably prosecuted.

The crisis off Bilbao began at 0556 hours on Tuesday 6 April 1937, when the British cargo ship *Thorpehall* radioed that the Insurgent armed trawler *Galerna* was firing at her ten miles off the coast. At that moment the Insurgent cruiser *Almirante Cervera* appeared. The destroyer HMS *Brazen* interposed itself between the *Thorpehall* and the Spanish cruiser. Commander Taylor of the *Brazen* later reported 'I informed the *Almirante Cervera* that the British Government did not permit any action being taken against the merchant ship'.[27] But what if the Spanish cruiser opened fire? Would the destroyer respond? Two destroyers, the *Blanche*, carrying Commander Caslon, the senior British naval officer in the area, and the *Brilliant*, steamed at full speed towards Bilbao. Fortunately the German pocket battleship *Graf Spee* arrived on the scene at the same time and probably gave some advice to the captain of the *Almirante Cervera*, which, accompanied by the *Galerna*, steamed away at 1100. However, despite the British captains' efforts to persuade the Insurgents that the *Thorpehall*, which was carrying a cargo of foodstuffs from Alicante, had been duly searched at Gibraltar for contraband, the *Almirante Cervera* returned to the scene. This time, the British destroyers *Blanche* and *Brazen*, now joined by the *Beagle*, prepared to fire torpedoes.[28] By 1415 hours, the *Thorpehall* was close to the mouth of the Bilbao estuary, and the destroyers turned away. The Admiralty commended the officers on their judgement and initiative. Caslon, however, included in his report the statement that the blockade was effective, and recommended that British shipping should be dissuaded from making for Bilbao.[29] This would be a solution. Britain would not be consenting to British ships being stopped, and the Navy would not be obliged to protect them.

The matter was complex. The Insurgents insisted that Spanish waters stretched six miles into the Cantabrian Sea, and that they had the right to stop cargo ships within that distance.[30] Britain insisted on the three-mile limit claimed by most nations and repeated that the Navy would assist British merchant ships up to that boundary.

The Insurgents claimed that their fleet, albeit small, was capable of maintaining a blockade. This was the international convention for respecting it, but only if the navy exercising that right was recognised as a belligerent.[31] Admiral of the Fleet Chatfield, First Sea Lord and Chief of Naval Staff, was of the view that, once Franco had control of the sea, it was contrary to established practice to deny his navy belligerent rights.[32] The Foreign Office investigated precedents. In the only analogous case, the American Civil War of 1861–1865, the southern Confederacy had indeed been recognised as a belligerent although it was also in rebellion against the internationally-recognised government of the United States. Yet legal advice said that, in civil wars, belligerency was not automatically recognised the moment a war began, as was the case with international conflicts.[33] Anthony Eden, the Foreign Secretary, stated that Britain was not going to grant belligerent rights to Franco 'for a variety of reasons'.[34] Eden probably stalled in order to counterbalance Germany and Italy's active support for Franco.

Admiral Chatfield thought that Britain needed a friendly Spain. He was unconcerned that a Spain under Franco would have an obligation to Italy, a potential enemy of Britain. He feared that if the Republic won the civil war Spain would ally itself 'with another power'.[35] When two senior French officers, Admiral Darlan and Rear-Admiral Decoux, had visited London on 5 August 1936 to try to persuade Chatfield of the risk of Italian expansion in the Western Mediterranean which would draw the Balearics into the Italian orbit, Chatfield had flatly rejected their concerns. Franco would not give anything away, he insisted.[36] But this was not the danger, which was that a Spanish government friendly to Italy and Germany would endanger French and British strategic routes. Chatfield and his political master, Sir Samuel Hoare, First Lord of the Admiralty, were convinced that the mutinies in the Spanish fleet betokened the real danger, which was revolution. They feared that a revolutionary Spain, given victory by Soviet and French Popular Front aid, would imply real danger for British interests. And, as Franco's victory began to seem more likely, the British admirals' insistence grew that Britain should not antagonise its future Spanish friends.[37]

Now, off the Biscay coast, what in practical terms was to be done?

On Wednesday 7 April, the day after the stand-off with the *Almirante Cervera*, the cabinet met.[38] Food for besieged Bilbao was now as valuable as armaments. The Francoist authorities saw the Royal Navy as intervening openly on the Basque side by escorting cargo ships through to Bilbao, but while the Insurgents looked on the Basques as mere 'Reds and Separatists', British opinion favoured them as a people fighting for their autonomy. Hoare insisted that the freighters had been only recently registered as British, specifically to claim entitlement to Royal Navy protection.

That same afternoon, a sub-committee on the matter met. It heard that abandoning the protection of British merchant shipping might block the supply of high-grade iron ore, a vital raw material now that Britain was beginning to rearm.[39] Besides, support for the Basques was widespread in Britain. It would look very bad if Britain were to concede that the Insurgents could be allowed to starve Bilbao into surrender. So, were British guns to fire at Spanish Insurgent warships? What would be the effect of such a clash? The committee and the government took the optimistic view that a Spanish Insurgent captain would not risk such an encounter and that the cool heads of British naval captains would avoid a clash also. That morning, Sir Roger Backhouse, commanding the Home Fleet, had suggested that cargo ships be advised not to try to approach Bilbao.[40] When Eden learned of this, he noted with annoyance that the navy seemed to be trying to bounce the government into a position whose advisability was as yet not decided.[41]

The cabinet conceded, however, that merchantmen should be warned of the dangers of trying to enter Bilbao. A message to that effect went out at 0538 hours on the next day.[42] Because not all merchant ships had radio, the matter of advising merchant masters was left to the tact of British destroyer captains who might meet cargo ships making for Bilbao. At the same time, the Insurgent authorities would be firmly warned against trying to impose a blockade. On the evening of Friday 9 April, Franco threatened that any attempt to convoy ships into Bilbao would be 'resisted by Insurgent warships by all possible means, '*even at the risk of a serious incident*'.[43] This was an intolerable threat, and so on Saturday 10 April, ministers came back from their country weekends and did the only thing they could: show that Britain could muster irresistible strength. The most powerful warship in the world, the battle-cruiser *Hood*, would race from Gibraltar to the Bay of Biscay. Besides the *Hood*, the cruiser *Shropshire* and four destroyers, the *Blanche*, *Brazen*, *Beagle* and *Brilliant*, would be on watch. Nevertheless, British merchant ships were still to be advised, although they could not be directly ordered, to anchor in Saint Jean de Luz, just over the French frontier. Five freighters did so, the *Marie Llewellyn*, the *Olavus*, the *Sarastone*, the *Hamsterley* and the *Leadgate*.

Warnings from Royal Navy captains, however, seem to have been more in the nature of orders. Commander Caslon had signalled cargo ships: 'You are not to leave Saint Jean de Luz for any port in the hands of the Spanish Government in the North of Spain.'[44] In reality, Royal Navy captains had no such authority over merchant skippers. Possibly the Insurgents knew this, but it is doubtful whether they understood subjectively the power of British public opinion and the limits of the authority of a democratic government.

Finally, another message was composed.

His Majesty's Government cannot tolerate any interference with British shipping at sea. They are, however, warning British shipping that, in view of conditions at present prevailing in the neighbourhood of Bilbao, they should not, for practical reasons and in view of the risks against which it is impossible at present to protect them, go into that area as long as those conditions prevail.[45]

This message was copied to the Insurgents in the hope that it would restrain them, and Prime Minister Baldwin announced it in the Commons on Monday 12 April. The Admiralty had prepared some notes to help the government, saying that the Insurgent blockade was effective (a condition for it being recognised), and that the coastal defences of Bilbao were ineffective. Major Attlee, the Labour leader, rose to insist that commercial traffic was safe inside the three-mile limit, while Baldwin spoke about a situation 'in constant change'. The Opposition had got the bit between its teeth and demanded a debate on a motion of censure for Wednesday 14 April. The previous day, 13 April 1937, Baldwin received a message from Aguirre, the Basque President, who insisted that there was no danger at all within territorial waters. There were no mines. Ships were entering and leaving Bilbao freely. Insurgent armed trawlers were unwilling to face the Basque Auxiliary Navy, and Insurgent warships feared the searchlights and the coastal artillery.

By the morning of 14 April, Aguirre's message was known to the Opposition. If its content was accurate, there was no reason to dissuade British merchant shipping from making for Bilbao, save the risk of interference from an Insurgent warship.

Sir Samuel Hoare tried to avoid conceding that the Royal Navy would protect a British freighter outside the three-mile limit if an Insurgent warship did try to stop it. Other ministers thought that protection should be clearly promised. Finally, it was decided that merchant ships would be warned of the dangers, while Eden wanted to leave the Insurgents in no doubt that the Royal Navy would protect British ships. It was decided to repeat the message to the Insurgents, warning them also that they would be liable for compensation for damage.

That afternoon, an irritable House of Commons assembled for the debate. Just before 4 pm Major Attlee, leader of the Labour opposition proposed:

> That this House, taking note of the statement of the Prime Minister on the situation at Bilbao, deplores the failure of His Majesty's Government to give protection to British merchant ships on their lawful occasions.[46]

The government had a large majority and the motion of censure was defeated. The crisis, however, had not been solved.

Evidently, the official position was to prevaricate as far as possible. Britain had made it clear that the Royal Navy would protect British merchant shipping, but at the same time was doing what it could in order not to put the Navy in a position where it would have to do so. The Insurgents were also relieved from having to make good their boast that they would do whatever they had to, to stop shipping entering the Basque port. So all were satisfied, except the merchant captains, whose cargoes

Republican cruiser *Miguel de Cervantes* at Cartagena, with revolutionary sailors giving clenched fist salute

were going bad, and the Basques who were short of food. On 17 April, Sir Henry Chilton telephoned from Hendaye to tell the Foreign Secretary that he had learned from the local Insurgent authority on the French frontier that 'Franco was very pleased with our attitude and probably would not interfere with our shipping'.[47] On the same day, Ralph Stevenson, British consul in Bilbao, cabled the Foreign Office that Insurgent warships were staying out of range of the coastal artillery.[48]

Nevertheless, Chilton was wrong. Unable apparently to fathom Franco's mind, he thought that the Insurgent general saw the parliamentary victory of the British government as a clear indication that merchantmen should not make for Bilbao, and that obviously they would do what they were told. But, far from definite, the situation was still fluid. In any case, the harbour at St Jean de Luz was small, and the skippers wanted to sell their cargoes in Bilbao.

As the days passed, the British freighters anchored in St Jean de Luz began to suspect that they ran no danger if they made the overnight run into Bilbao. On Monday, 19 April, Hoare was forced to admit in the Commons that two British ships had left Bilbao with iron ore. Mr Attlee rose to ask sarcastically what the specific difficulty was that prevented the arrival but not the departure of merchant ships.[49]

At ten pm on Monday 19 April 1937, the *Seven Seas Spray*, belonging to the Veronica Steamship Company of Cardiff and under the command of Captain William Roberts, with a cargo of 3,600 tons of foodstuffs from Alicante, steamed out of St Jean de Luz ignoring signals from a British destroyer. Roberts, accompanied by his daughter, probably did not know that the battle-cruiser *Hood* was shadowing him in case the Insurgents tried to intervene.[50]

The following morning, the *Seven Seas Spray* entered the Bilbao estuary and sailed past the wharves in an apotheosis of cheering from crowds of civilians, '*Vivan los marineros ingleses!*' '*Viva la Libertad!*' Captain Roberts was entertained by the Basque government and presented with a silver cigarette case inscribed with the thanks of the Basque People.[51] One of the partners of the Veronica Line, Alfred Pope, told journalists:

> My steamer has shown that Franco's blockade is nothing but boast and tommy rot [...] I hope that it has shown the rest of the vessels in St Juan de Luz the way to Bilbao.[52]

The triumph of the *Seven Seas Spray* overshadowed the failure of another ship and its captain. This was Captain David Jones of the *Marie Llewellyn*, owned by Claude Angel of Cardiff, with a cargo of potatoes. There were three Welsh sea-captains in St Jean de Luz, so he was known as 'Potato Jones', while 'Corn Cob' Jones commanded the *MacGregor* and 'Ham and Egg' Jones the *Sarastone*. 'Potato Jones', white-moustached and reddish-faced, sounded off bellicosely to the reporter of the Cardiff *Western Mail* in tones which echoed British prejudices and made him the hero of his native Swansea.

> Spanish navy! Never heard of it since the Armada. It makes me sick, thinking of these Spanish Dons strutting about the quarter-decks of their miserable ships intimidating the British Navy and interfering with shipping![53]

At 4 pm on 15 April, 'Potato Jones' weighed anchor without notice. Since he was sailing directly across the course of the Insurgent battleship *España*, his chance to imitate Elizabethan seamen and 'do battle with the Dons' might have come sooner than he wished had he not been turned back by HMS *Brazen*. Two days later, the *Marie Llewellyn* set sail again, this time for Alicante where Potato Jones unloaded his now elderly and sprouting potatoes.

The success of the *Seven Seas Spray* led British shipping circles to think that it was safe to try to run into Bilbao. Ministers abandoned their opposition when Vice-Admiral Blake, aboard HMS *Hood*, expressed the view that with a powerful British naval force in the area the Insurgents would not try to stop British ships.

After discussion with Admiral Blake it was decided that the *MacGregor*, the *Hamsterley* and the *Stanbrook*, with 8,500 tons of food between them, would sail for Bilbao on the evening of 22 April. The next morning, inside the ten-mile limit, the Insurgent cruiser *Almirante Cervera* fired a shot across the bows of the *MacGregor*. The *Hood* warned the *Almirante Cervera* to stop firing, which it did under protest. As the *MacGregor* crossed the three-mile limit the Insurgent armed trawler *Galerna* fired at it. The destroyer *Firedrake* issued a warning and aimed its guns at the *Galerna*. The *Almirante Cervera* moved towards the British destroyer. The entire policy of non-intervention depended on the cool reactions of Admiral Blake, the captain of the *Firedrake* and Captain Moreu, commanding the *Almirante Cervera*. Would shells from the 152mm guns of the Spanish cruiser crash into the British destroyer before the colossal firepower of HMS *Hood* blew the Spanish ship to pieces? Admiral Blake continued to signal 'Stop firing. Our merchant ships are five miles from the coast…four miles from the coast'. On board the *Almirante Cervera* Captain Moreu insisted that the limit of territorial waters was six miles, while Admiral Blake repeated that his government did not recognise this limit. But just in time the Basque coastal batteries opened fire. The Insurgent warships turned away. Captain Moreu no longer had to decide whether to capitulate or to lose his ship, albeit with honour, to the 42,000 ton *Hood*. On 23 April Admiral Blake reported to Admiral Chatfield that the blockade was not effective.

In the following week, the *Stesso*, the *Thurston*, the *Sheaf Garth*, the *Backworth*, the *Marvia*, the *Thorpehall*, the *Sheaf Field*, and the *Portelet* docked at Bilbao. The *Jenny* and the *Oakgrove* reached Santander. Several of these ships had been stopped by the Insurgents and protected by ships of the Royal Navy. Another twelve ships entered Bilbao in May.

Forcing the merchant ships through the Insurgent blockade was in a sense intervention in the Spanish Civil War, but to have dissuaded British ships from carrying foodstuffs to Bilbao and Santander would also have constituted intervention, but on Franco's side. Nevertheless, the worry continued. If the merchant ships were not really British, should the Royal Navy protect them? The law was clear. If the ships were British there was no need for the captain or the crews to be of that nationality. On 4 May, a government spokesman, at Question Time in the Commons, insisted that the Stanhope Shipping Company, one of the largest lines, had been the property of Jack Billmeir, a British citizen, since 1934, that is before the Spanish civil war began. Most of the other forty-seven ships which had begun to fly the Red Ensign were of under 1,000 tons and not involved in the Spanish trade.[54] Even so, a number of the other companies running the blockade had indeed been only recently constituted.

Yet to rule that the Royal Navy should protect only those ships belonging to lines already existing before the conflict and which had a proportion of British citizens in their crews would have been out of the question for a country which depended so greatly on its merchant marine. While in 1914 Britain's share of world merchant shipping had been a massive forty-one per cent, by 1938 it had declined to twenty-six per cent. In time of war Britain could not call on as many ships as before. The decline in tonnage indicated that the Royal Navy could not afford to be snooty about the activities and the masters and crews of cargo ships provided they were on the British register.[55]

VIII The Royal Navy Protects Refugee Ships

As the Insurgents neared Bilbao and bombing became more intense, the widely-reported destruction by the Condor Legion of the town of Guernica on 26 April 1937, graphically described by the journalist George Lowther Steer in *The Times* on 28 April, galvanised British public opinion.[56]

At dawn on Thursday 6 May 1937 a British naval force, including the battleships *Resolution*, with its two accompanying destroyers, and *Royal Oak*, on which Rear Admiral Ramsay flew his flag, and the destroyers *Faulknor* and *Fortune*, assembled off Bilbao, just as the 10,000 ton liner *Habana* and the steam yacht *Goiceko Izarra*, both packed with children, sailed for France and the hospitality of French trade unions.

The *Almirante Cervera*, one mile north of the *Royal Oak*, signalled:

I got (*sic*) orders from my Government to stop any Spanish ship leaving Bilbao. I protest if you stop me in the exercise of my rights.

At 0732 hours, Admiral Ramsay replied:

These ships are carrying non-combatant refugees certified by British consul. I have orders from my Government to protect these ships on the high seas. I have noted your protest and will inform my Government.

The *Almirante Cervera*'s 152 mm guns were no match for the *Royal Oak*'s 381 mm artillery. In addition, the Spanish cruiser had condenser problems and could not develop its full speed, so it moved away. That was the end of the incident.[57] The *Almirante Cervera* had received orders which were impossible as well as unwise to try to carry out.

The enormity of the bombing of Guernica forced the British government to protect the evacuation of a large number of refugees from the Basque capital and to receive nearly 4,000 children as refugees in Britain.[58] Two British capital ships escorted ships carrying refugees to France and in one case, the 10,000-ton liner *Habana*, to Southampton with 4,000 children. Pressure of public opinion had weighed heavy on an unwilling Admiralty. British warships continued to protect ships trading with the northern Republican Zone, and to escort refugee ships. It was hard for the Admiralty, nevertheless, to maintain its enthusiasm. While the Basques enjoyed great sympathy in Britain, naval officers empathised with their Spanish Insurgent opposite numbers. It is no surprise to find, among the reports of the *Almirante Cervera*, a message from a British destroyer which was escorting a ship with a cargo of iron ore,

I hope Bilbao will fall soon. When do you think? I've been for around a week and I hope you will kill a lot of Reds in this time.[59]

IX Sinking of the *Espana*: The Campaign in the North Ends

On 30 April, the Insurgent navy suffered a major loss when the battleship *España* sank. This ship and the destroyer *Velasco* were blockading Santander. As they tried to intercept the British-registered *Knitsley*, out of Newcastle, the *España* hit a mine, laid by the Insurgents. The battleship heeled over and the engine rooms were flooded. The captain ordered 'Abandon Ship!' The *Velasco* came alongside, rescuing all the crew save seven.[60] A British destroyer had witnessed an air attack on the *España* at the same time as it hit the mine. The Admiralty, which doubted the ability of aircraft to sink capital ships, and the Air Ministry, which wanted it to be thought that aircraft could certainly do so, hurriedly sent the naval attaché from Paris to make enquiries. The Admiralty suspected that the *España* had sailed too close to a minefield.[61] Yet aircraft were certainly involved. These were Gourdou-Leseurre-GL32 bombers, some of six that the Basques had bought in France. If these had indeed been responsible for sinking the *España*, it would have been the first time that a major warship had been sunk by aircraft in real war conditions, and the possibility caused grave concern to the Admiralty. The enquiry established that aircraft had in fact attacked the battleship, but whether they had alone been the cause of its sinking was doubtful. Possibly, the manoeuvres of the *España* to escape the aircraft took it into the minefield.

X Santander and Asturias. The Campaign Ends

British warships continued to protect merchantmen flying the Red Ensign. By 19 July 1937, the Royal Navy had protected nine ships evacuating 16,091 refugees from Santander.[62] Retired Lieutenant Commander Harry Pursey, who had risen to commissioned rank from boy seaman, and had reported from Spain on Insurgent 'bluff' about the presence of mines outside Bilbao, rowed refugees from Santander out to a British destroyer.[63] The British attitude was changing, however, because there seemed to be some truth in the Insurgent accusations that men of military age were being evacuated. The high sums of money exacted by merchant captains also caused outrage. Furthermore, the commander of a destroyer flotilla told the Admiralty that if the cruiser *Almirante Cervera* waited five miles outside Santander, as it had to do because the limit of territorial waters was calculated from the longest cape on the coast, it might be able to capture the merchantmen, since Santander's coastal artillery was not as powerful as that of Bilbao.[64] Thirteen British cargo vessels were taken over by the Insurgents between June and August 1937.[65] This seems to indicate a loss of enthusiasm on the part of the Royal Navy for protecting merchant shipping.

The imminent fall of Santander led the Spanish Republican Navy Minister to order the destroyers *Císcar* and *José Luis Díez* to sail westwards to Gijón, the last city in Republican hands along the northern coast. The *Almirante Cervera*, the two minelayers *Júpiter* and *Vulcano* and the armed trawlers now faced three submarines and two destroyers, which ought to have been able to constitute a grave threat. But their discipline and training was poor, the destroyer captains were young and inexperienced and two of the three submarine commanders were disloyal.. On 28 August, Lasheras and Ferrando left with the *C2* and the *C4* for France.[66] This left only the *C6*, with its Russian commander. Gijón was under constant air attack, short of food and with leaders who were desperately bribing skippers to take them on board.

The *José Luis Díez* sailed to Falmouth in Devon, trying to avoid Insurgent ships. The *C6* attempted to torpedo the *Júpiter* on 15 October, but its torpedoes were defective. Shortly after, the submarine was scuttled to keep it out of enemy hands. The destroyer *Císcar* was sunk by a bomb on 19 October, although it had received orders to leave and make for Cartagena. Prieto would later accuse the Russian advisers of delaying the execution of the order, with the result that the *Císcar* was in El Musel, the port of Gijón, when it was hit in an air raid.[67] Just as probable was a quarrel between the Republican commanders, each trying to protect himself and their respective staffs. A later report claimed that 'each feared that the rest would leave in the *Císcar*'.[68] The loss of this destroyer sowed understandable panic. There was no way out. Franco, with his courts-martial and his firing squads, was closing in. The navy staff and the now Rear Admiral Fuentes embarked on the *T-3* torpedo boat. Others sought anything that floated: tugs, lighters and fishing boats. About sixty boats tried to evade the barrier created by the *Almirante Cervera*, the *Velasco* and the rest of the Insurgent fleet.

When at last the refugees, soaked to the skin and sick after two days in choppy seas, reached French ports, the authorities quarantined them until finally they were allowed to disembark. Packed into wagons under lock and key they were dispatched by rail to the Catalan frontier and Republican Spain.

XI Republican Ships Abroad

Lieutenant Commander Pedro Prado, probably the only naval officer to hold a Communist Party membership card, was sent to take over command of the two submarines *C2* and *C4* in France. Ferrando and Las Heras, the previous commanders, then undertook a dangerous exploit. On night of 18 September 1937, with the connivance of Major Troncoso, Insurgent commanding officer at Irún, Lasheras, Ferrando and some French pro-Francoists, members of the extreme right-wing movement *La Cagoule*, tried to take over the *C2* at Brest.[69] They approached the submarine, moored at the Quai Malbert. Lasheras offered the crew a large sum of money to come over to the Insurgents. At 10 pm one of the twelve men not on shore leave, fired at the gang from the conning tower. The shot alerted the police and the group fled together with Ferrando and the chief engineer. Four men were arrested, Troncoso admitted that the Insurgents had offered Ferrando a sum of money to hand over the *C2*. The young lieutenant had agreed but the crew had resisted. It turned out that the group of civilians, members of La Cagoule, had already carried out sabotage and some terrorist acts on French territory, so the Minister of the Interior, Marx Dormoy, refused to repatriate Troncoso, who was found guilty of importing weapons and released after a trial in March 1938, counting the time he had spent under arrest.[70]

As for the destroyer *José Luis Díez*, its arrival at Falmouth created a headache for the British authorities. The Foreign Office decided that, since Britain had not recognised the Spanish Republic as a belligerent, it was not appropriate to intern the ship, but Britain had no obligation either to offer hospitality to a foreign warship. On the other hand, Britain could not allow the Insurgents to negotiate the surrender of the destroyer while it was in a British port. The best thing would be to allow the destroyer to have the minimum repairs carried out to allow it to leave.[71] On 4 September, Lieutenant Commander Agnew was sent to visit the *José Luis Díez*. He reported that the ship was dirty but ready for action and that despite the clenched fist salutes with which he was received, he was formally piped aboard. The sailors stood to attention when speaking to the officers but they called them by their first names. The commentary was fair and interesting, because it showed that informality had not completely demoralised discipline.[72] But it was not blind discipline. The crew was watchful and suspicious of the officers.

Two weeks later the senior engineer at Devonport confirmed that the starboard condenser needed a great deal of work.[73] When a few days later the Spanish Republic's naval attaché, Commander Fernando Navarro, arrived to organise the return of the *José Luis Díez* to Republican Spain, the officers took the opportunity to abscond, while sixty-eight crew members deserted, but were recaptured and imprisoned in Exeter. The *José Luis Díez* was put into quarantine because cases of typhoid had appeared. Finally the ship departed on 25 September under the command of Lieutenant Commander Horacio Pérez, brother of Virgilio whom the Insurgents had shot in Cádiz in July 1936. Arriving at Le Havre on the 27th, it spent many weeks there under repair.

Chapter 10

Non-Intervention and the International Patrol

I The Naval Patrol Plan 1937

Since the previous autumn, meetings between the ambassadors in London of the signatories to the Non-Intervention agreement of August 1936 had continued tediously. It seemed impossible to stop Germany and Italy aiding Franco or the USSR arming the Republic. But Britain and France aimed to prevent the Spanish war exploding into a European conflict. Therefore, in an attempt to prevent arms reaching Spain, Anthony Eden, the British Foreign Secretary, devised a plan for an international naval patrol around the Spanish coast and for observers to be stationed on the land frontiers.[1] Germany and Italy hesitated to accept this plan, hoping that the Condor Legion and the *Corpo di Truppe Volontarie* would ensure Franco's victory before the scheme came into operation.

The two Spanish parties refused to accept observers on their frontiers and in their ports, so a plan was devised to have cargoes inspected by onboard observers who would watch as ships were being unloaded in Spanish harbours.

The value of the plan was limited. Germany refused to allow observers to board ships in its ports. Furthermore, the plan did not allow the navies which would undertake the patrol to search a ship. They could merely check if the merchant ship had taken on an observer, in which case it would fly the Non-Intervention pennant (two black balls on a white background). The absence of the pennant or the observer would be a reason for suspicion. The naval patrol could warn the master, as well as reporting the ship to the government on whose register it figured. However, the patrols had no authority over non-signatories to the Non-Intervention Agreement, that is Spanish ships, those registered in other countries, and 'flag of convenience' nations such as Panama.

The deficiencies in the naval control scheme were obvious, but it was better than nothing. At least it kept Germany and Italy at the table on the Non-Intervention Committee. The plan was signed on 18 March 1937.

Apart from the observers along the Portuguese, French and Gibraltar frontiers of Spain, 330 would be recruited to sail on the cargo ships. Observers would board merchantmen at The Downs (off the Kent coast), Cherbourg, Brest, Le Verdon (Bordeaux), Lisbon, Gibraltar, Madeira, Oran, Sète, Marseilles or Palermo.

The zones were shared out as follows:
The Royal Navy would patrol from the French frontier at Hendaye along the Cantabrian coast to just west of Gijón. France would supervise westwards from there to the Portuguese frontier. Britain would patrol from the Portuguese–Spanish frontier at Huelva as far as Cape Gata, just east of Almería, where Germany would take over as far as Oropesa, north of Castellón. From here Italy would be responsible as far as the French-Catalan frontier. Italy would also watch around Minorca, and France around Majorca and Ibiza, as well as the Moroccan coast. Britain would patrol around the Canaries.

Thus the navies of Germany and Italy were to patrol the seas through which ships sailed to the Republican part of Spain. Britain would watch the Strait of Gibraltar because that was her major zone of strategic concern. But where was the Soviet Union in this? Against German and Italian wishes, Ivan Maiskii, the ambassador in London, insisted on his country's rights, especially since he claimed that Franco had detained eighty-four Russian merchant ships. Finally, the Committee agreed to invite the USSR to participate, but Maiskii rowed back, saying that there were no Soviet naval bases near enough to the northern coast of Spain where a small zone had been delimited for Russia (Italy had refused point-blank to tolerate Soviet warships in the Mediterranean).

Germany and probably the Royal Navy judged that Soviet naval efficiency was not up to what was required.[2] The Soviet Navy Minister, Admiral Orlov, had been against Soviet intervention in Spain, because of the obsolescence of the Soviet fleet, whose large ships, dating from Tsarist times, would have had a negative effect on the prestige of the USSR.[3] On the other hand, Moscow may not have wanted to take part in what it saw as no more than a method to keep Germany and Italy round the conference table rather than deal with them more forcibly.

When the plan came into force at midnight on the night of 19/20 April 1937, Britain deployed the battleship *Ramillies*, the cruisers *Galatea*, *Shropshire*, and *Arethusa*, and seventeen destroyers.

There was little possibility that the naval patrol would impede the traffic in war material. Skilled merchant captains could evade it. Italian transports to Spain were heavily escorted by warships. German ships would fly the Panamanian flag as well as change their names, while Russian cargo vessels had been largely replaced by Spanish Republican ships, which were not subject to checks.

The scheme, however, was welcomed by smaller countries. They hoped that their own licit traffic would be left alone by Franco's fleet, which had seized twenty-six Danish merchantmen, some not even bound for Spain. Danish, Norwegian, Finnish and Greek protests had been ignored. The Insurgents were acting little better than pirates, but short of an international attack on their ships or ports there was no way of stopping them which did not seem to bring serious risk of war.

In August 1937, Admiral Van Dulm, the Dutch senior administrator of the Plan, and Francis Hemming, Secretary of the Non-Intervention Committee, produced a report on the first three months of the control scheme. Observers had been recruited from seventeen countries. In the first six weeks of operation 323 cargo ships had been identified as belonging to the participating nations, but 79 vessels had not been identified and 415 were registered with non-participating nations. Twenty-four ships had set sail for Spain without taking an observer on board, but it could not be verified if they were carrying war material or what action had been taken against the owners.[4] By 17 September 1937, *The Times* was able to report that no infraction of the Non-Intervention regulations had been detected by the Naval Patrol, although it was well-known that a merchant captain had only to hoist a non-European flag to avoid being stopped.

The optimistic tone of these reports, however, was unfounded. German cargo ships continued to disguise themselves and to fly the Panamanian flag as they entered the English Channel in the course of ninety-six further voyages, as they carried men and material to Insurgent Spain.[5]

II Getting Past the Patrol

The Insurgents had successfully bribed a number of merchant captains to surrender their cargoes. For this reason a shipping line, called France-Navigation, was established by the French Communist Party on 15 April 1937. Its twenty-three ships, with trusted captains and crews, made a large number of journeys to Republican Spain, losing only two vessels and disguising their cargoes as agricultural or other machinery. France-Navigation took a significant part in evacuating refugees from Northern Spain in 1937. Like the German ships, France-Navigation masked its vessels with false funnels and new names.[6]

France-Navigation's first voyage was undertaken by the *Dairiguerme*, a small ship of 817 tons, on 30 April, from Gdynia to Bilbao with twenty million cartridges, while the larger *Plouzeblanc*, *Lézardrieux*, *Cassidaigne* and the smaller *Perros-Guirrec* sailed to Santander. However, between 14 December 1937 and 11 August 1938 twelve ships of France-Navigation, replacing Russian and Republican Spanish freighters, carried large quantities of war material, including aircraft, anti-aircraft guns, field artillery, howitzers and aero engines from Murmansk to Bordeaux.[7] The material was probably taken by road to Spain between 17 March and 30 June when the French government opened the the Catalan frontier.

Some ships were suspected by the patrol, however, but when in November 1937 HMS *Greyhound* took the *African Queen* into Malta and the *Euphorbia* into Gibraltar to be searched, nothing prohibited was found.[8] The British shipowner Jack Billmeir was, however, still being denounced by the Insurgents. One of his many ships, the *Stancroft*, on its way from Barcelona to Valencia on 9 May 1938, was stopped by the cruiser *Devonshire*, and taken to Gibraltar, where its master, Captain Scott, was prosecuted. Two eminent barristers, D. N. Pritt and Geoffrey Bing, Director of the Spanish Republican Press Agency in London, went out to the Rock to defend Scott.

The prohibited articles turned out to be seventeen boxes of cartridge and shell cases and nine aircraft engines described by Pritt as 'a jumble-sale lot'. Expert witnesses said that the material was in fact usable. Nevertheless, Pritt claimed that the act of Parliament which prohibited the carriage of arms *to* Spain in British merchantmen did not apply when the material in question was already *in* Spain. The case was dismissed, but the prosecution appealed to the Supreme Court in Gibraltar, which decide that the relevant act did apply in this case.[9] Defence counsel then appealed to the High Court in London, but when Captain Scott died suddenly, the matter came to an end.[10]

Given the failure of the Naval Patrol to prevent the arrival of war material in Spain, did it have any value? The Van Dulm-Hemming Report did not care to say that German and Italian ships were getting past the control, although British naval intelligence cannot have been unaware of this after the commanders of Royal Navy ships visiting El Ferrol and Vigo must have seen 'Panamanian' vessels unloading war material.

Nevertheless, even the German and Italian warships patrolling the Republican coastline did not report any infractions. As Alfred Duff Cooper, who had replaced Hoare at the Admiralty, remarked, the control scheme did not have to be *fully* effective to be successful. The point was not to stop the arms traffic, but to show that there was an active international response to it, including by Germany and Italy. It was, in fact, largely cosmetic.[11] Moreover, to be able to visit Royal Navy ships and be entertained in their wardrooms gave officers, particularly of the German navy which had been reduced to next to nothing after the First World War, the sense that they were participating in a task of international importance in partnership with the most respected navy in the world.

III The *Hunter,* The *Barletta,* The *Deutschland* and the *Leipzig*

With so many warships off Spain, accidental bombings by aircraft whose crews were not well-trained in identifying ships was unavoidable. British warships had already been bombed by Spanish aircraft of both sides, but now more serious attacks were to take place. On 13 May 1937, while on patrol off Almería, the British destroyer *Hunter* was seriously damaged by a mine, killing eight men and wounding several more. Spanish Republican ships towed the *Hunter* into Almería where doctors treated the wounded, who were then transferred to the hospital ship HMS *Maine*.[12] The cruiser *Arethusa* towed the *Hunter* to Gibraltar, where the bodies of the dead sailors were drawn through Main Street on gun carriages before burial. The Insurgents denied responsibility on the grounds that the *Hunter* was within six miles of the coast and thus in Spanish waters, and refused to pay the indemnity demanded, insisting that the mine had been laid by the Republicans.[13] Later, it was discovered that the mine had been laid by the torpedo launch *Falange*, acquired from Germany in February 1937, and had possibly become separated from its moorings.[14] Finally, after Italy, fearing for the safety of its own ships, protested, the Insurgents ceased to lay mines. However, bombings continued and would create a crisis at the end of May 1937.

In May 1937, a further shipment of Soviet Tupolev SB-2 bombers, flown by Russian pilots and known in Spain as *Katiuskas*, was supplied to the Spanish Republicans. They began to attack the Insurgent naval base at Palma (Majorca). This harbour was used by the Royal Navy, as well as by Italian and German warships in the intervals of their duties on the international patrol. While Royal Navy ships were welcome in all Spanish ports, the pro-Franco attitude of Germany and Italy prevented their warships anchoring in the Republican ports of Mediterranean Spain. Spanish Insurgent ships also anchored in Palma, including the cruiser *Baleares*, which suffered a small hit from a bomb on 23 May. On 26 May *Katiuskas* bombed Palma, hitting a number of ships. The heaviest loss was suffered by the armed Italian merchantman *Barletta* when it was hit by a 100 kg bomb which killed six officers.

Admiral von Fischel, commander of the German flotilla, was of the view that the Republican bombing was directed specifically at German and Italian warships, and decided that the pocket-battleship *Deutschland* and the destroyer *Leopard* should not anchor in Palma but in a roadstead off Ibiza. There, at 1910 hours on 29 May, two *Katiuska* bombers were seen approaching rapidly from the west. Two minutes later the aircraft released their bombs from a height of 1,000 metres. The German battleship suffered two direct hits. Many sailors were on the mess deck, which was destroyed causing large loss of life. The final casualty list was thirty-one men killed and seventy wounded. The *Deutschland* was able to reach Gibraltar, where the wounded were tended in the naval hospital. The dead were carried to the cemetery in military lorries, the coffins draped in the Nazi flag, and buried with military honours. On 11 June, the corpses were exhumed and taken to Germany for a State funeral attended by Hitler. In August, Admiral Carls visited Gibraltar and presented awards to people who had cared for the wounded. The German navy became popular in military and naval circles on the Rock.

The pilot and the bomb aimer of the *Katiuska* had little if any experience in identifying warships from the air. They assumed that, since notice had not been given to the Republican authorities that foreign warships were anchored at Ibiza, the large vessel there was the Insurgent cruiser *Canarias*.[15] The Republican authorities issued a statement that the *Deutschland* had been in an Insurgent area, and that Ibiza was in the French, not the German, patrol zone. Nor had notice been given that the *Deutschland* was anchored off Ibiza. They also claimed that the battleship had fired first. This was denied by Germany, but it is not unlikely that the battleship did fire at the *Katiuskas*, assuming that the gunners had time to reach their weapons. Nevertheless, the low level bombing proved for the Germans that the attack was intended, and not merely a reaction to being fired at.

The German Foreign Minister, von Neurath, passed hours with an enraged Hitler.[16] He telegraphed to Ribbentrop, ambassador in London, instructing him to inform the Non-Intervention Committee that Germany would cease to participate in the naval patrol until it received a positive guarantee that there would be no repetition of the incident. Germany reserved the right to take measures against the 'Red tyrants'.[17]

The Spanish Republic could not risk allowing foreign public opinion to work itself up against 'Red barbarity' employed against innocent sailors or to suggest that the Republic did not have control over its own air force, so allegations against Germany were required. It was a fact that the German naval commander had threatened to fire on aircraft which flew over his ships.[18] The Republican government insisted that aircraft had to fly over warships anchored in Insurgent ports in order to verify their nationality. This was all that the *Katiuskas* had been doing when they were fired on.[19]

If indeed the *Katiuskas* were only verifying the identity of the *Deutschland* or even trying to score a hit on what they thought was a Spanish Insurgent ship, their low flying was understandable. That the German crew were on their mess deck does not imply that the guns were not manned, as the Spanish ambassador in London told Eden, who repeated the statement to Sir Henry Chilton for him to tell the Insurgents.[20] Again, if indeed the German gunners had fired, there would have been right on their side, but in order to underline Spanish Republican responsibility, the Germans had to deny that they had fired, just as the pilots had to say they had been fired on in order to disguise their inability to identify ships correctly.

Hitler in his rage wanted his warships to bombard Cartagena and Valencia, but his naval chief Admiral Raeder convinced him that it would be very dangerous to attack harbours defended by powerful coastal artillery. Since the Republican battleship *Jaime Primero* was thought to be anchored at Almería, that port was chosen for an attack which would attempt to put the battleship's large calibre guns out of commission. On the night of 30 May, the battleship *Admiral Scheer* and four destroyers, the *Albatros, Luchs, Leopard* and *Seeadler*, were ordered to assemble off Almería. Admiral von Fischel told the German High Command that the *Jaime Primero* had unexpectedly sailed to Cartagena and that Almería was now undefended, save by small calibre artillery, but he was overruled, possibly for fear of Hitler's anger. Opening fire from eight miles at 0730 hours on 31 May, the *Admiral Scheer* fired 94 280 mm shells and 148 shots from its smaller guns, while the destroyers fired 33 shells.[21] The result was 19 civilians killed, 55 injured and 30 buildings destroyed. The coastal battery defended Almeria with 60 shots, none of which scored hits. Admiral Raeder later commented that the city was thus not undefended.[22]

Later that day Indalecio Prieto, the Republican government's Minister of Defence, proposed a general attack on the German warships of the international patrol, which might have led to a full-scale conflict. The Communist ministers in the Cabinet communicated urgently with Moscow, which instructed them to oppose the proposal, for it was not in the interests of the USSR, and Prime Minister Negrín agreed with them.

The shelling of Almería was a political error, because international obloquy shifted from the Spanish Republic to Germany, which now had to make decisions about whether to continue to participate in the naval patrol, having threatened to leave. That morning, 31 May 1937, at the meeting in London of the Non-Intervention Committee, the seats reserved for the German and Italian ambassadors were empty. A letter from Ribbentrop was read out, followed by a silence among the ambassadors and their advisers. Charles Corbin, the French ambassador, commented that the most important thing was to keep the Committee in existence. What guarantees could be offered to Italy and Germany to keep them involved in the attempt to corral the Spanish war so that no general conflict arose? In Berlin the French ambassador told von Neurath that the German reprisal for the bombing of the *Deutschland* had been 'within extremely moderate limits'.[23] On the same day, in contrast, Eden told the German embassy counsellor Woermann that the reprisal had been 'too extreme'. Britain had also lost lives through the bombing of its warships, but had not resorted to revenge attacks.[24] The German response was that the attack on the *Deutschland* had been 'premeditated' rather than accidental.

The arguments about guarantees went on until an agreed text was established on 12 June. Both Spanish parties would be asked to respect foreign warships even in territorial waters. If there were further attacks, the aggrieved country could take any steps which it considered appropriate, but a further set of agreements would be composed as far as was possible. This woolly set of sentences virtually gave Germany what it wanted. Germany and Italy returned to the naval patrol. In Berlin it was thought that danger to German warships was not great; the diplomatic victory was more important, as was the prestige that Germany earned by taking part in the patrol as one of the great powers.[25]

However, the diplomatic truce lasted for a short time only. On 15 June, Berlin claimed that torpedoes had been fired at the German cruiser *Leipzig*. The wakes of the missiles had not been seen but the hydrophone operators had heard them on their courses. Rumours that the *Leipzig* had been sunk had circulated, according to Berlin, 'in certain circles abroad'. On 18 June there was another attack some twenty miles north of Oran. This time the wake of the missile was seen. One of the torpedoes was said to have banged the hull of the cruiser. Since the Insurgent navy had retained none of the Spanish submarines, it was claimed that one of these, under Republican command, must have launched the torpedo. Germany was not prepared to tolerate the attack.[26] Ribbentrop demanded a joint naval demonstration off Valencia by the four powers involved in the naval patrol, and that Spanish submarines be surrendered to those powers. The French ambassador took a critical position on the German demands. Where was the *Leipzig* exactly? Who had circulated the rumours? Was it technically possible to be sure from sound detectors that torpedoes had been launched? Corbin had presumably been advised by his naval attaché to ask these questions. He seems to have suspected bad faith in the German charges. The Admiralty told Eden that the *Leipzig* might have been attacked, but the British authorities knew nothing of the presence of Spanish submarines in the area.[27] On 21 June, in a further cable, Ribbentrop let drop that even Germany had not confirmed that the submarine involved was Spanish.[28] Moreover, neither the French nor the British naval authorities nor even the Insurgent navy believed that there were Republican submarines in the area.[29]

Von Neurath instructed Ribbentrop:

> If in further discussions the official report of our commander with regard to what actually happened in the torpedo attacks should be doubted, such doubt should be most sharply rejected. You may make it clear that, if such doubt should persist, you would be compelled to leave the conference.[30]

Through the fog of diplomatic language, the German Foreign Minister's words might be interpreted as concealing his own hesitations about the truth of the matter. According to Spanish naval historians, writing much later, several Republican submarines had been lost, and three were known to be in the Cantabrian Sea. Only the *C1*, the *B1* and the *B2* were in the Mediterranean, but none of these were active in the area of the supposed torpedo attack.[31]

So, it is possible that the matter was fabricated on the basis of some other cause of the phenomenon interpreted on the *Leipzig* as a torpedo attack by the 'Red pirates', a description which Germany wanted to establish as the characteristic of the Republic's naval forces.

One further hypothesis remains. Von Neurath perhaps knew that two Italian submarines, the *Archimede* and the *Torricelli*, were in the service of the Insurgents under the names *Sanjurjo* and *Mola*. They had been handed over on the small Balearic island of Cabrera, for reasons of secrecy, and announced as the ex-Republican boats *C3* and *C5*. The former had been sunk, as is now known, by a German U-boat off Málaga on 12 December 1936, and the latter had disappeared off the Cantabrian coast at the end of 1936, possibly sabotaged by its captain. Perhaps the rumours about the torpedoing of the *Leipzig* were put about to suggest that the two submarines were still in the service of the Republic. In a memorandum of 22 June, von Neurath noted:

> It is absolutely certain that the attempt to torpedo the *Leipzig* was not made by White [i.e. Francoist] submarines.[32]

He did not say that Franco had no submarines, and his denial suggests the contrary and that the attack may have been carried out by the *Sanjurjo* or the *Mola*, thinking in error that the *Leipzig* was a Republican cruiser.

Finally, not having received the assurances demanded, on 23 June, von Neurath announced that Germany was leaving the naval patrol.[33] On 29 June 1937, France and Britain proposed that only they should continue to police the coasts of Spain.

However, events in the summer of 1937 were to bring about a new crisis in the Mediterranean, one which was to involve the Royal Navy and the French fleet heavily.

IV Nyon

Despite the naval control scheme, the Spanish Insurgents feared that quantities of war material would arrive in Republican Spain and have a decisive effect on the war. Consequently, on 3 August 1937, Franco's government sent an urgent message to its ambassador in Rome.

> All reports of the last few days agree in announcing strong Russian aid for the Reds consisting of 100 heavy, 500 medium and 2,000 light tanks; 3,000 motorised machine guns; 300 planes and tens of thousands of machine guns, all of them with maintenance personnel and command units.
>
> The report seems exaggerated, since the numbers appear to exceed the capacity of one nation to provide assistance.
>
> In case the report is confirmed, however, urgent action is necessary to stop the transports as they pass through the straits south of Italy and to block the route to Spain. This can be done by providing Spain with the necessary number of ships or through intervention by the Italian fleet itself. Any Russian assistance via the Mediterranean can be prevented by a number of destroyers operating along the Italian coast and harbours, either openly under the Italian flag or with a Spanish officer and several men on board, and hoisting the Spanish Nationalist flag during the capture […].
>
> Please transmit the above information and request to the Duce or Count Ciano with the utmost urgency […].

The Director of the Political Department of the German Foreign Office commented that Berlin knew nothing of increased Russian aid to the Republic and that Franco's demand seemed 'very strange'.[34] Nevertheless,

Mussolini and Ciano took it seriously. Nicolás Franco, elder brother of the General, arrived in Rome on 5 August accompanied by a senior naval officer, Commander Regalado, who was negotiating the purchase of Italian warships. He suggested that the Italian navy should not only block the channel between Sicily and Malta but should also keep an eye on shipping in the Aegean Sea and along the North African coast, and sink any ship trying to enter Barcelona, Tarragona, Valencia, Alicante or Cartagena at night.

Italy now prepared a massive array of warships, with two submarine flotillas to oversee the route out of the Dardanelles, and three more in the Sicilian Channel. A group of destroyers and submarines would block the route along the North African coast between Sicily and Oran and, finally, four submarines added to the two which had been ceded to the Insurgents, would patrol off the Spanish coast and the Gulf of Lion.[35]

The results of the Italian decision were very soon evident. Between 6 August and 7 September 1937 some thirty-one British, French, Greek, Spanish, Danish, Panamanian and Russian ships were attacked, machine-gunned from the air, torpedoed, or bombed or sunk by aircraft. The attacks took place off the North African coast, in the Aegean, the Dardanelles, the eastern and western Mediterranean, and off the Spanish coast.

Warships were not spared either. On 12 August at 2125 off Cartagena a submarine torpedoed the Republican destroyer *Churruca*, damaging its boilers. At 2150 hours on 31 August, between the Balearics and the Spanish coast, a submarine fired a torpedo which narrowly missed hitting HMS *Havock*, having probably confused it with a Spanish Republican warship of the same design. The *Havock* spotted the submarine which had launched the missile, but lost contact with it. An Asdic sweep during the night was unsuccessful and the submarine, which many years after was discovered to have been the Italian *Iride*, managed to slip away. The British vice-consul on Majorca, Lieutenant Commander (retd.) Alan Hillgarth, saw the *Iride* in dock, badly knocked about by the depth charges launched against it in the early hours of 1 September by the *Havock*, the *Hotspur*, and the *Hereward*, and later by the *Hardy* and the *Hyperion*. An ultra-secret report, probably proceeding from the British success in breaking the Italian codes, an achievement which could not at the time be revealed, confirmed the attack and the counter-attack.[36] This was the first time that Asdic had been used to track an attacking submarine, and its failure led to an order that enemy submarines should be attacked by depth-charges at once if seen at a relatively close distance.[37]

On 2 September the tanker *Woodford* was torpedoed and sunk eighteen miles off the Spanish coast. The *Woodford* was carrying oil to Republican Spain from Rumania and had been warned by the Insurgents that it was under observation. Rear-Admiral Somerville, commanding the destroyer flotillas, received information that on a previous voyage the *Woodford*'s captain had been bribed to take his oil into Palma but had not fulfilled his part of the bargain. The sinking was carried out in revenge.[38] The second engineer and several crew-members lost their lives. The press was indignant and several more British warships were dispatched to the area.[39]

Eden was meeting the senior British admirals regularly to discuss practical measures for tackling the submarine menace. The Admiralty was unwilling to take on the Italian navy when Britain required its fleets to cover the vast expanses of the Empire. It would, insisted the Admiralty, be better to grant Franco belligerent rights. Of course, the admirals said, the Royal Navy had to protect British shipping, but it should not be required to risk its warships and interrupt its normal training programmes to protect ships such as the *Woodford*, which had only just been put on the British register. On 26 July 1937, Captain Tait, commanding the cruiser *Shropshire*, sent a long dispatch to the Admiralty in which he remarked that 'changelings' as he called some ships flying the British flag, were not British in any way and of 'disreputable appearance'. Admiral Sir Dudley Pound, commanding the Mediterranean Fleet, concurred with the view that it 'would be a travesty of justice' if the Royal Navy were to defend a 'so-called British ship' operating under charter to one of the belligerents.[40] The phrase 'one of the belligerents' meant of course the Spanish Republic. This one-sided view failed to mention that German and Italian merchant shipping were carrying arms to the Insurgents and would certainly be protected by their navies against Republican warships if these were to try to impede them. Eden, nevertheless, was unwilling to concede rights to Franco, who was being openly aided by Italy, a nation which was disrespecting international norms of behaviour by its undisguised participation in the Spanish war. The only solution was to seek and sink the guilty submarines. On 18 August a signal went out to the Royal Navy in the Mediterranean. British ships should attack any submerged submarine within five miles of a torpedo attack on a British cargo ship.[41] There was to be an intensive campaign to sink 'unidentified' submarines, whose nationality was known because the Italian naval codes had been broken. Italy could not protest without admitting that it was her submarines which were responsible.[42] This plan led to massive joint action by Britain and France.

On 26 August 1937 the French government suggested a conference. Eden wanted a joint decision that any submarine sailing underwater should be sunk. Rapidly a conference was organised, to be held at the Swiss town of Nyon. Italy used the Soviet accusation that Italian warships had sunk the Russian merchantmen *Timiryasev* and *Blagoev* as an excuse not to take part. Germany, resenting the lack of international support over the incidents of the *Deutschland* and the *Leipzig*, also refused to attend.[43]

Italy's absence ceased to be relevant before the conference met, for on 4 September Ciano ordered the attacks to cease.[44] This was immediately known in London. Further information reported that there were no submarines in the Sicilian Channel and other critical locations and that the submarines in the Aegean had received orders not to attack ships.[45] Yet none of this information could be revealed, for fear of betraying the Admiralty's ability to decipher the Italian codes.

Thus the conference went ahead. Eden and Admiral Chatfield flew to Paris, dined with the British ambassador, and took the sleeping car to Geneva whence they and Yvon Delbos, the French Foreign Minister, drove to Nyon, fifteen miles along the shore of the lake, to be welcomed by the mayor before the first session of the conference. Agreement was swiftly reached. Eden and the French, accompanied by their naval experts Admirals Chatfield and Darlan, suggested that Britain and France should protect the Mediterranean to the west of Malta, leaving the east to other countries. The Balkan nations protested that they were unable to protect the Eastern Mediterranean, where there had been many attacks. Britain and France, however, refused to take over responsibility for the entire Sea. The thirty-five British and twenty-eight French destroyers finally allocated to the patrol would sink any submarine attacking a non-Spanish ship or seen close to where a ship had been sunk. Maxim Litvinov, the Soviet Foreign Minister, pointed out that attacks by submarines on merchant ships were in any case illegal, because survivors could not be rescued. He proposed extending action against surface warships and aircraft. Eden accepted his argument but said that the submarine menace was more urgent.

Aircraft and surface warships, however, created different problems. Aircraft, even if they were flown by Italian crews, bore Spanish Insurgent markings and to attack them would compromise the principle of Non-Intervention. To fire on Italian surface warships would bring with it the risk of a battle, Litvinov protested. Perhaps to try to appease him Britain and France agreed to assume responsibility for the entire Mediterranean, supporting the navies of Turkey, Greece and Yugoslavia.[46] The USSR would not, however, participate, a fact which the British Foreign Secretary put down to Russian unwillingness to incur the hostility of the other littoral nations.[47] However, the plan went ahead smoothly. All arrangements were complete by 14 September. When asked by journalists if Nyon meant the end of submarine attacks, Eden said 'If there's another attack, I'll eat my hat.' He knew, if the reporters did not, that Italy had already ceased her activities.

Despite the Italian refusal to participate, as a sop to her pride Italy was allocated the Tyrrhenian Sea, an area unused by traffic making for Spain. This was mere diplomatic play-acting, because the attacks had in any case ceased. In fact a message headed 'Most Secret Information' was sent on 14 September to the British naval delegation at Nyon reporting that some Italian submarines had already been ordered to cease offensive action.[48] On 20 September, Pound told Chatfield that a week had passed with no submarine activity.[49]

Ciano boasted that Italy, previously accused of piracy, was now a policeman, and that the Russians had been kept out.[50] He was deceiving himself. The USSR had not had naval ships in the Mediterranean during the Spanish war. Nyon was a diplomatic triumph for Eden and a blow for Italy.

A month later, the anti-submarine patrols were reduced. For the Insurgents Nyon was a serious setback. No non-Spanish ships could now be attacked on the high seas without observing the humanitarian principles governing such attacks. This meant that the Italian submarines *Archimede* and *Torricelli* and four more which had been lent to the Insurgents with crews and commanders, were no longer of value except within territorial waters, where they were now to be concentrated in order to discourage freighters which were approaching Republican ports at night and without lights.

The Insurgents came to an agreement with Britain. Suspected vessels would continue to be stopped by the Royal Navy and taken to Malta or Gibraltar to be searched. Within Spanish waters British warships would escort British freighters, and these would avoid anchoring in the vicinity of Republican warships.[51]

On 2 October, the Insurgents and the Italian Naval Mission also came to an agreement. Discretion and craftiness would have to be employed. Submarines would remain underwater during the day, surfacing at night to recharge batteries. They would attack suspicious ships at night, but only within territorial waters and in specific cases. During the day they could attack foreign ships, except British, United States, and French vessels, if they were known to be carrying contraband arms. This order was known in London by 13 November.[52] Lieutenant Commander Hillgarth, in close contact and on good terms with the Insurgent naval commander on Majorca, Rear-Admiral Bastarreche, in Hillgarths' words 'a most friendly little man', wrote that the submarines in question were hard to identify because the names were often repainted and sometimes a Republican letter and number combination was used.[53]

Another weak point of Nyon was that aircraft bearing Spanish Insurgent markings, often flown by German or Italian pilots based on Majorca, would bomb merchant shipping in the ports of Barcelona, Tarragona, Valencia and Alicante.[54] On 6 November 1937, Admiral Moreno telegraphed the Insurgent government that the French admiral in command off the Balearics had protested strongly about aircraft attacking ships and that Moreno was consequently restricting air attacks to targets on the Spanish mainland.[55] In September 1937, in view of the increase in bombing activity by Italian machines taking off from Majorca, the French Foreign Minister Minister, Yvon Delbos, had gone as far as to suggest, unsuccessfully, to his British opposite number, Anthony Eden, that Britain and France should occupy Minorca.[56] Admiral Cervera, Franco's Navy chief, told the Insurgent admiral Moreno that his reply to British and French protests should be that he had to do everything he could to hinder ships arriving in 'Red' Spain. On 19 November a further note from Cervera told Moreno to do the impossible. He should act energetically and at the same time help Insurgent diplomatic efforts.

The Insurgents had been taken aback by the rapid and determined international reaction to the Italian attacks during August 1937 on often innocent shipping. Insurgent diplomacy as well as the orders given to their forces in the air and at sea had now to be very carefully formulated. The relatively minor details of conflicts arising from the activities of merchant shipping echo the diplomatic atmosphere of the moment. The British *Margaret-Rose*, for example, was reported to have taken on a cargo of small arms at Antwerp, hidden in sacks of beans and lentils destined for Gijón. A message giving this news had been picked up by Insurgent radio operators on 19 September. Flashed to the Insurgent cruiser *Almirante Cervera*, the latter's captain informed the senior Royal Navy officer in the Cantabrian Sea, who relayed the details to London. From London he was told that the Insurgents had received incorrect information. The *Margaret-Rose* had taken on an observer as required, who had watched the ship being loaded at Antwerp.[57]

On 9 October, an Insurgent seaplane narrowly missed torpedoing another British merchantman, the *Cervantes*, of the MacAndrews Line, carrying a Dutch observer for the Non-Intervention Committee. Protected by the destroyer *Firedrake*, the *Cervantes* reached Valencia. As was frequent, the British channel of communication was Hillgarth, based in Palma, to whom Admiral Bastarreche, the senior Insurgent naval officer, admitted that the seaplane was German and had been armed with torpedoes against orders. The pilot had been arrested. Hillgarth told London that this information had been reported confidentially. Of course, the Insurgents were not going to admit officially that they had German pilots and that, moreover, they often disobeyed orders.[58]

The *Jean Weems* was another British merchantman, sailing from Marseilles to Barcelona with grain and skins. It carried two Non-Intervention observers. The *Jean Weems* was bombed and sunk on 30 October by an aircraft sixteen kilometres off Palafrugell, on the Costa Brava. The aircraft had radioed a warning before bombing, which gave the crew time to take to the lifeboats and to reach the present-day tourist resort of Calella. The attack, however, had taken place outside territorial waters, though this was denied by the pilot, who was Spanish rather than German or Italian. No attempt had been made to establish whether or not the freighter carried contraband.[59] The sinking would have been unacceptable even if the aircraft had belonged to a recognised belligerent, which Franco was not, and so Britain presented a formal diplomatic protest. Admiral Moreno apologised and promised to prevent any more attacks.[60] There were no more for some considerable period of time.

The *Jean Weems* was typical of numerous incidents that would occur from then onwards. A merchant ship would be bombed. Occasionally, there would be deaths. London would usually protest that the ship was not carrying war material and that it was outside Spanish territorial waters. If the ship were within the three-mile limit, the protest would say that no resistance had been offered. The Insurgents would insist that the ship was inside territorial waters (which for the Insurgents stretched six miles out to sea) or that the pilot of the aircraft had made an error. Privately, they would tell Lieutenant Commander Hillgarth that the pilots were Italian or German and that they were disobeying orders. In this case, the *Jean Weems* was fulfilling a contract for the Spanish Republican government, so that the Insurgents had some right to claim that the ship was in enemy service though only if their status as unrecognised belligerents in rebellion against an internationally-recognised State were ignored.

However, the submarine menace had disappeared and on 10 November the Admiralty told Admiral Pound, C-in-C of the Mediterranean Fleet, that a considerable reduction of patrols was acceptable.[61] Tension relaxed somewhat. Britain now recognised the Insurgents unofficially on 16 November 1937 by an exchange of diplomatic agents, Sir Robert Hodgson and the Duke of Alba. As suitable preparation for the event the following British freighters, captured during previous months, were released: the *Mirupanu, Caper, Seven Seas Spray, Stanwold, Dover Abbey* and *Yorkbrook*.[62]

The Insurgents had to take care but were still going to be able to attack and sink Republican ships. The armed merchantman *Cabo Santo Tomé*, for example, coming from Odessa with aircraft and artillery, was destroyed twenty-four miles off the Algerian coast by two Insurgent gunboats, the *Cánovas* and the *Dato*, on 10 October 1937. The *Cánovas* fired a shot over the bow of the merchantman, which stopped. The gunboat, thinking this meant surrender, sailed close and, at 400 yards the freighter uncovered its gun. A short combat ensued. The *Cánovas* was hit under its waterline. The *Dato* fired its 101 mm artillery at 4,500 yards. The *Cabo Santo Tomé* made for the coast, ran aground and exploded. The crew, meanwhile had taken to the boats. The 11,600 ton *Cabo Santo Tomé* was one of the largest Republican freighters and its loss was a serious blow.

By the end of 1937 twenty-eight Republican cargo vessels had been sunk, 106 captured and seventy recovered for the Insurgents largely by being sequestered in port or surrendered intentionally, so that the Insurgents had more than 400,000 tons of shipping at their disposal.[63] Finally, on 6 December, 1937, the Insurgents declared a close blockade of the coast. The Republican government reacted by issuing a statement that the Insurgents did not have the warships to declare a blockade along 700 miles of coast. The next day, Hillgarth radioed London from Majorca that the Insurgents were not intending to blockade in the strict sense of the word. The measure was not directed against British ships on the high seas or even in port, although British shipmasters should realise that they were at risk of bombing when the harbours were the target of raids.[64] On 22 December, *The Times*'s correspondent, from his vantage point in the Insurgent zone of Spain, reported that the Francoists reserved the right to stop vessels on the high seas if they were suspected of carrying arms. How the suspicions were to come about was not mentioned.[65] And what did the Insurgents claim was contraband? Was it only war material as listed in the laws passed in any one of the 27 signatory countries? Was it anything that could possibly contribute to the fighting? Or was it also food, medical supplies and the like which would enable the Republic to continue the struggle? What about exports, which provided the Republic with valuable foreign exchange in order to make purchases on the international market? Furthermore, direct attack, sinking by bombing or aerial torpedo was not permitted even to a recognised belligerent especially if the aggressor did not assure the safety of the crew of the ship. Bombing a neutral ship was not permitted even inside enemy ports. But on 27 December 1937 the Insurgents declared that, except for visiting warships, they no longer recognised the safety areas in which neutral ships had moored. Such areas in the harbours of Barcelona and Valencia had in general been respected.[66] The British government had for that reason not threatened to extend its protection to British merchantmen within territorial waters. This had been the standard reply to those who had accused the Royal Navy of protecting cargo ships which were not really British and which were in it 'only for the money'.

In future, sailing to Spain would be ever more risky for merchant shipping, exposed as it was to bombing by aircraft flying from Majorca, and to the patrols of the energetic Insurgent fleet, now concentrated in the Mediterranean and reinforced by 'legionary' submarines supposedly

Spanish but actually Italian, as well as some older destroyers bought from that country. In the last three months of 1937, fifty-three merchantmen were stopped by the Insurgents. Some were British-registered, but others were Greek, Swedish, Norwegian, French, Danish and Russian. All were carrying coal, general cargo, fruit and other foodstuffs.[67]

But what of the still powerful Republican fleet with its numerous fast destroyers? On 10 December 1937 the three Insurgent cruisers *Almirante Cervera*, *Canarias* and *Baleares* shelled Alicante for fifteen minutes.[68] The Republican fleet either lacked a capable information service or did not want to take advantage of this opportunity to mount an attack with all the forces it could muster.

Chapter 11

Two Spanish Navies in Contrast

I New Officers for the Republican Fleet

The problem of the lack of professional officers in the Republican navy had been exacerbated by the disloyalty of some of the few who had remained, or in some cases had been saved from court martial and the firing squad or from murderous mobs of mutinous sailors, and had agreed against their will to command ships or take up senior positions in the bureaucracy and on naval staffs. This was one reason, though not the only one, why the Republican fleet, its one battleship, three cruisers, numerous destroyers and twelve submarines, as well as smaller gunboats and armed merchantmen, had been hesitant to tackle the exiguous Insurgent navy.

Furthermore, Britain and other countries' refusal to recognise the Republican regime as a belligerent had meant that, after the first few days, Republican warships had ceased trying to blockade Insurgent ports. Nor, with the exception of the German *Palos* in 1936, had Republican warships attacked or even stopped Italian and German cargo ships, either escorted by warships or disguised as neutrals, as they brought war material to Francoist forces. Nevertheless, to the credit of the Republican fleet had been the safe arrival of major shipments of arms, particularly from the USSR.

However, if the Republican navy was to make a determined effort to attack the modern Insurgent cruisers *Canarias* and *Baleares*, the older *Almirante Cervera*, the armed cargo ships and the Italian submarines under Spanish Insurgent command which were now roaming the Western Mediterranean, a better strategy was required and above all more suitable men had to be found for command responsibilities.

In March 1937, Indalecio Prieto, the Socialist Minister of Marine and Air, set up a training academy, the *Escuela Naval Popular* or ENP, following the model of the *Escuelas Populares de Guerra* which had been established earlier by the Prime Minister and Minister of War Francisco Largo Caballero to supply the Republican Army with a new corps of officers.[1] The word *popular*, though it means 'People's', should not be taken to mean communist or even socialist, but merely as recruiting young men of adequate education and political reliability for emergency officer-training courses. On 22 March 1937 applications for entry to the new naval college were invited. The explanatory part of the decree referred to the 'well-deserved aspirations of all personnel' (*'merecidas aspiraciones de todo el personal'*). The exclusive nature of the naval officers' corps had been one of the major causes of resentment among the senior petty and warrant officers, who could not achieve commissioned rank. The entrance tests for the ENP consisted of examinations in Spanish grammar, that is to test if the applicant could express himself clearly and correctly, and three long pages of mathematical problems.[2]

The ENP had a political officer or *Comisario Político*. This was the parliamentary deputy Ginés Ganga. Concerned that pre-war rivalries between the ranks and the branches of the navy should not be repeated, Ganga insisted that all should henceforth wear the same uniforms and that the instructors should all be professional officers. Yet a booklet that the socialist Ganga wrote displayed a strangely counter-revolutionary tone. In a section titled *Formas de Cortesía* or simply 'Good Manners', Ganga wrote:

Wearing a hat and gloves is an attribute of elegance and good manners in a cultivated man.

This was certainly so in the Spain of the 1930s, which is why the Republican government tried to recreate such gentlemanly values and to display, especially to foreigners, that the Republic was not revolutionary. In the Republican army, militia overalls for officers had long been replaced by insignia of rank, highly-polished boots and elegant uniforms. Ganga ended his text with a reference to 'the refined manners of the Spanish gentleman (*'la educación esmerada del hidalgo español'*). It was important that foreign naval officers, especially the Royal Navy, should not think that courtly manners were restricted to the Insurgents.

In the *Escuela Naval Popular*, there were four levels. The first three would train future navy officers, while the fourth would prepare for staff work and higher level appointments requiring specialised knowledge and skills. These courses evidently were intended to produce professional officers, assuming that the Republic would win the war, yet the real shortage was urgent, so some short courses for artillery and torpedo officers were introduced. These men graduated as sub-lieutenants (*alféreces de navío*) and, after three months at sea would become lieutenants. The first thirty-two graduates passed out at the end of April 1938. In September there were fifty-eight of these junior officers, that is two cohorts of graduates. The third course did not reach graduation before the war ended.

Could a naval officer be trained in such a short time? The question was asked by Eugenio Rodríguez Sierra, a long-service engineer warrant officer, in the Republican navy paper *La Armada* of 16 October 1937. His answer was positive. He claimed that in the Great War Britain had trained destroyer captains in six months. Moreover, he added

> … we do not have a 'Home Fleet' but just a few ships which have to face a couple of cruisers and know how to defend themselves from submarines.

By 1938 some new officers were directing fire, navigating and serving as seconds-in-command. However, the Republican navy's problems were at the higher level of tactical skill and the still higher one of strategic vision. These were the responsibility of the Minister and the fleet and flotilla commanders.

II Professional Naval Officers

There was a great shortage of these officers. On 18 May 1938, the naval officer list of the Republic, not counting the specialist branches, was composed of only fifty-two men. The needs of the fleet were calculated as a vice-admiral, a rear-admiral, 4 captains, 19 commanders, 24 lieutenant-commanders, 42 lieutenants and 64 sub-lieutenants, 155 altogether.[3] The navy was also short of engineer and artillery officers. The minute group of academy-trained officers had to occupy a series of senior posts, and followed each other in them in a game of musical chairs.

COMMANDERS OF THE FLEET
Commander Fernando Navarro (20 July 1936)
Lieutenant Commander Miguel Buiza (1 September 1936)
Lieutenant Commander Luis González de Ubieta (25 October 1937)
Lieutenant Commander Miguel Buiza (28 January 1939)

CHIEFS OF STAFF OF THE NAVY
Lieutenant Commander Luis González de Ubieta (27 May 1937)
Commander Valentín Fuentes (25 October 1937)
Lieutenant Commander Miguel Buiza (1 January 1938)
Lieutenant Pedro Prado (19 April 1938)
Lieutenant Commander Julián Sánchez Erostarbe (28 January 1939)

CHIEFS OF STAFF OF THE FLEET
Lieutenant Commander Luis Junquera (11 November 1936)
Lieutenant Commander Horacio Pérez (21 October 1937)
Lieutenant Commander José Núñez (27 November 1938)

COMMANDERS OF DESTROYER FLOTILLAS
Lieutenant Vicente Ramírez de Togores (10 August 1936)
Lieutenant Commander Federico Monreal (12 July 1937)
Lieutenant José García Barreiro (25 December 1938)

Lieutenant Commander Junquera was appointed to head the Escuela Naval Popular, and Buiza was moved on 27 October 1937 from the post of C-in-C of the Fleet to heading the Mobile Coast Defence (*Defensa Móvil de Costas*) in the rank of Vice-Admiral.

In order to remedy the shortage of personnel, on 7 May 1937 a number of officers who had been subject to court-martial were appointed to head sections of the naval Under-Secretariat of Defence and, according to one historian of the naval war, 'would stay with the enemy' (*quedarían con el enemigo*), that is they would be considered by the victorious Insurgents to have been helpful to them and deserved to continue their naval careers after the war.[4] A British diplomat who visited Cartagena reported that the sympathies of the naval officers were with the Insurgents. He wrote that they were known as 'radishes' (*rábanos*) because they were red outside but inwardly white.[5]

After the first few months of the war the Insurgent commanders noted that the Republican fleet did little to impede Insurgent activities, but that its morale and technical ability had improved markedly. This was due, according to a report sent to Franco, to the 'foreign elements' in the Republican navy, by which must have been meant the Soviet officers. While the seventy-seven Russian naval officers who at some time acted as advisers to the Spanish Republican fleet may well have contributed significantly to an improvement that the Insurgents noticed, it may also be true that the new and younger destroyer commanders in particular played a part in giving an impression of competence and energy.

III Political Commissars and their Work

In the Republican navy social and political matters were attended to by political officers, known as *comisarios políticos*.[6] Their responsibilities included attention to the leisure time of sailors. The navy commissars edited ships' newspapers and libraries. On the cruiser *Méndez Núñez*, for example, there was a library with five hundred books, including the *Espasa* encyclopaedia ('much consulted'). Six hundred loans per month were made to the crew. The smaller destroyer *Lepanto* possessed 270 volumes.[7]

Shore leave, however, was what the sailors looked forward to. Here the Antifascist Women's Committee of the major base of Cartagena organised an event in the Salon Sport of the city to inaugurate a library 'intended to offer intellectual pleasure, strengthen education or increase the skills of our sailors' ('a *proporcionar un placer spiritual, a robustecer la cultura o a capacitar a nuestros marineros*').[8]

The language used, as can be seen in the next quotation with reference to the opening of a sailors' *hogar* or 'home from home' club in the premises of the previous businessmen's club, the *Unión Mercantil de Cartagena*, was lofty and removed from the urgency of the moment, but it contained a note of humanity and nobility as well:

We are far from our homes, without the love of our mothers, partners and children. Like wandering birds we must find a way to compensate [...] and to acquire education [...] thus we have decided to open this *Hogar del Marino* far from depravity and occupied with conversation and reading [...] so that our minds may be strengthened with healthy principles...[9]

In the *Hogar del Marino* at Cartagena a lecture was delivered every Thursday. For example, a member of the crew of the *Libertad* spoke on 22 December 1937 about the need for political unity. On another occasion a judge sitting in the People's Court of Murcia, capital of the province, spoke on the poet Federico Garcia Lorca, murdered by the Insurgents. The commissars published the newspaper *La Armada*. Financed by contributions from the crews, it proclaimed itself to be 'the official organ of the sailors of the Republic' and was edited by the chief fleet commissar, Bruno Alonso. It began publication in March 1937 with the slogans 'For education and freedom!' 'For morality and discipline!' *La Armada* is not very interesting to read today because it suffered from unbearable verbosity. Nevertheless, it contained educational and technical sections of some interest. It insisted on discipline and political unity, major problems in the Republican forces, but it exhibited a powerful note of egalitarianism which clashed with the general tendency after the departure of the Caballero government and the appointment of Juan Negrín in May 1937.

Educational work and the creation of the *Hogar del Marino* were important as part of the campaign against sexually-transmitted diseases often contracted in port by sailors. On 1 January 1938 *La Armada* published a warning by the commissar for health services in the Cartagena naval base, requiring sailors going on shore leave to report to a clinic to be given condoms.

IV Discipline

The question of discipline came up frequently. This was unavoidable, given the origin of the Republican navy in a mutiny. Major efforts were made to enforce the correct wearing of uniform, prevent drunkenness, restrict political activities and maintain secrecy about fleet movements.[10] The efforts produced some results. The commander of the British destroyer *Gipsy* reported that Spanish Republican sailors were smart and saluted their officers. Nevertheless, the navy issued many circular orders which indicate that problems were arising, even if they were not general. For example, the staff of the destroyer flotilla forbade anyone to go on shore to take shelter during air raids.[11] It was also frequent for sailors to fail to report to their ships before they left harbour. The question of penalties was difficult, because they could not be those of the pre-war navy. During the civil war commanders and commissars took the decision to impose fines or deprive offending sailors of shore leave. The only serious punishment was to send a man to a penal unit on land. The problem became so serious that in late 1937 the fleet C-in-C, Lieutenant-Commander González de Ubieta, telegraphed the Ministry asking permission to send any man who missed his ship, whatever his age or rank, to a unit engaged in building fortifications.[12]

V Political Proselytism

It was difficult and perhaps impossible to separate the specific duties of commissars from campaigning for one political view or another. The Republic's ideological panorama included the powerful anarcho-syndicalist movement, the *Confederación Nacional de Trabajo*, which had been influential among the sailors, and the equally powerful Spanish Socialist Party, the *Partido Socialist Obrero Español*, as well as the Spanish Communist Party, whose influence and size had grown rapidly because, following the Stalinist adoption of the Popular Front policy, it took a counter-revolutionary position in defence of the liberal and parliamentary Republic. The aid provided by the Soviet Union had brought prestige to the communists. In May 1937, as described by George Orwell in his *Homage to Catalonia*, the revolutionary and anti-Stalinist POUM was crushed by the communists and the Republican-Socialist government.

Bruno Alonso, the senior naval commissar, fought against political proselytism, but he found himself the target of criticism. Never using one word when several would do, Don Bruno, as he was known familiarly, complained against 'layabouts, dodgers, schemers, chatterers, the indisciplined and the malcontents' ('*vagos, remisos, intrigantes, charlatanes, indisciplinados y descontentos*'). He meant those who did not accept the reorganisation of the fleet, but he was probably also thinking of communist political penetration.[13]

Bruno Alonso's major problem, however, was with the command, among which he claimed, in his post-war book, the old hierarchical arrogance had spread.[14] For example, Lieutenant Commander González de Ubieta refused to let Alonso read outgoing messages.[15] Commissars on the destroyers told him about the incompetence of their commanding officers. Such tensions were inevitable. Bruno Alonso had an impossible task, so it was not surprising that when a decree of 25 December 1937 extended an army regulation to the navy, and required commissars of military age to hold their office only aboard warships and not on shore, Alonso protested and offered to resign in sympathy with the commissars at the Cartagena base. On 11 February 1938 a decree required Alonso to abandon his functions in the base and restricted his jurisdiction to the fleet. A few months later, when González de Ubieta refused to allow him to read transmitted and received messages, Alonso resigned, although finally and under pressure from Dr Negrín, the Prime Minister and Minister of National Defence (Prieto had left the government in April 1938), Alonso withdrew his resignation.

Insufficient evidence is available to say whether the naval commissars impeded the command in its proper functions and rendered the Republican fleet less active and aggressive, or if on the contrary, the commissars were, to quote the mural newspaper of the destroyer *Alcalá Galiano*, responsible for the

> [...strengthening of discipline, the increase in morale and political awareness, [...]creating will and determination stronger than those of the enemy[...] [the struggle against provocation, espionage and disorganisation that might have been present in the auxiliary services such as ammunition, medicine, supply [...] and good relations between command and crews.

> ([...] *fortalecimiento de la disciplina y la elevación de la moral y conciencia política, [...] creando [...] una voluntad y un temple superiores a los del enemigo [...] la lucha contra la provocación, el espionaje y la mala organización que pueda haber en los servicios auxiliares: municiones, sanidad, intendencia [...] que haya relaciones cordiales entre el mando y los marineros.*[16]

VI Restructuring the Insurgent Navy

Producing new officers was not as acute a problem for the Insurgents. Nevertheless, and with an eye on the post-war years, Admiral Cervera, the Chief of Staff, began to reorganise the San Fernando (Cádiz) naval academy. The most urgent task was to complete the training of the forty-nine cadets who were already serving aboard warships and to prepare a naval reserve composed of merchant navy personnel. Cervera was concerned that the cadets should be thoroughly trained despite the present emergency. In November 1937 Commander Manuel Ferrer was appointed Director of the Naval Academy.[17] The cadets left their ships and returned to the lecture-hall. Sixty-six vacancies were advertised for the naval reserve on 26 March 1938 and eighty more in September. Lower ranking navy personnel were entitled to apply and would be admitted as cadets after the war.[18]

Parallel to the Republic's concern to avoid the conflicts which had led to so much bad feeling between the senior petty officers and the commissioned officers, Admiral Cervera wrote to his colleagues on 3 November 1936 to persuade them that the status and treatment of the lower ranks should be examined.[19] This question was debated later in the Higher Naval Council. 'Every word was discussed', wrote Cervera later, 'and the matter was shelved to be looked at after the war.'[20] However, some temporary reforms in making the system more responsive to the needs of the wartime navy were introduced.[21] In a letter of 21 March 1937 Franco reminded Admiral Cervera that volunteers coming from the *Falange* Fascist Party and the *Comunión Tradicionalista* or Carlist Catholic militia were to be permitted to wear their insignia and that the Roman salute should be permitted.[22] Behind this lay a struggle between navy professionals and the enormously increased power of the two political movements, forcibly united by Franco who appointed himself their head. The tension was evident in a letter of a senior naval captain:

I have been fighting my worst battle aboard ship because of officers who confuse concepts and ideas and create discord in the crew. What happened yesterday is a true picture of my mood[...] My reiterated orders that all crew and officers should salute in the same way [...] were openly disobeyed. I reacted not angrily but energetically and reproved the crew.

(*'Vengo sosteniendo a bordo la peor de las luchas que jamás he sostenido, y ello se debe a la incomprensión de algunos oficiales empeñados en confundir conceptos e ideas y fomentar discordia entre la dotación. Lo ocurrido*

*ayer es un fiel reflejo de mi estado de ánimo[…] Mis reiteradas órdenes,
uniformando el saludo a bordo entre el personal que viste el uniforme[…]
fueron desobedecidas abiertamente y ante este hecho reaccioné, no airada
sino energéticamente, reprendiendo a la dotación.')*[23]

The letter reveals an unsuspected aspect of the politicisation of the
Insurgent navy. Though for different reasons, politics created problems
in both navies which fought the Spanish civil war at sea.

VII Insurgent Commanders

There were far fewer changes in the Insurgent naval command than
in the Republican structure. Nevertheless, there is evidence of tension
between the Chief of Naval Staff, Vice-Admiral Cervera, and the
C-in-C of the Fleet, Captain Francisco Moreno Fernández, who was
promoted to acting Rear-Admiral in the *Boletín Oficial de Estado* of 11
November 1936 and to Vice-Admiral on 11 October 1937. Cervera had
been the most senior of the admirals, while Moreno had been halfway
down the seniority list of *capitanes de Navío* (equivalent to Captains RN).
Furthermore, tension between Cervera and General Franco can be read
between the lines of the admiral's memoirs. Cervera complained about
the *'mamparos estancos'* or 'waterproof compartments' of Franco's staff and
how difficult it was to persuade Franco to give missions to the fleet which
he feared to risk losing.[24] Disputes arose about personnel matters which
reflected the hostility between the *Cuerpo General* and other branches of
the service, which Cervera blames on what he called *'consejeros áulicos'* or
'Court Counsellors' who were biased against the *Cuerpo General*.[25]

The command structure was amended on 10 October 1937 when
acting Vice-Admiral Francisco Moreno was appointed Head of Blockade
Forces in the Mediterranean, with authority over air and land forces in
the area and a staff of loyal and enthusiastic officers which contrasted
with the penury of reliable equivalents in the Republican fleet. Admiral
Bastarreche, who had held command on Majorca, was transferred to the
base at Cádiz. The squabbles mentioned by Cervera do not seem to have
had any effect on the solidity and determination of the group of Insurgent
naval leaders. Lieutenant Commander Hillgarth, source of information
for the Royal Navy from his post on Majorca, claims that Bastarreche

was moved precisely because he did not work well with the local army commanders, which shows how important this cooperation was judged and explains why Admiral Moreno was given overall command.

VIII More Ships For Franco

The Insurgent fleet was completely without destroyers in the Mediterranean. After the skirmish on 25 April 1937 (see Chapter Eight), where the imbalance revealed the danger in which the Insurgent capital ships were without destroyer escorts, long negotiations took place to acquire destroyers from Italy. Modern, powerful and high speed cruisers like the *Canarias* and the *Baleares* could not be wasted in convoying captured merchantmen to friendly ports and be at risk of being torpedoed by the many destroyers of the Republic. On 4 April 1937 the cruisers avoided combat with four enemy destroyers off Almería because they were highly visible and risked being hit at ranges of between three and four thousand yards, even given the unreliability of the torpedoes in use.[26]

In addition, the lack of Insurgent submarines meant that a sustained war against merchant traffic could not be undertaken. The first Italian submarine campaign had ended abruptly in February 1937, after which Italy transferred the *Archimede* and the *Torricelli* to the Insurgents. They were named *C3* and *C5* to suggest that they were the recovered real ex-Republican submarines *C3* and *C5*. On 30 May the '*C3*' torpedoed the *Ciudad de Barcelona*, a passenger vessel belonging to the *Compañia Transmediterránea*, causing the deaths of hundreds of international volunteers who had embarked at Marseilles for Barcelona. The same submarine damaged the tanker *Campero*. The '*C5*' sank the *Granada*, loaded with war material, in the Gulf of Lion. In August the '*C3*' took part in sinkings in the Aegean before the Nyon agreement came into force. On 26 June the '*C5*' sank the merchantman *Cabo de Palos*, on its way from the USSR to Valencia.

Cargo ships making for Republican ports followed the North African coast until they reached a point which gave them the shortest route over international waters to Spain. The Insurgent Higher Naval Council, meeting on 22 and 23 July 1937, concluded that two submarines were insufficient. All along the North African coast there were many ports in which a merchant ship could shelter, watch for Insurgent ships, and then steam fast for Republican Spain. It was very difficult to trace them, especially if they sailed by night.[27] The meeting decided to acquire older Italian warships and two modern submarines, as well as newer artillery and fire direction equipment for the *Baleares* and the *Canarias*. Non-Intervention had made it impossible to acquire plans from the partially British SECN to build destroyers in El Ferrol, but the building of new minelayers was to be accelerated and it was decided also to repair the old cruiser *República*, now in dock at Cádiz, and put it into service.

Negotiations to buy Italian ships were the last recourse. Germany and even Japan had already been approached and had refused.[28] But Italy's unconcealed intervention in the Spanish war encouraged it to provide warships to Franco Spain.

It seemed that the Insurgents were anxious about the Republican navy. The latter's technical ability was increasing all the time, and the Insurgents thought that the torpedoed cruiser *Miguel de Cervantes* would soon re-enter service (in fact it did not emerge from Cartagena dockyard until 4 March 1938). In contrast, the Insurgent commanders were aware that their own firing was inaccurate.[29]

So far, continued the Higher Navy Council, the Republican navy had been passive, but this was unlikely to continue. Here one must consider the German criticism of Insurgent passivity. The previous month, a joint conference of Spanish Insurgent, German and Italian naval commanders, held on board the *Deutschland* while this battleship was under repair at Cádiz after being bombed at anchor off Ibiza, had concluded that the Insurgent cruisers should act more aggressively against Republican merchant shipping.

In fact, the real problem for the Insurgents was the international reaction to their attacks on neutral shipping. It was this which would always place a limit to the various tactics invented by the Insurgents to hamper merchant shipping making for the Republican coast.

Italian aid was thus indispensable. Italy had been generous already, sending radio and electrical material and supplying artillery for the three Insurgent cruisers, together with telemeters, ammunition, boilers, accumulators and other technical material.[30] In order to help the Insurgent armed merchant ships which patrolled the Sicilian Channel, Italy had provided an anchorage on the Island of Favignana, west of Sicily, bases on other islands and at Cagliari, where more than 15,000 tons of oil were stored.[31] But more was needed. Lieutenant Commander Arturo Génova returned to Italy, where he had negotiated the transfer of Italian submarines months earlier. He now arranged for the sale of two small counter-torpedo ships, the 858 ton *Alessandro Poerio* and the *Guglielmo Pepe*, together with two destroyers, the *Aquila* and the *Falco*, with speeds of twenty-nine knots, and the 1910 cruiser *Taranto*, of 4,550 tons and nineteen knots. These ships were, however, old and slow and of little use in tackling the Republican destroyers. The Insurgents thought the fifty million liras that Italy wanted 'prohibitive'.[32] Finally, however, Mussolini made a personal decision, ignoring the opinion of Count Ciano and the opposition of the Minister for the Navy, to sell the ships to the Spanish Insurgents for forty million liras. The aged cruiser *Taranto* was not sold, but the transfer of the other ships was worrying for the Italian Foreign Ministry, for it could hardly be concealed or denied. The *Aquila* and the *Falco*, now renamed *Velasco-Ceuta* and *Velasco-Melilla*, sailed for Spanish waters on 12 and 13 October 1937, reaching Sóller on Majorca after a voyage which revealed many difficulties in handling these craft, which dated from 1916 and 1919 respectively.[33] The *Guglielmo Pepe*, now the *Huesca*, and the *Alessandro Poerio*, now renamed *Teruel*, were transferred to the Spanish Insurgents in November. They suffered frequent breakdowns and there was a shortage of engine-room personnel who were able to handle them.[34] The Insurgent naval staff was soon complaining about these ships, which it described as 'old iron' ('*chatarra*').[35]

However, high quality Italian naval reinforcements for the Spanish Insurgents also arrived. At the end of August 1937, four submarines docked at Sóller, as Hillgarth reported to London.[36] These were the *Galilei*, the *Ferraris*, the *Iride* and the *Onice*, which were renamed *Sanjurjo 2*, *Mola 2*, *González López* and *Aguilar Tablada*. These submarines were crewed and commanded by Italian naval personnel, although they carried a Spanish officer on board.[37] The *Sanjurjo 2* and the *Mola 2* belonged to the 600 series, with less displacement, speed and armament than the *Archimede* and *Torricelli*, which had been previously transferred to the Insurgents.

These submarines began operating on 17 September 1937. The Italian crews of the first two submarines transferred were replaced by Spanish personnel on 18 October and those of the second series on 27 January 1938.[38] Mussolini had insisted that they should attack only Spanish Republican traffic and leave British, United States' and French vessels alone at all times, and attack those of other flags only if within territorial waters. They should also keep well away from the routes laid down for merchant ships by the Nyon agreement.[39] In fact, these submarines carried out only thirteen missions, making a total of ninety by Italian submarines in the entire war, most of which were seen by the Italian naval command as part of the training of crews as much as collaboration with the Spanish insurgents.[40] However, when the *Sanjurjo* and the *Mola*, the original Italian submarines which for some time had been described as the Republican *C3* and *C5*, until they had been identified on the surface, sank the Dutch freighter *Hannah* on 11 January 1938 and the British *Endymion,* carrying coal, on 31 January, the international outcry led to a reinforcement of British patrols in the Mediterranean. Consequently, Italy withdrew its 'legionary' submarines on 5 February 1938. There would be no further undersea attacks on British ships. The Insurgents would now rely on aircraft to block traffic to Barcelona, Valencia, Alicante and Cartagena.

IX The Battleship Jaime Primero

The Insurgents had lost the battleship *España*, sunk by a mine on 30 April 1937. A few weeks later, the Republic in its turn lost its only battleship, the *Jaime Primero.* Damaged by air raids, it had been taken to Cartagena for repair, reaching the base on 28 May. At 1500 hours on 17 June, while under repair in the dockyard, an explosion in one of the powder magazines caused 179 deaths, and a large number of injured.[41] Fire ran rapidly from one end of the ship to the other, decks collapsed, funnels were blown off and the ship foundered. The subsequent enquiry concluded that the explosion was probably caused by careless use of a welding lance too close to the powder store. Whatever the cause of the explosion, Rear-Admiral Valentín Fuentes, commanding the base since the beginning of the year, was dismissed and replaced by the dockyard commander, the senior warrant officer Alfonso Játiva.

X Mobile Coast Defence

The approaches to the ports of Republican Spain were well-defended. The Republican navy, now better-led and organised, created a number of anti-submarine flotillas. The first was to patrol off the Catalan coast.

The flotilla was an autonomous naval unit, coming directly under the orders of the naval staff and the mobile coast defence. It consisted of three deep-sea trawlers, a customs cutter (the *L1*) and a couple of other minor units. On 31 July, the Almería anti-submarine flotilla was created, also using small vessels; on 17 August a flotilla began to scout the waters off Valencia, using the gunboat *Laya*.

The Insurgents had understood from the beginning that even small and slow ships had a useful function. However, they had abundant trained officers whereas the Republic employed men who, while competent, had, with rare exceptions, not enjoyed command. Nevertheless, the anti-submarine flotillas kept vigilant watch. Their vessels were small, of no more than three or four hundred tons each, armed with Vickers 101.5 guns salvaged from the *Jaime Primero*. Some were provided with Russian depth charges. Their presence contributed to the lack of success of the Insurgent-Italian submarines in those waters.

In fact, mines were potentially a graver problem than submarines for merchant ships. According to the memoirs of Admiral Cervera, mines were laid from Cape Gata, just east of Almería, as far north as Cape Creus, on the French frontier, but with little success.[42] Republican mine-sweeping was efficient, clearing mines twice daily from a mile wide channel a mile from the coast, with ships serving as minesweepers based at Port de la Selva, Rosas, Palamós, Blanes, Barcelona and a series of ports, small harbours and seaside resorts all the way down to Almería.

The Soviet naval attaché, Commander Kuznetsov, was surprised at the absence of fast motor boats, of which the Soviet Navy possessed about 300. He requested some, and four arrived in May and June 1937 on two Spanish freighters.[43] The well-informed Royal Navy reported their presence on 14 June.[44]These eighteen-ton launches developed a maximum speed of 53 knots and possessed two torpedo tubes. They were accompanied by the Soviet specialists Alexei Batrakov, Vassili Likholiutov and Yakov Osipov.[45] However, the Insurgents, fearing the powerful coastal artillery at Cartagena, did not venture near enough to constitute good targets, and the Russian motor launches were unemployed for much of the time.

XI Clashes at Sea

Neither of the two Spanish navies seemed particularly eager to attack the other. Sometimes combat came about by accident. On 20 May 1937, the cruiser *Baleares*, now with its artillery fully installed, and heading for the Moroccan port of Melilla to escort a convoy of troops and equipment to the Peninsula, spotted two enemy destroyers. The *Baleares* fired, but at 7,000 metres and in poor visibility it scored no impacts.[46] The Insurgent Higher Naval Council, in its report of 22 and 23 July, criticised the 'frankly inefficient firing of our large and medium calibre cruisers'.[47]

Another combat took place on 12 July 1937 off Valencia, when the *Baleares* fired at four Republican destroyers, the *Lepanto, Churruca, Miranda* and *Valdés*. Using their high speed and manoeuvrability, and making smoke, the destroyers escaped the powerful artillery of the cruiser. Meanwhile, two more destroyers, the *Gravina* and the *Sánchez Barcáiztegui,* successfully escorted a tanker into Valencia. There was an hour of shelling. The *Baleares* discovered that after fifty shots the barrels of its 203 mm guns overheated. The commander of the Republican destroyer flotilla, Vicente Ramírez de Togores, was not successful in positioning his ships so as to be able to fire torpedoes at the *Baleares*. This cost him his post, in which he was relieved by Federico Monreal. Ramírez de Togores was dismissed to calm the widespread criticism of the passivity of the Republican fleet. The navy newspaper *La Armada*, in its issue of 17 July 1937 published an article headed 'For those who wonder what the Republican navy has usefully done' ('*Para los que se preguntan qué ha hecho de eficaz la Marina republicana*'). The paper explained that the destroyers had gone to sea with insufficient ammunition, without air cover and sometimes without anti-aircraft guns. They had begun the war with no staffs. Admittedly, there had been indiscipline. Seamen had thought they could do what they liked. Yet great progress had been made.

XII The Battle of Cherchell

One major combat took place on 7 September 1937. Four Republican freighters, the *Aldecoa*, the *Antonio Satrústegui,* the *Mar Blanco,* and the *Mar Caribe* were returning from the USSR laden with war material and were off Algiers about to turn north to dash across to Cartagena. Such an important convoy required a powerful escort, which was provided by the cruisers *Libertad* and *Méndez Núñez* (the *Miguel de Cervantes* was still under repair), the destroyers *Lepanto, Gravina, Valdés,* the brand new *Jorge Juan,* and the *Miranda, Escaño* and *Almirante Antequera*. This fleet sailed out of Cartagena setting course for Algiers. By chance, at the same time the *Baleares* was making for the base at Cádiz to have some repairs carried out. At mid-morning, just north of Cherchell on the Moroccan coast, the *Baleares* spotted the Republican fleet and opened fire on the *Libertad* (the *Méndez Núñez*'s lower speed left it behind the *Libertad*, which was making thirty knots) in poor visibility and at distances of between 13,000 and 16,000 metres. The Republican cruiser scored a hit, killing five men and wounding a number of others. The report of the *Baleares* underlined the accuracy of the fire of the Republican cruiser, which was the flagship of the fleet commander Miguel Buiza. The combat was broken off, to be renewed twice during the course of the day.

So, while the artillery of the *Libertad* performed well, the *Baleares* was less competent, though technical faults were also responsible. However, the Republican destroyers, possibly under orders not to neglect the four merchant ships, did not attempt to manoeuvre in order to launch torpedoes. A British admiral's view was that two or three destroyers would have been sufficient to protect the convoy, thus allowing the other destroyers to attack.[48] This might have been true with experienced commanders and well-trained crews, with a full provision of torpedoes in first-class condition, but none of this held good for the Republican destroyers. In fact the Insurgents were successful, because the freighters, alarmed, changed course and made for the Moroccan coast. The *Aldecoa* ran aground and another ship was interned by the French authorities.

XIII Serious Losses

The *Jaime II* and the *J.J. Síster* were sailing from Barcelona to Port Mahon on Minorca with a cargo of mortars, explosives and other war material. They were escorted by the destroyers *Antequera*, *Gravina*, *Sánchez Barcáiztegui* and *Escaño*. The Insurgents detached the *Canarias* to search and destroy or capture the convoy. At 2140 hours on 17 September 1937, the *Canarias* saw the convoy off Calella and opened fire at 5,000 metres. The *Antequera* responded by firing torpedoes, while the other destroyers zig-zagged as they tried to take up position to fire. The *Sánchez Barcáiztegui* was hit. The *Canarias* took the two merchant ships in to Palma. Both Admiral Moreno, the Insurgent commander, and Bruno Alonso, the Republican Commissar, criticised the incompetence of the destroyers.[49] Neither writer may have known that Federico Monreal, the destroyer flotilla commander, had orders to save his ships in the last instance, and to abandon, if he had to, the freighters. It is also questionable if the crews of the destroyers had the necessary training and capacity to respond to orders with the speed required in the brief moments when they might have launched torpedoes without exposing the ships to the overwhelming firepower of the *Canarias*.

As a consequence of these losses of freighters carrying large quantities of armaments (see Chapter Eight for the *Cabo Santo Tomé*), the mobile coastal defence forces were reinforced and put under the command of Buiza. The Soviet adviser Kuznetsov's view of Buiza was that:

> He had neither the experience nor the knowledge necessary for such a responsible post. He was courageous in the face of a strong adversary but, as later circumstances would show, he could not demonstrate gifts in command of a large fleet.

Yet there is no indication that the Russians imposed Buiza's successor, Luis González de Ubieta, as C-in-C of the fleet, since Kuznetsov writes that he also lacked the necessary aggressive attitude.[50]

On 10 October 1937 the command structure of the Insurgent fleet was reorganised. The new structure was:

CRUISER DIVISION (Rear-Admiral Manuel de Vierna)
Baleares, Canarias, Almirante Cervera

DESTROYERS (Commander Regalado)
Velasco, Ceuta, Hueca, Melilla, Teruel

GUNBOATS
Datio, Cánovas, Canalejas, Lauria

MINELAYERS
Júpiter, Vulcano

SUBMARINES (Lieutenant Commander Abárzuza)
Sanjurjo, Mola, and four Italian submarines which would remain until February 1938

MOTOR TORPEDO BOATS (Lieutenant Commander Pérez de Guzmán)

Requeté, Oviedo, Toledo, Badajoz, Cándido Pérez, Sicilia, Nápoles

The Mediterranean blockade forces also had about thirty Italian and German seaplanes, as well as the captured armed merchant ship *Mar Cantábrico* and nine others.[51]

Thus, with its two modern cruisers and six submarines and with loyal and efficient commanders and sufficient trained officers, the Insurgent navy could consider itself superior to its foe in all ways except in destroyers, where it possessed only elderly and slow ships.

A senior United States naval officer visited Spain in October 1937. In the major base of Cartagena, he wrote, the dominant note was apathy together with quite open expression of sympathy for the Insurgents. As for the destroyers, the strongest suit of the Republican navy, the *Churruca*, which had been torpedoed, would not return to service for many months. The new *Jorge Juan* and *Ulloa* were almost finished, but little progress had been made on them since the start of the war (actually, the former was in service and the latter would enter service in December 1937), the *Císcar* had been lost, the *José Luis Díez* was still under repair in Le Havre. The *Escaño* and the *Alcalá Galiano* were also in dock. The only destroyers in operative condition were the *Sánchez Barcáiztegui*, the *Almirante Antequera*, the *Almirante Valdés*, the *Almirante Miranda*, the *Gravina* and the *Lepanto*, as well as the older *Alsedo and Lazaga*. The American officer thought that the submarines *C3* and *C5* were in Insurgent hands, which shows the great success of the lie that Italian submarines loaned to the Insurgents were really captured Republican ones.[52]

The actual position with Republican submarines was disastrous. The *C1* was being repaired, the *C2* and the *C4* were in Bordeaux and Brest respectively, and the others had been sunk, the *C3* off Málaga, the *C5* in the Cantabrian Sea and the *C6* at Gijón, the last city and port on the northern coast to fall to Franco. The *B1* and the B3 had collided with ships and were inoperative in Cartagena, the *B2* could not dive, the *B4* had been seriously damaged by a bomb and the *B5* and *B6* had been sunk in 1936. In other words, only the *C1*, *C2* and *C4*, while under repair, were potentially capable of taking part in operations.[53]

Thus the reports indicated clear advantages to the Insurgents, though the efficient mobile coastal defence forces would not allow them a rapid victory. Nevertheless, 1938 would see a steady strangulation of merchant traffic making for Republican ports, together with the emasculation of the Republican fleet.

Chapter 12

1938, Testing the Limits of British Tolerance

I Merchant Shipping Attacked…Without Consequences

After the attacks on the *Cervantes* and the *Jean Weems* on 9 and 30 October 1937 respectively, Admiral Moreno had decided to refrain from stopping and searching British merchant ships, but the pause was short-lived. At the end of the year the Insurgent naval forces unleashed a torrent of attacks on merchant traffic. On 31 December 1937 the British *Bramhill* was shelled off Burriana, north of Valencia. On New Year's Day 1938 the French *Guarija*, sailing to New York from Marseilles, was bombed and driven aground. On 11 January the Dutch *Hannah* was torpedoed and sunk seven miles off Cape San Antonio. On 18 January the *Nantucket Chief*, flying the United States flag, was forced to accompany an Insurgent warship into Palma. On 20 January the British *Thorpeness*, with a cargo of coal for Tarragona, was bombed in port, leaving two men dead and five missing. British and French warships freed other ships which the Insurgents had stopped.[1]

Since several British freighters had been searched at Gibraltar and been found to be carrying foodstuffs and coal, which were not listed as war material by the Non-Intervention Committee but which undoubtedly helped the Republic to continue fighting, the Insurgents considered that the bombing and shelling were justified. 'The British think that it is in order to supply the Reds with petrol' ('*consideran las autoridades inglesas que proveer a los rojos de gasolina es tráfico leal*'), wrote Admiral Cervera with curious blindness about the over three million tons of oil imported by the Insurgents with the help of the Texas Oil Company.[2]

The series of detentions of ships and attacks came to a head when the British cargo ships *Endymion* and *Alcira* were sunk. A submarine, which was identified later as the *Sanjurjo I*, one of the first Italian submarines which had been transferred to the Insurgents, torpedoed and sank the *Endymion* on 31 January 1938. The *Endymion* was sixteen miles from the coast, sailing from Gibraltar to Cartagena with coal, and with a Non-Intervention observer on board. Twelve members of the crew lost their lives. In London, it was noted that this was the first sinking by submarine since the Nyon agreement of September 1937. In the House of Commons, members laughed sarcastically when Eden said that further talks were to be held with Italy. Didn't everybody know that the *Endymion* had been sunk by a submarine provided for the Insurgents by Italy? Eden had no reply. He had come to the end of his efforts to persuade the Chamberlain government that until Italy complied with its obligations over Spain no more concessions should be made, and on 20 February 1938, he would resign from a government which was not willing to challenge the Fascist regime but had resolved to keep it away from an alliance with Hitler even at the cost of allowing it to aid Franco openly. The Admiralty, seeing that the Insurgents had responded to the British protest about the *Endymion* by dismissing Lieutenant Commander Suances, commander of the *Sanjurjo I,* and that the Italian 'legionary' submarines had left Spanish waters, preferred to view the sinking of the *Endymion* as an unfortunate accident, and did not wish to do anything that 'could affect the intimate and cordial relations which up to now have existed between the Navy and the Insurgent authorities in Palma, which have had great value'.[3] The British chiefs of staff had frequently expressed the view that relations with Italy should be improved, and that Italy should be kept at least neutral while the rearmament plan was strengthening the British position in the Mediterranean. The assumption was that the war in Spain should not be allowed to interfere with this overall desideratum.[4]

On 4 February 1938, however, something else happened to demonstrate that, despite the Insurgent Admiral Moreno's having command over air, land and sea operations in the Mediterranean, he did not have entire control over the Italian and German air forces based on Majorca. The British *Alcira*, with a cargo of coal, was bombed and sunk twenty miles off Barcelona, despite carrying a Non-Intervention observer. The aircraft gave the crew five minutes' notice to abandon ship, and then dropped its bombs. The Republican navy's coastal defence force rescued the seamen. Responding to the British protest, Moreno claimed that the *Alcira* was in territorial waters. The Admiralty, basing itself on the evidence of the master, retorted that the *Alcira* was flying the British flag and that the aircraft concerned was a Heinkel 59 belonging to a squadron which had been responsible for at least three recent attacks.[5] The internal Insurgent enquiry admitted that the *Alcira* had not been in territorial waters but insisted that its master had not followed the agreed procedure for identification and had refused to sail for Palma for inspection as the aircraft had ordered. Internal Insurgent correspondence reveals tension between Admiral Moreno, the Insurgent government, the Chief of Staff Admiral Cervera and the German air command, whose pilot said he thought the *Alcira* was the Republican *Aldecoa*.[6] Questioned in the House of Commons, Prime Minister Neville Chamberlain admitted that the Insurgent reply to the British protest was not satisfactory and that the government reserved the right to demand compensation.[7]

The Insurgents were evidently testing the limits of British tolerance. Their submarines had ceased torpedoing merchant ships because it provoked an immediate response from the Royal Navy. In addition, the Republican coastal defence force and the anti-submarine patrols were proving so efficient that the Insurgents had to rely more and more on attacking merchant ships from the air. Even here they had to restrict themselves to territorial waters and to bombing ships in port. The Insurgents had already cancelled their agreement to respect zones for merchant ships in Republican harbours. Thus on 15 March, the *Stanwell*, unloading coal in Tarragona, was bombed, killing the Danish Non-Intervention observer and some crew members. The survivors insisted that the British flag was flying and must have been visible to the aircraft which had bombed them from 300 feet. The usual protest was made.[8]

In the spring of 1938, as Franco's forces surged through Aragon, reaching the Mediterranean at Vinaroz on 15 April, Russian, Greek and other ships were being bombed or captured.[9] While, however, taken in context, losses were only a minority of the 140 merchant ships calculated as sailing in and out of Spanish Republican ports, from the diplomatic point of view the situation was intolerable. British merchant ships were about their legitimate business and Britain did not seem able to protect them. In early May the masters of twelve British cargo vessels anchored in Valencia with four hundred crew aboard sent London a telegram of protest about the bombings.[10] This was at the same time as Admiral Moreno was assuring the Admiralty that he had forbidden attacks on British, French, United States' and Japanese vessels, and that aircraft crew had been ordered to make sure of the nationality of ships before attacking them.[11] He blamed the attacks on the *Euphorbia* in Barcelona on 14 May, and on the *Greatend*, *Penthames* and *Thorpehall* in Valencia on pilot indiscipline or lack of skill in identifying ships.[12] Nevertheless, the Insurgents had little more to fear than protests. At the worst, according to *The Times* of 2 June, the Insurgents could expect 'stronger' protests. But what else was to be done? Bombings were continuing daily, on the *St. Winifred* on 6 June, the *Thorpehaven*, the *English Tanker* and the *Thurston* on the 7th, the French *Brisbane* on the 8th, the *Isadora* on the 9th, the *Thorpehaven* again on the 10th, the *Thorpehall* and two French merchant ships on the 15th, the *Thorpeness* and the *Sunion* on the 22th, and the *Arton* and the *Farnham* on the 27th. Insurance premiums shot up.

Given that from the beginning of the Spanish war the British government had refused to allow the Republican navy the right to blockade, all Labour MPs and many Conservatives thought that Britain was favouring Franco against the spirit of Non-Intervention. How could we tolerate the bombing and sinking of British ships and the deaths of sailors? The immense majority – 113 out of 140 – of merchantmen which traded regularly with Spain were British and had always been. Granted, the profits were high, but the risks were great also and in any case they were carrying coal and food, not war material as such. Why, it was asked, could Britain not withdraw its unofficial diplomatic agent from Franco's capital, Burgos, and insist that Italy remove its air force from Spain. Could the Royal Navy not station aircraft carriers in Spanish ports so that fighters could take off and attack aircraft trying to bomb British merchant shipping?[13]

The government's argument was that any such action would risk a European war. The cabinet was heavily influenced by the Admiralty, which despised the merchant skippers whom they considered profiteers, and favoured the Insurgents over the Republicans, whose original sin had been the mutiny and the murders of officers in 1936. Captain Blagrove, for example, of the cruiser *Sussex*, in his report of 17 June 1938, wrote that the merchant masters and the owners knew the risks they were taking, and were making fat profits.[14]

Pro-Francoist prejudice at government level arose, from among other causes, from a growingly sophisticated Insurgent propaganda offensive.[15] The advice that the government received suggested that a Franco victory was inevitable. Certainly Britain should maintain the Non-Intervention policy, and protect merchant shipping on the high seas, but it would be better not to antagonise Franco.

Chamberlain's attitude arose from his view that Hitler was the major peril, and that Britain could neither afford nor did it need to be on bad terms with Italy over Spain. For Eden, Italy's withdrawal from Spain had been a condition for the better relationship with Italy that Chamberlain sought. The British premier could see no way to stop the bombing of merchant ships which would not interfere with his policy.

The difficulty of the situation in which the British government found itself did not escape the notice of Franco's allies. The parliamentary debates on the subject led to much diplomatic correspondence between Berlin, Rome and Burgos. It was later discovered that Germany and Italy were alarmed about the apparently weak Insurgent authority over their expeditionary air forces. German aviators received strict orders to obey Spanish instructions not to attack British ships.[16] This had some effect and, on 15 June, *The Times* reported that a relieved Chamberlain was able to tell the Commons that he had been assured that aircraft in Franco's service would not attack British merchant shipping on the high seas and avoid bombing them in port as far as possible, and that ports without military installations would be listed for them to drop anchor.

In effect, attacks from the air did become less frequent, although during the first days of the last major battle of the Spanish civil war, the battle of the Ebro, which began on 25 July 1938, the Norwegian merchant ship *Tirranna* was attacked, the British *Dellwyn* and *Eleni* were sunk at anchor in Gandía and Aguilas and the Danish *Bodil* in Palamós, none of which were military targets. In August the British *Lake Lugano* was sunk and the *Stanforth* damaged. In general, however it can be said that the Franco government, which had taken the policy of attacking commercial traffic to the limit, had realised that that limit had been reached.

II In Northern Waters

However, on 24 November 1937 Admiral Somerville, aboard the cruiser HMS *Galatea*, had been informed by the Insurgents that a number of ships were carrying war material to Republican Spain through the Baltic, the North Sea and the English Channel. Could the Royal Navy intercept them? Somerville reminded the Insurgents that the stopping and search of the *Euphorbia* had required large amounts of fuel and that it had not been found to be carrying war material. The Royal Navy could not be expected to embark on many more of 'these expensive wild-goose chases'.[17]

Nevertheless, it was true that ships were sailing from Baltic and Soviet ports through the North Sea and the Channel to Le Havre and Bordeaux. The cargo was transferred to trains which entered Republican Catalonia by rail or by another ship from Marseilles to Barcelona. Consequently, the armed Insurgent merchantmen *Ciudad de Alicante* and *Ciudad de Valencia* began to intercept traffic from the USSR while it was still in northern waters.[18] The delicacy of the international situation – the Czech crisis was at its height – made it advisable not to employ warships but only auxiliary armed merchant ships and not to attack British ships or those of France-Navigation, but only Spanish ones such the *Río Miera*, which the *Ciudad de Alicante* captured on 30 October as it was emerging from the Humber where it had taken on cargo.[19] The *Ciudad de Valencia* captured the *Cantabria* after an exchange of fire off the North Sea port of Cromer on 2 November. *The Times* warned that Franco could not expect to be granted the rights of a belligerent if he did not respect the rules of war. The newspaper also published a letter in contrary spirit from a representative of the pre-war Spanish owners of the ships, claiming that the crews had mutinied at the beginning of the war and had no legal right to the vessels.

III The Sinking of the *Baleares*

In reality there had been few battles between the two Spanish navies. The *Canarias* had sunk the Republican destroyer *Ferrándiz* in 1936, an Italian submarine had seriously damaged the cruiser *Miguel de Cervantes*, the two battleships of the pre-war navy had been lost accidentally, and most of the Republican submarines had been sunk or rendered inserviceable. However, now there was to be a major loss. On 6 March 1938 Republican destroyers sank the new Insurgent cruiser *Baleares*.

In general, the Insurgents had avoided a clash with the Republican destroyers. Their cruisers were being overworked, needed frequent attention in the dockyards, and could not be risked. They had acquired Italian destroyers, but these were older and slower than the new

Republican ships. The 'Legionary' submarines had been withdrawn. In addition there was always the risk that the Republican destroyer *José Luis Díez* and the submarine *C4*, under repair in France, could return to the Mediterranean. When, at last, after its long-delayed repair, the cruiser *Miguel de Cervantes* rejoined the Republican fleet on 4 March 1938 it seemed highly likely that the Republican navy was going to take an aggressive stance.

At the beginning of March, the Republican Staff issued an operational order. Three of the fast Soviet motor torpedo boats would take on fuel at Alicante, and speed fourteen miles eastwards to meet the first Republican destroyer flotilla – the *Jorge Juan*, the *Escaño*, the *Almirante Valdés* and the *Ulloa*, at sea. During the night of 5 to 6 March the MTBs would make for the small Balearic island of Formentera where, refuelled by the destroyers, they would sail to Palma, where the Insurgent ships were in harbour. The MTBs, which it was hoped could get through the anti-submarine protection of the anchorage, would launch their missiles at 0030 hours on 6 March. To reinforce the operation, the cruisers and the second destroyer flotilla would remain north-east of Cape Palos.

The use of the Soviet MTBs may have been at the insistence of the Soviet senior adviser Commander Nikolai Piterski, who replaced Kuznetsov in November 1937. However, the operation was cancelled because the MTBs were forced to return to their base by heavy seas. This was considered a pretext and the C-in-C, Lieutenant Commander Luis González de Ubieta, demanded the dismissal of the Russian officer in command.[20]

Meanwhile, at 1500 hours on Saturday 5 March 1938, the three Insurgent cruisers left Palma and at 1736 hours they took over escort duty of two ships laden with cargoes of war material and bringing eighty-five Italian artillery specialists. They made for Cape Tres Forcas, north of Melilla on the Moroccan coast, past which it was considered that there was no danger in continuing to Cádiz. However, Italian aircraft on Majorca had been grounded because of British complaints. In addition, the recently acquired Italian destroyers were all undergoing repair. For lack of adequate Intelligence, the cruisers, the *Baleares* (Captain Fontenla), with the flotilla commander, Rear Admiral Manuel de Vierna, aboard, the *Canarias* (Captain Estrada) and the *Almirante Cervera* (Captain Agacino), were sailing at nine knots – the speed of the merchantmen – without destroyer or submarine protection and unaware of the movements of the enemy, who was rapidly approaching.

The Republican cruisers *Libertad* and *Méndez Núñez*, and the destroyers *Sánchez Barcáiztegui*, *Almirante Antequera*, *Lepanto*, *Gravina* and *Lazaga*, were also unaware of the movements of the Insurgent convoy. Once it was known that the Russian MTBs had returned to base, Luis González de Ubieta, C-in-C of the fleet, ordered the main body of Republican ships to 'carry out an exploration eastwards to protect the first flotilla and attack the enemy if found'.[21]

At 0036 hours on 6 March, the Insurgent ships were spotted by the Republican destroyers on the port bow at 2,000 metres distance. The *Sánchez Barcáiztegui* (Lieutenant Alvaro Calderón) reacted at once, launching two torpedoes which missed the *Almirante Cervera*, which was the target. The Insurgent cruisers changed course immediately, trying to get out of torpedo range and to a position where their more powerful artillery could be effective. One hour later they returned to their previous course and made for the Strait of Gibraltar. In the meantime, the Republican ships described a wide circle to the south and west which would bring them across the course of the Insurgent convoy. Nikolai Piterski, the Soviet adviser who had replaced Kuznetsov, claimed later that he had had to persuade González de Ubieta to attack but, charitably, says also that the latter was concerned not to endanger his ships.[22] Admiral Vierna, trying to return to protect the merchant ships, made a 180 degree turn. He spotted the enemy and fired flares, allowing the Republicans to identify his ship, the new cruiser *Baleares*, which now offered a spectacular target for the *Sánchez Barcáiztegui*, the *Lepanto* and the *Almirante Antequera*. Between 0217 and 0220 hours the destroyers launched twelve torpedoes at a range of 2,000 to 3,000 metres. Two of the torpedoes hit the *Baleares* in the ammunition holds, which exploded in a fireball rising 1,000 metres into the night sky, while fire ran along the sides of the stricken ship and pieces of its structure fell into the sea, watched in awe by the sailors on the destroyers. The engine rooms were flooded, electric power was cut and the *Baleares* could not move. The bridge had been destroyed. Admiral Vierna and many other officers were killed. The other two cruisers, *Canarias* and *Almirante Cervera*, sailed off at high speed, as was their duty in order to avoid being hit by torpedoes and to escort the two merchant ships, while the Republican flotilla returned to Cartagena, although Piterski, who was aboard the *Libertad*, claimed later that González de Ubieta was unwilling to risk his ships.[23] This would have been an appropriate decision. Given that the destroyers had exhausted most of their supply of torpedoes, González de Ubieta was correct in not exposing his ships as day broke to the artillery of the *Canarias* and the *Almirante Cervera*. The surviving two Insurgent cruisers, for their part, feared the loss of the two cargo ships which they were escorting, and thus convoyed them as quickly as they could out of the area of danger.

The British destroyers in the vicinity, *Kempenfelt* and *Boreas*, spotted the flares and heard the roar of the explosion. They raced to the scene, arriving at 0425 hours. With valour and skill, thanked later by the Insurgents, the *Kempenfelt* (Captain McGrigor) came alongside the stricken *Baleares*, which was listing heavily and whose screws were out of the water. Captain McGrigor skilfully steered the *Kempenfelt*'s bow between the cruiser's two propellers.[24] The cruiser sank suddenly at 0508 hours. The destroyers, playing their searchlights on the water, strove to rescue the Spanish sailors trying to keep afloat and at risk from the burning oil. 469 men were saved, despite some bombing by Republican aircraft at 0800 from 10,000 feet. It may be that the aircraft hindered the humanitarian labour of the *Kempenfelt*, killing a British sailor, but the report of the pilots published in the Madrid *ABC* of 8 March, and a note published by the Ministry of National Defence in *ABC* of 12 March supports the claim that the pilots thought that the *Baleares*, which was still afloat, was the identical and untouched *Canarias*.

Of the *Baleares*'s crew of 1,206, 790 were lost, among them Rear-Admiral Vierna, Captain Fontenla, the chief of staff of the cruiser division, the second and third in command, the deputy chief of staff and twenty-five other officers. Among the dead was one of Admiral Cervera's four sons.

Contributing to the loss of the *Baleares* were the poor information available about Republican movements, the absence of destroyer and air protection, and taking a course too close to the areas where Republican destroyers patrolled rather than sailing close to the shores of North Africa. Another mistake was to sail at night when the advantage was with the low-profile Republican destroyers rather than the easily spotted Insurgent cruisers. Another reason for the disaster was the overuse of flares.

Lieutenant-Commander Hillgarth, who watched the British destroyers bringing the dead sailors into Palma, wrote later that the *Baleares* and the *Canarias* were a 'designer's compromise'. Their poor protection made them very vulnerable.[25] It might be added that the Insurgents did not expect the professional, if junior, captains of the Republican destroyers to launch their torpedoes, which they had rarely done before. A comment by the Insurgent naval staff, commenting on the skill with which the enemy fleet was handled, insists that the Republican ships were certainly not in the hands of the few professionals who were serving the 'Reds' ('*Desde luego se puede asegurar que los mandos de los barcos enemigos no estaban en manos de los pocos ex-jefes y oficiales españoles que tienen los rojos*').[26] One last explanation for some of the heavy loss of life was that neither Spanish navy required crew to wear life-jackets.[27]

IV The Republic is Split in Two

Franco's forces reached the Mediterranean on 15 April 1938, dividing the Republic into two: firstly, the Central-South Zone, a triangle with Madrid at the apex, and Valencia and Cartagena at the two other angles, and secondly Catalonia, with the city of Barcelona now the temporary capital. In June, Republican forces established a heavily fortified defensive line about eighty miles north of Valencia which Franco could not pass. Between late July and November 1938, Republican forces would fight the heaviest battle of the Spanish war, the battle of the Ebro, launched across that river from the Catalan zone. After nearly three months they would finally be forced back into Catalonia.

As a result of the disaster of the spring of 1938, Indalecio Prieto, Minister of National Defence, left the government. His portfolio as Minister of National Defence was taken by Juan Negrín, the Prime Minister. Negrín appointed Alfonso Játiva, in charge of the Cartagena dockyard, to be Under-Secretary for the Navy. Miguel Buiza was succeeded as Chief of Staff by Pedro Prado, the only communist professional naval officer.

The return to active duty of the cruiser *Miguel de Cervantes* and of the three submarines, *C1*, *C2*, and *C4*, all of which had been under lengthy repair, led to an increase in Insurgent air activity, as the Francoists strove to limit Republican ability to keep the sea routes to Minorca and Catalonia open. Convoys between Cartagena, Port Mahón, Valencia and

Barcelona were escorted efficiently by anti-submarine patrols, usually by night, along the mine-swept channel, and sometimes flew the flags of one of the Non-Intervention Committee's participants, or so the Insurgents claimed.[28] For fear of losing another capital ship, Franco himself ordered the Insurgents to avoid the coast.[29] This was one of the points made by the Generalíssimo in his speech to naval officers at Vinaroz on the Mediterranean coast on 31 May 1938. *The Times* suggested that this call for avoiding risks was in fact an acceptance that the Insurgents no longer dominated the sea. There had indeed been very little attempt to disrupt sea communication between the two zones into which the Republic had been split by Franco's blitzkrieg-like advance that spring. Orders to the Insurgents' Blockade Command had been limited to escort duties, exercises and the like, on the assumption that the enemy was sheltering in Cartagena. The Italian ships and the old cruiser *Navarra*, now back in Insurgent service, inspired no confidence. But the Republican fleet, despite its triumphant sinking of the *Baleares*, was paralysed. From then on, Republican warships would leave the harbour of Cartagena only at night in order to shelter from the regular Insurgent air raids. Its three remaining submarines would do little.

V Republican Ships Return from Abroad

Three Spanish submarines returned to service with the Republic after long repairs. The lack of loyal officers to command them was remedied by the arrival of a number of Soviet submarine specialists Their appointments should not be put down to communist machinations, but to the shortage of Spanish officers with submarine experience.

The *C1*'s Spanish commander, Sub-Lieutenant José Martínez Montero, who was suspected of disloyalty, was replaced by Russian Lieutenant-Commander German Kuzmin (alias 'Carlos Murato'). Kuzmin was accompanied by another Russian officer, Sergei Prokofyevich Lisin (alias 'Sergio Leone'). Kuzmin commanded the *C1* throughout the summer of 1938. His report expresses amazement at the poor level of training of the crew and the frequency of breakdown caused either by poor dockyard workmanship or sabotage. He complained about slow repairs in Cartagena, and about lack of support from the naval hierarchy. In general the officers tended towards defeatism. The crews, nevertheless, were often extremely loyal and spoke of going to the USSR if the Republic were defeated. Kuzmin found it difficult to persuade the fleet commander, Luis González de Ubieta, or Pedro Prado, the chief of staff, to attend to the problems he brought up. On the *C1* Kuzmin experienced opposition from the commissar, who did not wish to take risks with an unreliable vessel. The submarine patrolled but apart from keeping the Insurgents alert, had little strategic importance. After the *C1* was sunk in an air raid on Barcelona on the night of 9–10 October 1938, Kuzmin returned despondent to the USSR. He would lose his life in the Second World War.

On 14 April 1938, having finished its repairs, the *C4* left Bordeaux. By the 23rd it was in Cartagena, and a Russian officer, V.A. Egorov, alias 'Juan García', was given command. On 25 December the *C4* ran aground. The immediate subordinates of the commander sent a radio message to naval headquarters, which was retransmitted to the Ministry of National Defence, complaining about the incompetence of the Soviet commander. The only Spanish submarine officer within the regulatory age limits available was Sub-Lieutenant Sebastián Gallo, to whom command of the *C4* was transferred.[30]

The third submarine to return to duty was the *C2*. This boat left St Nazaire on 17 June and arrived at Cartagena on the 26th under the engine-room warrant officer Antonio García Alcaraz.[31] In August command was assumed by the Russian 'Juan Valdés'.[32]

VI The Adventures of the Destroyer *Jose Luis Diez*

This destroyer's movements would at times occupy the front pages of the British press as it tried to make its way back from Le Havre to Cartagena. On 8 August 1938, when the destroyer had completed repairs, Pedro Prado, chief of staff of the Republican navy, informed the C-in-C, Luis González de Ubieta, that all was ready for the *Díez*, as it was called for short, to return to Cartagena.

The *Díez* was commanded by Juan Antonio Castro Eyzaguirre, who had been a second year midshipman when the war began. At the age of 26 he was one of the youngest men to command a destroyer in the Spanish war. In July 1936 he had been on leave and had fought for the Republic in the battle for the frontier town of Irún and then made his way to Cartagena. After serving as second in command of the cruiser *Méndez Núñez*, he had commanded the destroyer *Císcar* before being transferred to the *Díez*. He was one of the few naval officers of undoubted loyalty to the Republic. While he was in France supervising the repair of his ship, Salvador Moreno, the Insurgent Deputy Chief of Staff, who had been his superior officer when Castro was a first year midshipman, wrote an emotional letter to him suggesting that he should 'invent' a malfunction in the engines and surrender the ship at sea. This was perhaps known to the Republican authorities, who recalled him from France to Barcelona. The Interior Minister was unwilling to allow him to return to Le Havre, but the Chief of Staff and the Under-Secretary of the Navy, Alfonso Játiva, together with the Secretary General of the Ministry of National Defence, Julián Zugazagotia (later handed over by the Nazis to Franco, who executed him), were convinced of Castro's loyalty.[33] They would be proved right.

The plan for the *Díez*'s safe return to Cartagena from Le Havre was to spread the rumour that it was going to Murmansk, but the intention was that the destroyer should traverse the Strait of Gibraltar on the night of 25 August 1938. On 20 August the *Díez* raised anchor. The secret was badly kept and Insurgent command got wind of it. Major intervention was planned. The cruiser *Almirante Cervera* was at anchor at Ceuta. On 21 August the destroyers bought from Italy, now named *Ceuta* and *Melilla*, left El Ferrol for the Strait. Admiral Moreno sailed for the Strait with the *Canarias* and the aged cruiser *Navarra*. The *Díez* captured two fishing boats which were looking out for the destroyer on behalf of the Insurgents, as had been learned from radio messages. On 23 August the Republican C-in-C informed the chief of staff that the Insurgents knew that the *Díez* was not making for Murmansk.[34] The destroyer would have to do its best to run the gauntlet through the Strait, and for security reasons the fishermen could not yet be released. A tragic fate awaited them.

Six warships were ready to stop the *Díez*, for if it got through to Cartagena Republican morale would be hugely strengthened.[35] But where was it? Had it perhaps made for Casablanca, to wait for a better opportunity? The Insurgents watched this Moroccan port, but without result.

Finally, on 26 August, at 2200 hours, Sub-Lieutenant Castro began the perilous course through the narrow Strait of Gibraltar. He ordered full speed ahead and strove to avoid the searchlights sweeping the sea from Ceuta and Tarifa, on either side of the Strait. Although the night was clear, Castro had a good chance of success, but the Insurgents had an ace up their sleeves.

A radio-telegraphist on board had offered to reveal the *Díez*'s position to the Insurgents, and had been provided with a code in order to do so. The speed at which the destroyer was travelling, the fact that it had painted on its side the number and letter D15, corresponding to the British destroyer *Grenville*, that it had the British flag painted on the bow gun turret and that the bands painted on the funnels corresponded to those of the relevant British flotilla, suggest that only a message from the *Díez* itself could have alerted the Insurgent warship *Ceuta* to the Spanish ship's presence a mere 2,000 metres away, at 0110 hours on 27 August.[36] The *Díez* was now seven and a half miles off the port of Ceuta, and already beginning to emerge from the Strait. The *Ceuta* informed the *Canarias*. As the *Díez* fired at the *Ceuta*, an explosion in one of its guns and a technical problem in another reduced its firepower.[37] At 0257 hours the *Canarias* opened fire. One of its 203 mm shells hit the mess deck of the *Díez*, killing the twenty-four fishermen who had been taken aboard. Yet, even with the damage, Castro managed to avoid the *Canarias*'s powerful artillery. With several dead and wounded, he brought the *José Luis Díez* into British waters and anchored in Gibraltar at 0815 hours.

Moreno's account, however, trying to minimise the very junior Castro's skill, suggests a rate of knots that the *Díez* was probably not able to reach. There were so many Insurgent warships in the area and so much light from searchlights that the *Díez* would have been visible. The British naval command in Gibraltar confirmed that the *Díez*'s torpedoes were badly maintained and not ready for launching. Evidently, the Republican destroyer had intended to pass through the Strait unseen, so the British opinion that the *Díez* had missed a great opportunity to torpedo Insurgent ships was misplaced.[38] This would have been possible if the Republican fleet had been ordered to the Strait en masse. But orders not to risk the fleet to save one destroyer had come from high up.[39]

The correspondent in Algeciras of the Seville (Insurgent) edition of the newspaper *ABC*, who had crossed the bay to Gibraltar to have a look at the damaged *Díez* and its crew, had no hesitation in telling his readers that some of the officers and crew of the ship 'will be the subject of much discussion at the Non-Intervention Committee's next meeting' ('*darán mucho juego para la próxima reunión del Comité de No Intervención*'). By their appearance, he judged that many of the crew were foreign. This echoed the Francoist conviction that courage was a characteristic only of the Insurgents or of foreigners. However, the reporter had also said that nobody was allowed near the *Díez*, so one may wonder how he reached his conclusion since, apart from Castro, the political commissar was Bernardo Simó, from Cullera (near Valencia), the second in command was Rafael Menchaca Alcalde, a veteran of the Basque Auxiliary Navy, and the navigation officer was Ernesto Hernandoarena, all of course Spanish, as the Madrid edition of *ABC* retorted on 31 August. The Insurgents did not understand that the desire to gain favour was so great among prisoners that a Republican sailor, who had been blown overboard and rescued by the Insurgents, told his interrogators that there were fifty-three French sailors and two Czechoslovaks on board the *Díez*. Yet reliable British reports, although not in general sympathetic, do not mention any non-Spaniards among the crew of the *Díez*.

The presence of the *Díez* in Gibraltar raised several diplomatic questions:

First, who was going to repair the four metre long hole in the port bow extending two metres below the waterline? The Gibraltar dockyard workers could not, because this would imply open intervention in favour of the Republic (though it had not bothered the French who had repaired the same ship). Only the Bland company had the skills to carry out the repairs, and their commercial life was closely linked to the Insurgent Zone, so they refused. In any case, many of the dockyard workers came over the frontier from La Línea, and the Insurgents soon threatened anybody who contributed to the repair of the *Díez*.

Then, what about the crew? The British authorities, who were on the whole in favour of the Insurgents, preferred to keep the crew on board rather than let them into the colony since they would probably cause unrest. However, conditions aboard were very cramped for the 162 crew members, as a Royal Navy officer who visited the destroyer reported.[40]

Again, what was to be done with the *Díez* if and when it was repaired? Should it be interned or expelled? The Insurgents, through their

Destroyer *José Luis Díez* of the Republican Navy, in dock at Gibraltar for repair between 27 August and 30 December 1938. (*Evans Collection, courtesy of Nick Evans*)

representative in London, the Duke of Alba, demanded that the Gibraltar authorities intern the destroyer. But since the Republic did not enjoy belligerent rights there was no official war and the *Díez* could not legally be interned. The international situation was highly delicate. Britain and France were dealing with the Czech crisis. While on the one hand Britain was hesitant to react to the provocations of the Insurgent aircraft which were bombing British freighters in Spanish Republican ports, on the other hand to expel the unrepaired *José Luis Díez* as a prey to waiting Insurgent guns would be an act of open hostility against the Republic and would raise awkward questions in Parliament. And the circle of problems came round to the beginning again. There were no facilities willing to repair the *Díez* in Gibraltar, although the crew might perhaps be repatriated as had been the case with the sailors of the Insurgent cruiser *Baleares* whom the *Kempenfelt* and the *Boreas* had rescued.

Messages flew from London to Gibraltar and back. On 18 October London granted the ship three weeks' grace before it would have to weigh anchor. But the Gibraltar authorities were unwilling to allow any repairs to be done although it recognised that if the ship were forced to leave in its present state it was tantamount to exposing it to instant destruction.

On 21 October a senior Spanish naval engineer left Cartagena for Gibraltar, followed the next day by Commander Fernando Navarro, the naval attaché in the Spanish Republic's London embassy. The attitude of the Admiralty is revealed by the strange comment of the Director of Naval Intelligence, who claimed that Navarro was not a commissioned officer![41] The Republic clearly intended to bring workmen from Cartagena to repair the *Díez*. Attitudes changed, perhaps conditioned by the international situation, and London allowed seven weeks for the repairs. The Insurgent ships, waiting off Gibraltar for the crippled *Díez* to emerge, left.

On 6 December 1938, two barges arrived from Oran with equipment to help raise the bows of the *Díez* sufficiently to be able to cover the hole with iron sheets. The Duke of Alba claimed that the barges were bringing munitions, that they were towed by a tug, the *Mistral*, with French sailors aboard and that the French Navy was going to protect the departing destroyer. The Gibraltar authorities were able to assure London that this was fantasy.

VI The *Jose Luis Diez*: Departure and Disaster

Repairs were finished on 15 December 1938. The *Díez* was allowed to take on fuel from a British tanker.[42] The Admiralty calculated that the ship had enough fuel to reach a Republican port even if Castro had to sail it at uneconomical speeds. Castro, Major Carlos Lago, the naval engineer, and Commander Navarro were arrested at Europa Point, at the southernmost end of Gibraltar, and accused of misusing the radio, which they had been allowed merely to test. The next day the magistrate fined them for illegal use of radio, given that Gibraltar was a fortress. Lago and Navarro had been rehearsing the possibility of transmitting the exact positions of Insurgent ships the next day.

The *Díez* was ready. It had to leave by 5 January 1939. Probably trying to deceive the Insurgents, Castro planned to leave on the night of 29–30 December 1938. He had asked for support from the Republican fleet, which did not come, at least not close enough to tackle the Insurgent vessels that Castro could see from Europa Point.

Meanwhile the Insurgents maintained their watch with the coastguard cutters *Arcila* and *Xauen*, the minelayer *Júpiter* and the gunboat *Calvo Sotelo*. Finally, at 0045 hours on 30 December, the *José Luis Díez* weighed anchor and sailed out of Gibraltar. Insurgent agents fired flares from the Rock Hotel and the Yacht Club, receiving acknowledgments from across the bay in Algeciras. The *Calvo Sotelo* reported this to the *Júpiter* and the two new minelayers *Marte* and *Vulcano*, which would be able to concentrate fire on the *Díez* from the south-east. The *Díez* turned east after passing Europa Point and, still in Gibraltarian waters, exchanged fire with the *Júpiter*. The *Vulcano* collided with the *Díez* amid intense machine-gun fire. Shells penetrated the destroyer's engine-room. Castro ordered all his six torpedoes to be launched but four missed and two did not explode. The *Díez* went aground on the beach at Catalan Bay, on the east side of the Gibraltar peninsula. Coming alongside the *Díez* to save lives, the British destroyer *Vanoc* signalled the Insurgent vessels to cease firing in British waters. The crew of the *Díez* were evacuated and the destroyer was towed to an anchorage point in Gibraltar, where it would remain until the war ended, while the crew were lodged in the uncomfortable naval prison until they were repatriated to Almería. None of them had accepted the offer to go to the Insurgent zone. On 1 January 1939, from gaol, Castro wrote his report by hand. The Spanish consul countersigned it.[43] From the Republican government came bitter protests about the treatment of the 153 officers and men. Negrín himself telegraphed to Castro:

> You should oppose fiercely the use of force against the heroic crew of the *José Luis Díez*. Accept only if physically forced [...] Behave with complete propriety but do not treat as gentlemen those who do not deserve to be so called ('*Opongan viva resistencia a acto fuerza tratan consumar con heroica tripulación* José Luis Díez.*y someterse solo reducidos físicamente [...]Manténgase sin embargo en la más estricta corrección pero negándose a dar trato de caballeros a quienes no lo merezcan.*')

There were certainly reasons for complaint. The Insurgents had attacked the destroyer in British territorial waters. Their agents on the Rock had signalled the departure of the *Díez* with flares. Castro and his men had been obliged to see their flag hauled down and had been kept in bad conditions in a military prison.

This was the tragic end of the destroyer *José Luis Díez*, whose young commander and poorly-trained crew had fought twice with valour.

Chapter 13

Surrender, Evacuation and Flight

The effect of the Munich agreements, concluded on 29 September 1938, had been to encourage Germany to send large amounts of war material to Franco to enable his forces to push the Republicans back over the Ebro, begin the invasion of Catalonia on 23 December and bring the war against the Spanish Republic to a swift and victorious end. The hope, cherished by the Soviet Union, of a pact of collective security against the Axis, the alliance between Hitler's Nazi Germany and Mussolini's Fascist Italy, was dashed. There was little point in the Soviet Union shoring up the Spanish Republic now. Nevertheless, Stalin agreed to the request of the Spanish government, transmitted by the commander of the Republican Air Force, General Ignacio Hidalgo de Cisneros, for a shipment of a large quantity of material. These arms arrived, however, too late to stave off Franco's advance.[1]

On 23 December 1938, Franco's massed armies poured into Catalonia. Their opponents were two broken Republican armies, one of which had fought desperately for weeks in the battle of the Ebro. They conducted a fighting retreat, but within a few weeks, on 26 January 1939, Barcelona fell. A massive exodus of military and civilians ensued, making their way to the French frontier. The President of the Republic, Manuel Azaña, together with the government under Juan Negrín, crossed into France on 5 February 1939.

The British cruiser HMS *Devonshire*, commanded by Captain Gerard Muirhead-Gould, who would play an important part in the surrender of the island of Minorca, was ordered to help to evacuate the British consulate-general, which was now at Caldetas on the Costa Brava, north of Barcelona. A ton of archives were packed with the help of the crew, and the staff, accompanied by some political refugees, were taken to Marseilles on the destroyer *Greyhound* on 24 January.

I Minorca

As the Republican leaders began their flight, Republican Lieutenant Commander Luis González de Ubieta was given command of the Balearic island of Minorca, with its naval base at Port Mahon. He was seconded by the energetic Baudilio San Martín, who had defended Málaga to the end almost two years earlier. González de Ubieta was replaced as fleet C-in-C by Miguel Buiza.

Minorca had played virtually no role in the war, once Palma had been established as an important naval base for the Insurgents. There were rumours that some of the garrison on Minorca wanted to surrender the island to the Insurgents.[2] The rumours came to the knowledge of Lieutenant Commander Alan Hillgarth, based on Majorca.[3] Britain had no consular representation on Minorca, but Hillgarth received information from Royal Navy ships which visited Port Mahon and reported back to him. Diplomatically speaking, it would have been improper for Hillgarth to suggest meddling in internal Spanish affairs, so he told the Foreign Office that the idea of a negotiated surrender of Minorca had been suggested by a Spanish Insurgent officer. This was Fernando Sartorius, Count of San Luis, who headed the Air Region over the Balearics. Sartorius (usually referred to as San Luis) had consulted Franco, who had approved his initiative. The Foreign Office also approved the proposed negotiation, provided that no foreign troops, in other words Italians, landed on Minorca. At a meeting on Sunday 5 February 1939, Hillgarth, Captain Muirhead-Gould of the *Devonshire*, Admiral Moreno and San Luis agreed that no British person, even Hillgarth, should take part in the negotiations, although these should take place on the *Devonshire*, and that there should be no naval or air activity while the cruiser was at Minorca. Admiral Moreno and San Luis assured Muirhead-Gould that he might evacuate refugees and officers considered 'criminals' by the Insurgents, but only if this was an absolute condition for surrender.

Given that negotiations were to take place on the *Devonshire* it would seem that forbidding any British participation was unreal. Two enemies were to meet on a British warship, so great responsibility would fall on Captain Muirhead-Gould, who was described significantly by San Luis as 'Intelligent, diplomatic, and favourable to our cause' (*'Inteligente, diplomatico y adicto a nuestra causa'*).[4]

The *Devonshire* dropped anchor in Port Mahon at 0910 on 7 February, 1939, clearly identifying itself as British lest the powerful coastal batteries of the base suspected it was an Insurgent vessel and opened fire. Muirhead-Gould expected to see General José Brandaris, who had until recently been in command of the large garrison. In fact he met the recently appointed González de Ubieta. Through his interpreter, he explained why he had come to Minorca and asked Gonzalez de Ubieta if he was willing to meet the Franco representative. Muirhead-Gould had to insist several times, which indicates that, contrary to the literal sense of his orders, he did indeed take a major part in the negotiations. González de Ubieta insisted that he had to get the agreement of his government before speaking to San Luis. However, the Republican ministers, on the road or possibly in France and without proper facilities for communication, were going to be difficult to locate. Muirhead-Gould persuaded González de Ubieta to come on board the *Devonshire* at 1330. Some 'stimulant' was offered and taken. González de Ubieta refused to see San Luis at first but in the end was persuaded to do so. San Luis begged Muirhead-Gould to remain present. The British captain did not know Spanish, but reported what the interpreter repeated later about the substance of the conversation. San Luis's report, however, claims that Muirhead-Gould spoke French well, which means that he did speak directly to the Spaniards rather than only through the interpreter. After one hour and forty minutes the meeting ended. Not having received a communication from the Republican government, Ubieta said he would make a decision at 0700 hours the next day. It proved impossible for Ubieta to get a reply from General Miaja, who was the supreme commander in the remaining territory of the Republic, but he did receive a reply from Buiza, now in command of the fleet. Buiza said that he could not get a reply from the government about surrendering Minorca but that he was confident that González de Ubieta would 'resolve the matter with his customary valour and loyalty' (*'sabrá resolverlo con su probada hombría y lealtad'*).[5]

On Wednesday 8 February the Republican commander came out again to the *Devonshire*. The sticking-point was the safety of persons whose lives might be in danger when the Insurgents arrived. San Luis advised Muirhead-Gould that if he promised to evacuate refugees a surrender was certain. González de Ubieta suggested that there might be fifty or so people who required to be evacuated. Muirhead-Gould was hesitant and insisted that their passports carried the French consul's stamp so that they would be allowed to disembark in Marseilles. At this Ubieta agreed to the surrender, after which he was entertained to lunch in the *Devonshire*'s wardroom.

All seemed to be going smoothly when from 1330 hours onward Italian aircraft began to fly low over Port Mahon and drop bombs. Negotiations ceased until absolute assurance was received from Palma that the raids would be stopped.

On the next day, Thursday 9 February, after an uprising by the military garrison of Minorca in favour of surrender, large numbers of people approached the ship before dawn demanding to be evacuated. Muirhead-Gould had not expected this but, probably when he learned that Franco's supporters were beginning to carry out a savage repression, he allowed all 452 refugees to come on board. The *Devonshire* weighed anchor at 0500 and set course for Marseilles. That afternoon three troop transports brought Franco's forces to Minorca. In Palma, Admiral Moreno apologised to Hillgarth for the bombing while the *Devonshire* was at Port Mahon and formally requested the withdrawal of Italian aircraft from Majorca.

The Minorca episode ended with an exchange of thanks between the Insurgents and the British government. Opposition MPs needed to be pacified, given that Britain had had a hand in surrendering a piece of Republican Spain, but the news of the dismissal of the Italian officer responsible for the bombing and the evacuation by the Royal Navy of so many people calmed tempers and was perhaps seen as a model for future behaviour when the rest of the territory of the Republic was surrendered. But this was not to be.

II Uprising in Cartagena

After fleeing to France, Republican Prime Minister Juan Negrín, some of his government and the highest-ranking communist militia officers in the Republican Army, flew back on 9 February 1939 to what was left of the Republican zone and tried to encourage further resistance. This was against the wishes of most of the Republican career army commanders, who saw no chance of forcing Franco to accept a truce but hoped that a surrender would lead to generous terms. Negrín, for his part, though aware of the parlous state of the Republican forces, hoped that resistance would allow the Republic to survive until the European war which he thought imminent would subsume the Spanish conflict. Then, he hoped, the Germans and Italians would leave and Franco would be abandoned.

The Republican navy was still largely in being and essential for escorting imported war material, food and other essentials. However, on 9 February the now Admiral Buiza had announced that he was going to insist that Negrín take a decision.[6] At a decisive meeting of the senior Republican military leaders on 16 February 1939 at Los Llanos airfield, four miles south of Albacete, in the centre of the Republican zone, Buiza threatened to sail the fleet away from Spain if peace were not made quickly.[7] He alleged that the crews themselves and the officers in the major base at Cartagena, supported by the recently-appointed General Bernal, commander of the port, had said they were not prepared to tolerate daily bombing against which their anti-aircraft defences were insufficient. Cartagena, as was revealed in a long report by the Spanish Communist Party dated 15 August 1938, was a nest of pro-Franco sympathisers, a large number of whom were acquitted in post-war courts-martial and continued their careers in the navy. Similar accusations had been made by the socialist political commissar of the navy Bruno Alonso to the Defence Minister, Prieto, on 23 June 1937. 'My impression', wrote Alonso, 'is that many Fascists are well-entrenched in the base' (*'La impresión que tengo es que en la base [...]están incrustados muchos fascistas'*).[8] Military Intelligence also had detected subversive attitudes among civilians, army and naval officers in Cartagena.[9]

On 2 March, aboard the cruiser *Miguel de Cervantes*, Buiza chaired a meeting of cruiser captains and most of the destroyer commanders and political commissars, together with the flotilla commanders and their chiefs of staff. Buiza wanted to hold the fleet together while Negrín made approaches to the Franco side for peace. A number of the destroyer captains, among them those of the *Jorge Juan*, the *Escaño*, the *Gravina*, and the *Lepanto*, the chief of staff of the flotillas, and the commander of the cruiser *Libertad* openly advocated surrender, but no disciplinary action was taken against them.[10] This was reported to Negrín who sent one of his ministers to try to persuade the naval officers that resistance was still possible and desirable.

Following this meeting Negrín replaced General Bernal in command at Cartagena with the communist Colonel Francisco Galán. Similar appointments of reliable men who advocated continuing the war were made for the ports of Alicante and Almería. On the same day, Saturday 4 March, Buiza, Bernal, the ex-commander of the Cartagena dockyard, and the chief of staff at the base, cabled General Matallana, Chief of the General Staff, declaring that they were prepared to oust Colonel Galán. It seemed that the loyalty of the fleet was at least doubtful, and that an uprising of the naval officers would follow any attempt by Galán to dismiss them if that was his intention. As a result, an infantry brigade was sent to support Galán.

The ensuing events in Cartagena took place against the background of an uprising on 5 March 1939 against the Negrín government headed by Colonel Segismundo Casado, commander of the Army of the Centre. The uprising was supported by most of the career officers still serving in the Republican Army. Within a few days they defeated the counter-insurgency led by the leading communist militia officers and set up a new government, called the National Defence Council (*Consejo Nacional de Defensa*) which began abortive negotiations for peace with Franco, on the assumption that they could achieve an generous settlement, particularly for the professional officers who had held commands in the Republican forces.

One of the uprisings in Cartagena was pro-Casado, and led by naval lieutenant Vicente Ramírez, chief of staff in the city, and Lieutenant Colonel Norberto Morell, commanding the dockyard, and backed by the officers of the powerful batteries of coastal artillery. There were other movements led by officers who wanted to surrender the base to the Francoist Insurgents. Over the night of 4–5 March the Republican commander, Colonel Galán, was arrested and the coastal artillery regiment under Colonel Armentia rose in revolt. The situation was highly confused. Was the uprising intended to surrender the base to Franco or to dismiss the Negrín government and negotiate peace, using Cartagena as the ultimate redoubt of the resistance and an escape route for refugees?

So far, the fleet had remained at anchor. Buiza, aboard the *Libertad*, could not obtain any information. Who had been arrested and who was in charge? He suspected a pro-Franco insurrection and threatened to shell military headquarters in the city.

Meanwhile, the commander of the 206 Brigade, sent post-haste to Cartagena to support Colonel Galán, and who had driven to Cartagena ahead of his men, was detained by a patrol which used the password 'For Spain and for peace!' (*Por España y por la paz!*'). The specific words used, avoiding '*República*', made him suspect that a pro-Francoist insurrection was taking place. He managed to escape. His suspicions were deepened when he learned that a naval officer who had been dismissed for attempting to surrender his ship to the Insurgents, had taken over the fleet's onshore radio station and was broadcasting the monarchist anthem and pro-Franco slogans.

Colonel Casado appointed the retired General Barrionuevo as commander of the Base. What was the fleet to do? Officers and men wanted to put to sea, although some wanted to sail to another Republican port, and others to a neutral harbour or to one in Franco's hands, such as Palma or Málaga. The war was lost and nobody wanted to engage the Insurgent fleet. The Republican professional officers wanted to make it clear to the court-martials which they would face when Franco won the war that they sympathised with the Insurgents and had served the Republic unwillingly and that they were concerned to preserve the large fleet that was still in their hands.

At 1130 hours on 5 March, Italian bombers raided Cartagena and scored hits on three destroyers. Shortly afterwards, the commander of the coastal batteries gave Buiza fifteen minutes to sail out of Cartagena. Buiza knew that the Republican infantry brigade was approaching and would suppress the uprising, but in the meantime the ships were at the mercy of the fifteen-inch coastal guns. General Barrionuevo issued an ultimatum. If the ships were not moving by 1230 hours he would order the batteries to bombard them. Colonel Galán, who had been released but was unable to control events, hastened to the dock and boarded a cruiser. At 1208 hours the cruisers *Miguel de Cervantes*, *Libertad*, and *Méndez Núñez*, and the destroyers *Ulloa*, *Jorge Juan*, *Lepanto*, *Almirante Miranda*, *Almirante Valdés*, *Gravina*, *Almirante Antequera* and *Escaño*, together with the submarine *C4*, sailed out of harbour, carrying a few hundred refugees and families of the sailors, leaving the rebels in control of the Base and the dockyard.

Insurgent headquarters had prepared a plan to land troops in Cartagena. On 5 March, Admiral Cervera ordered heavily-loaded troop transports to sail at once, without waiting for a convoy to be formed or escorts to arrive.[11] Cartagena had to be occupied before it was retaken by Republican troops.

In Cartagena, the rebels anxiously awaited Franco's troops. General Barrionuevo radioed Burgos, Franco's capital, that the coastal artillery would not fire at the transports as they approached the port. Where, however, was the Republican Fleet and what would it do?

The 206 Brigade of the Republican army now reached the city. It took control and on Monday 6 March it overwhelmed the coastal battery of La Parajola. At 0730, as the Francoist troop transports *Mar Negro* and *Mar Cantábrico* approached, La Parajola opened fire but was itself targeted by a battery on the other side of the bay.

During the day, the transports arrived loaded with Insurgent troops. The officers commanding the transports had insufficient information. The expedition had been put together too hastily, without preparation for an offensive and particularly without plans and equipment for destroying coastal batteries. All the following night, the transports, crammed with men, remained at sea. No reliable information came from the city. It seemed evident that some of the coastal batteries were under Republican control, as were the anti-aircraft batteries. It would be unwise to attempt a landing in the port. Moreno discussed with Franco's headquarters the possibility of a landing at Portman, a few miles to the east. This was agreed, but too late. By 7 March the 206 Brigade had suppressed the Cartagena rebellion. The landings would be cancelled. Some of the transports, however, were still on their way and a few did not even have radio. This led to the event with the greatest loss of life at sea in the Spanish war. The *Castillo de Olite* did not see and was not seen by the other transports, which it thought were now in Cartagena. Hit by a shell from La Parajola, its ammunition exploded. The *Castillo de Olite* sank at once, and 1,477 men, most of whom probably came from inland Spain and could not swim, were drowned. Another ship, the *Castillo de Peñafiel*, was also hit, but managed to limp back to its base on Ibiza.

If it had not been for the tragedy of the *Castillo de Olite*, the attempted landing might have been justified, given the strategic importance of the naval base, and the danger that, if recovered by the Republic, it would have constituted a last redoubt. It was true that General Barrionuevo's earlier messages had claimed success for the pro-Francoist rebellion.

Nevertheless, it was irresponsible and hasty to dispatch men on vessels without escort, radio, or any means of defending themselves.

III The Fleet Takes Refuge in Bizerta

Soon after midday on 5 March 1939, the Republican warships left Cartagena. At 2110 they heard a message to say that fighting was still continuing in the city. At 0017 they learned of the formation of the National Defence Council in Madrid. Some officers wanted to return to Cartagena in order to put the Council and its leader, Colonel Casado, into a position of some strength when he negotiated terms with Franco, but Admiral Buiza was under pressure from those of his officers who wanted to surrender the ships to Franco and try to escape the consequences of the inevitable courts-martial which they would face, as well as from the crews who were accompanied by many of their families, and refused to return to port. At 0021 hours, however, a message was received from the anti-submarine flotilla off Valencia:

> I have received the following teletype from *Posición Yuste* (Negrín's headquarters. MA) 'Minister of Defence to Commander of Fleet. Situation at Cartagena under control, return to Base'. (*De posición Yuste […]recibo el siguiente teletipo: 'El Ministro de Defensa nacional a jefe flota. Dominada situación creada en Cartagena, disponga que flota se reintegre a la base.*)[12]

According to Benavides, a message arrived at 0021 from Cape Palos with the words 'Highly urgent. All quiet with the Republic' ('*Urgentísimo. Tranquilo con la República*') and reports a message of similar nature arriving at 0221. Were these all the same message?[13] There was yet another similar message at 0320 and from Portman another one at 0428 purporting to retransmit the same order that Negrín was said to have broadcast at 0021. The messages may have been genuine or from pro-Casadists, but Buiza would have rightly been suspicious. At 0554 hours he changed course and made for Cartagena but changed again shortly after, when his radio operator captured a message from General Barrionuevo to Franco saying that he was in control of the shore batteries.

Buiza now ordered the fleet to set course for Algiers, a decision which was logical, given the need that would arise to refuel and to disembark the civilians on board, the uncertainty of the situation in Cartagena, and the reasonable chance that, if the Casado Junta needed the Fleet, the French authorities in Algeria would be unlikely to intern it and it could return to Spain. Always present among the officers was the need to preserve the ships and use their behaviour in doing so as a defence when facing a post war court-martial.

On the morning of Monday 6 March 1939, the Spanish Republican fleet was lying outside Algiers. The French authorities instructed Buiza to continue to Bizerta where there were more appropriate facilties. As they entered Bizerta that evening, Buiza circulated the following order:

> The commander of the fleet urges all commanding officers, given that their ships are about to enter a foreign port, to ensure that crews maintain perfect discipline, uniform, and behaviour. (*El mando de la flota encarece a todos los de los buques que, dado el próximo fondeo en un puerto extranjero, se mantenga por las dotaciones de los mismos un perfecto estado, de disciplina, uniformidad y corrección.*)[14]

In Bizerta, caretaker crews were allowed to remain on the Spanish warships, while the rest of the men were taken by train to a camp. On 26 March, nearly three weeks later, the deputy chief of the Insurgent naval staff, Rear Admiral Salvador Moreno, sailed to Bizerta on the destroyer *Císcar*, now refloated and repaired after being sunk in Gijón in October 1937, to recover the ships of the Spanish navy. France had recognised the Franco government, so the navy was formally handed over on 30 March, the same day that Colonel Casado, after failing in his attempts to win favourable terms for surrender, left Spain on a Royal Navy warship. On 2 April, 1939 at 1830 hours, Moreno radioed that he was leaving Bizerta to return to Spain.

4,300 persons, about 3 per cent of whom were civilians and family members of the crews, had arrived in Bizerta. Of them, 2,278 opted to return to Spain. About 2,000 preferred to remain where they were, among them five ships' commanders.[15] On 4 April, as they passed the site of the sunken cruiser *Baleares*, those sailors who had decided to return to Spain and face the consequences were ordered to salute the dead.

IV Evacuations. Despair at Alicante. Final Activities of the Royal Navy at Gandia

Juan Negrín later claimed to have organised sufficient shipping from French companies to evacuate the 40–50,000 people who ran the greatest risk from Franco's reprisals. He blamed the Casado movement and Franco's blockade, declared on 9 March, for impeding their departure. More than anything, he blamed Buiza for depriving the refugees of the protection of the fleet.[16] The Insurgent navy had threatened to fire on any ship in Spanish territorial waters which did not stop when ordered, which meant that few merchant vessels would risk taking on refugees. Unlike the protection given by the Royal Navy in 1937 to refugees from northern Spain, the British position now, announced by the Prime Minister in the Commons on 8 March, was that the Navy was unable to help without clear agreement of the Spanish government, which was now the Franco regime, recognised by Britain on 27 February.

In the last days of March 1939, thousands of desperate people arrived on the quays of Alicante, 170 kilometres south of Valencia. They hoped that ships would be provided, having learned that France-Navigation's vessel *Lézardrieux*, carrying members of a French delegation assembled to help evacuations, had taken off 380 people. Casado had optimistically claimed that he had already made arrangements for ships to evacuate some 10,000, which seems to have been completely untrue. Importantly, Casado had also advised that the best port for ships to go to was Alicante. It would take longer for Franco's troops to get there than anywhere else on the coast and Casado falsely claimed that Franco had agreed not to oppose evacuation.[17] In Valencia, the main city left to the Republic, desperate people had been told that they could find ships to board at Alicante. Lorries full of men, women and children were dispatched to that port.[18] There they waited in vain for ships to rescue them from Franco's vengeance, until Alicante was taken and they became prisoners.

The last ships to leave Alicante were four British cargo vessels, the *Stanbrook*, the *Maritime*, the *Ronwyn* and the *African Trader*, carrying 5,426 refugees. The largest number, 2,638, boarded the 1,383 ton *Stanbrook*, which had belonged to Jack Billmeir's line. The master, Captain Archibald Dickson, allowed all who could find a place to board his ship, which was low in the water. The decks and the holds, the lifeboats and

Stanbrook at Oran – Fundación Pablo Iglesias.

any other place which could be occupied were crammed with people, including a number of seriously wounded soldiers. Even as the anchor was being hauled up men climbed the ropes securing the *Stanbrook* to the shore. Fortunately, during its two day voyage to Oran, nothing untoward happened.[19]

At the end of March 1939, having failed to win the conditions he sought for a surrender, Colonel Casado drove 60 kilometres from Valencia down the Mediterranean coast to the port of Gandía, whose installations were British property and which had been regularly visited by Royal Navy ships during the Spanish war.[20] Gandía had become the port through which, with the cooperation of the Royal Navy, Italian prisoners of war who had fought for Franco and International Brigaders captured while fighting for the Republic, had been exchanged through the agency of the Red Cross and later in 1938 by the mostly British Commission headed by Field-Marshal Sir Philip Chetwode. The events at Minorca in February 1939 had seemed to indicate that the Royal Navy would be allowed to take off small numbers of important persons, particularly if they were considered to be in immediate danger, and provided that there was some sort of benefit for British policy, particularly that the Spanish war should be ended without a massacre of Francoists or other prisoners in the Republican zone, and that there should be some sort of exchange. On 16 February, well before Casado's uprising, the Foreign Office had cabled Mr. Goodden, the British consul in Valencia, to say that if the Republican government surrendered or fell, he was authorised to provide facilities for evacuating members of the government and their families if they requested, if there was room on Royal Navy ships after British subjects had been evacuated and if he was sure that the Spaniards were in imminent danger. At the same time, Goodden was not to guarantee evacuation to everyone because this would only encourage them not to surrender. A Foreign Office mandarin, Sir George Mounsey, showing his bias, asked why insistent Liberal and Labour MPs did not simply charter a ship and take the refugees off to Russia where he was sure that they would be well-received.[21] However, on 28 March, Goodden was told specifically that he might allow a small group of Spanish Republicans to embark on a Royal Navy warship.[22] At 0600 hours on the morning of Wednesday 29 March, the destroyer HMS *Nubian* entered Gandía to find almost 200 Spanish Republicans, who were joined later by a group of armed soldiers who it was feared would become aggressive. An unarmed detachment of Royal Marines was landed and remained there, with their weapons in a boat, until the evening in case firing began.[23] The Republican soldiers later moved on to Alicante 'under the false impression given to them by Mr Apfel, [the manager of the British harbour installations at Gandía] that there were some ships waiting there to evacuate them'.[24]

Casado himself and his sizeable group had gone to Gandía having possibly received indications that they would be evacuated from that port, though the hesitation of the Foreign Office to confirm this until the last moment suggests that Casado may have taken too literally the assurance that he had received from consul Goodden that he could embark on a British warship.[25] Alternatively, the fact that Gandía was probably not being closely watched by Franco's navy and that his ships would not fire on a British warship was an important factor in his calculations. On 29 March HMS *Galatea* was lying off the port, and Goodden was consulting the captain and Rear Admiral Tovey, the senior British naval officer in the area. Not till late that afternoon did the Foreign Office radio that the consul should interpret his instructions 'in the most prudent and generous way possible'. At 5 pm Mr Goodden told Casado that he and his group might embark. That night, twenty-five Spanish Republicans went aboard, including Casado, who was ill and later transferred to the hospital ship *Maine*. The others embarked, making a total of 194, early next morning, Thursday 30 March 1939.[26] In Admiral Tovey's report, some of the refugees were said to be of 'the lowest criminal type', though on what basis he made this judgement is unclear.[27]

V The Fate of the Defeated

Most of the men of the pre-war Spanish navy who had reason to fear the vengeance of the victors because they had been in some way involved in the mutiny and the massacres of officers in 1936 probably decided not to return to Spain. A number of officers, among them the ex-commander of the destroyer *Almirante Miranda*, Lieutenant Gasca, did meritorious work in looking after the interests of their erstwhile subordinates who were subjected to forced labour under harsh conditions in French North Africa.[28] Admiral Buiza was admitted to the French Foreign Legion as an officer. When the Allies landed in North Africa in late 1942 he re-enlisted in the Free French forces, commanding a company formed mainly of ex-sailors of the Republican fleet who now liberated Bizerta, the naval base where they had been forced to haul down the flags of their fleet four years earlier. Buiza was awarded the Croix de Guerre. After the war he and other ex-Republican sailors took part in smuggling survivors of the Nazi concentration camps into Palestine. Later he lived in France where he died on 23 June 1963.[29] Buiza's predecessor as commander of the Republican fleet, Luis González de Ubieta, wrote a series of letters from his exile where he was employed as first officer aboard a freighter sailing between Venezuela and California. He explored in vain the possibilities of returning to Spain. He died in a storm in 1950. Several other officers, including Vicente Ramírez, Chief of the General Staff in Cartagena, and a number of commanders of warships such Diego Marón, and Alvaro and Eugenio Calderón also lived for years in exile in Latin America. Pedro Prado went to the USSR where he lived through the siege of Leningrad. He returned to Spain after the death of Franco. Juan Antonio Castro, commander of the destroyer *José Luis Díez*, wrecked in the Strait of Gibraltar when attempting to rejoin the fleet at Cartagena, escaped to Britain after the defeat of France in 1940. He commanded a destroyer of the Free French navy. After the war he rose to the rank of *Capitaine de Vaisseau*, equivalent to Captain RN, commanded the Toulon base and became head of meteorological services in the French Navy.

As for those who returned to Spain, most of the officers were dismissed from the navy and, unless they could adduce extremely meritorious services for the Insurgents, were also sentenced to terms of imprisonment of various lengths. Two belonging to the *Cuerpo General*, Sub-Lieutenant Enrique Manera and Commander García Freire, remained in the Navy.[30] Death sentences were handed down on Admiral Molíns, who had commanded the Cartagena base in 1936, and on Lieutenant Commander Horacio Pérez, whose responsibilities do not seem to have been any graver than those of others. He was, however, the brother of Virgilio Pérez, who had been shot by the Insurgents in Cádiz at the outset of the war, and personal questions or known attitudes may have had a part in the vengeance of the victors. Major Baeza of the Marines, Benito Sacaluga, senior engineer officer of the *Jaime Primero*, and General Berenguer of the Legal Corps, who had probably presided over courts-martial of captured Insurgent officers, also faced the firing squad. Altogether, 192 officers appeared before court-martials, of whom 80 were acquitted and 112 found guilty. Ten death sentences were imposed, of which two were commuted, as well as six of life imprisonment, and others of varying terms. The majority received sentences of under three years, which meant, according to legislation of the time, that they were not dismissed from the service, though many were pensioned off.[31] As for other ranks, 153 death sentences were handed down of which 115 were carried out.[32]

Conclusion

S everal reasons can be adduced to explain why the Spanish Republic's fleet, which at the beginning of the civil war of 1936–1939 was so superior to Franco's Insurgent navy in numbers and in variety of warships, and which retained all twelve Spanish submarines, failed to dominate the sea and to carry out an aggressive campaign to support the Republican army which fought Franco for two years and eight months.

Bases: Control of the Strait of Gibraltar

The Republican navy controlled only one major base. This was Cartagena, on the south-east coast of the Peninsula. Cartagena lacked protective measures against submarine attack, and was very vulnerable to attack from the air, particularly once Palma had been developed as a major air base. Furthermore, the dockyard of Cartagena became almost a byword for slowness, inefficiency and probably sabotage. In contrast, from the outset the Insurgents controlled the base of El Ferrol in north-west Spain. Unlike the Republican base at Cartagena, El Ferrol was at the end of a long estuary and totally secure from attack. Franco's uprising had also taken Cádiz in the extreme south. This well-equipped base, overseeing the approach from the Atlantic to the Strait of Gibraltar, reduced the freedom of movement of Republican warships once they had failed to use their strength to block Insurgent forces crossing the Strait from Spanish Morocco. Furthermore, the immediate takeover by Franco's Insurgents of the ports of Ceuta and Melilla, on the Moroccan coast, and of Algeciras, on the other side of Gibraltar Bay, put the Republican fleet in an inferior position in the Strait and impeded its movements between the northern territory of the Republic, along the Cantabrian Sea, and its Mediterranean coast. In the Mediterranean, after the Republic had abandoned the attempt to retake the Balearic island of Majorca, the Insurgents developed its capital, Palma, into its third naval base.

New Cruisers

The Insurgent fleet, at the outset with no more than an old battleship, a cruiser and a destroyer and some smaller craft, could look forward to the completion of two new cruisers, the *Canarias* and the *Baleares*, which were nearing completion and would dominate the sea. Their characteristics were such that no Republican force dared to engage them except by accident.

Mutinies, Indiscipline and Lack of Officers

Undeniably, the mutinies in the navy were a source of Republican inefficiency and indiscipline, especially at the beginning of the war. Distrust of the officers who remained was also a major factor. Nevertheless, by the end of the war the Republican navy had been to some extent cured of its mutinous and revolutionary stance, first by the abolition of the sailors' committees by Indalecio Prieto, the Minister for the Navy and Air, and later National Defence Minister, and possibly by the pressure of the Soviet advisers, although their influence is difficult to judge.

The mutinies meant that Republican ships were very short of officers, particularly of higher rank. Many of those few officers who did accept commands, often following menaces if they refused, were either unwilling or inexperienced both for command and for staff responsibilities. The relative mildness of most of the sentences imposed by Franco's post war courts martial on naval officers who served the Republic, compared with the general harshness of the repression, is an indication of the success of foot-dragging and even sabotage on the part of a substantial proportion of the Republican naval command and bureaucracy. Whether even a minimum number of the naval officers who were imprisoned and assassinated in the Republican Zone would have served the Republic loyally had they been offered the chance, is at least doubtful.

The Insurgents, on the other hand, had a plentiful supply of officers whose loyalty to their cause was not in doubt. Discipline was rigid, but they had to go to sea often in command of half-trained seamen as a result of the dismissal, imprisonment, execution, and sometimes the sheer distrust of a proportion of the crews by their officers. German criticisms of lack of aggressiveness on the part of the Insurgent ships have to be understood in this context.

German and Italian Support

The Insurgents had the benefit of systematic German and Italian help, not only because the materials and technical aid which the two dictatorships supplied allowed the Insurgents to complete the two new cruisers and other ships, as well as make older vessels serviceable, but also because Italy and Germany made it clear that they would not tolerate interference with their supply ships. The Republic, in contrast, was obliged to provide its own escorts for freighters bringing arms from the USSR because the Soviet navy had no presence in Spanish waters. It thus became vital to preserve the cruisers and destroyers of the Republic for these escort duties. Thus the mere threat of action by German and Italian warships, both surface and submarine, which were present in the western Mediterranean throughout the war, inhibited the potential aggressiveness of the Republican navy.

Loss of Ships

Another significant point was the loss of a number of Republican warships, beginning with the destroyer *Ferrándiz*, sunk in September 1936 by the new Insurgent cruiser *Canarias*, while the *Almirante Cervera* severely damaged another destroyer, the *Gravina*. The Republican cruiser *Miguel de Cervantes* spent many months under repair after an Italian torpedo attack. In addition, most of the Republican submarines were sunk, sabotaged by their commanders or otherwise put out of action. The Republican command was imbued with the concept of 'the fleet in being'. So long as the ships were at sea they constituted a threat to the enemy. In the face of its losses, consequently, the Republican command grew ever more unwilling to risk its ships in combat.

The Insurgents, whose naval commanders had undergone the same training as the Republican officers and indeed often knew them personally and had served with them in the past, also believed in the concept of 'the fleet in being', but in contrast they were confident that the mutinous crews of the Republican navy lacked the skill and the morale to fight. Thus the Insurgents adopted an aggressive stance from the beginning. Personal factors were also in play here. The Insurgents included high-ranking and energetic officers, convinced of the rightness of their cause, and able to act with autonomy, given that in Insurgent Spain the old bureaucracy of Minister and Under Secretary no longer existed. In the Republic the survival of governmental institutions, however chaotic, was often itself a cause of inertia.

Strategic Errors

The Republican navy lost control of the sea, and ended by merely reacting to the situation in which it found itself. Yet the Republican fleet might have been able to repeat its accidental victory in sinking the new Insurgent cruiser *Baleares*. Possibly, an attempt by the Republican fleet to blockade Palma, and to try to interrupt the sea communications of the Insurgents in general, might have had an inhibiting effect on the enemy. In reality, the Insurgent victory at sea was never absolute until the Republican fleet, having taken shelter in Bizerta, was surrendered.

Reaction to the Casado Coup: March 1939

Had Colonel Casado's uprising in March 1939 against the Negrín government not taken place and had Admiral Buiza not decided to abandon Cartagena, perhaps unaware that it had been retaken from pro-Francoist rebels, and had he not sailed the fleet to Bizerta to be interned, the Republic might have been able to fight on for a few months until the expected European war had subsumed the civil war and Germany had abandoned Franco.

Counter-factual propositions, however, are of limited value. Casado did rebel, the Negrín government did leave Spain, the Republic did surrender, and 20,000 refugees were abandoned on the quays of Alicante by the fleet which could have evacuated them or protected friendly merchant ships which might have done so.

International Questions: Merchant Marine Traffic and Blockade

The international importance of the sea in the Spanish Civil War lay mainly in the question of merchant marine traffic and arms supply. After the first few weeks, the Republican navy did not even attempt to stop German and Italian cargo ships laden with armaments and making for

Insurgent-held ports. This was a question of diplomatic realism. In 1936 the Republic was the legally and internationally recognised government of Spain, confident that it could suppress the Franco uprising, which had not managed to take control of large parts of the country. The Republican government could permit itself the luxury of respecting international norms of behaviour and even accept the decision by Britain, the principal naval power, to refuse to recognise the State of War and the naval blockade declared by Madrid over Spanish coastal waters. The Republic needed the support of other countries and could not afford to antagonise them by insisting on rights at sea which they did not wish to recognise. The Insurgents, in contrast, had no alternative. For them success was a question of life or death. At all costs, they had to prevent armaments, raw materials and food reaching the Republic. Thus the Insurgents, though not granted belligerent rights, went to the limit and even beyond the limit of provocation in stopping, searching, sequestering and often sinking foreign merchant ships en route to Republican Spain, and bombing vessels in Republican ports.

Foreign Reactions, Britain, the Royal Navy and the Spanish Civil War

The British reaction proved that the Insurgents gauged the situation accurately. This was because Franco enjoyed the support of the two powers, Nazi Germany and Fascist Italy, whom Britain and France, the democracies with the major navies in the Western Mediterranean, wanted to appease. In particular, it became ever more clear at sea, as well as on land and in the air, that Britain would tolerate a large amount of Italian support for Franco because London's policy was to keep Italy away from an aggressive alliance with Nazi Germany.

German aid at sea consisted of sending war material, but more than anything else Germany safeguarded its cargo ships by disguising them and by threats, which became real in the case of the German freighter *Palos,* whose capture by Basque ships was followed by an fierce German reaction which in theory nations such as Britain, whose freighters were also attacked, could have adopted against the Insurgents but did not for fear of setting off a major war. If Britain had reacted as energetically as Germany to interference with its seaborne traffic to Spain it would not only have avoided the loss of so many merchantmen, but the Insurgents would not have been able to gain that psychological advantage over their opponents which became so evident.

Thus neither side in the Spanish war completely achieved the aims of naval warfare: to dominate the enemy and destroy his power at sea, cut his communications, dry up the sources of his commercial power and close his ports, though the Insurgents came close. The latter realised that the way to victory was to inhibit Republican traffic, a strategy which the Republicans could not or chose not to employ.

For Britain, the Spanish war at sea, coming as soon as the Abyssinia crisis of 1935–1936 was over, was seen as a tiresome distraction from the Royal Navy's other responsibilities and its training schedules. The question of how to tackle Franco's attempts at blockade became uppermost. While the navy of course obeyed the orders of the British government, its hostility towards the Republican navy, which it considered to have been born out of mutiny and murder, was hardly concealed, as was its enmity towards the owners and masters of the increased number of cargo ships which came on to the British register in order to enjoy the support of the Royal Navy and to earn high profits from supplying Republican Spain.

One British decision remained constant. Britain would not grant belligerent rights to either side in the Spanish civil war to stop neutral traffic at sea. The Republic was undoubtedly entitled to have those rights and Franco was not, but Non-Intervention, a device created out of fear that the Spanish war would descend into a general European conflict, created a new and difficult situation. Neither Franco nor the Spanish Republic would be permitted to stop neutral traffic on the high seas. But, while Franco's interference with commercial sea traffic was endured though under protest, Britain would not allow 'unidentified' submarines – though they were known to be Italian – to attack cargo ships at will. As a result, the Anglo-French reaction to Italian submarines sinking merchantmen in August 1937 was immediate, energetic and successful. Perhaps a similar reaction to the bombing of merchant ships by Insurgent aircraft might have achieved similar results.

Lessons Learned

The Spanish civil war was of little technical interest for the Royal Navy, but it did perhaps have some influence on the perennial question of whether capital ships were at risk from bombing. The chiefs of staff produced several reports on this perplexing issue.[1] By 1936, the Royal Air Force and the Royal Navy were competing fiercely for funds. The Royal Navy was ill-prepared to deal with air attack.[2] Most Royal Navy officers were sceptical but some thought that air attack could be serious if it were concentrated and synchronised, and if anti-aircraft defences were not improved. The use of aircraft to target shipping in the Spanish civil war made the question more urgent. The Joint Intelligence Committee produced a report on 'Air attack on ships' which argued that the Spanish war demonstrated that air attack could be very serious and that defences, both on warships and cargo vessels during wartime, should be strengthened. In the Spanish war eighty attacks had been made on warships from the air. No warships had been sunk but seventeen had been damaged. There had been eighty-one attacks from the air on merchant ships, sinking six and damaging twenty-nine.[3] A report by a sub-committee of the Committee of Imperial Defence on the Vulnerability of Capital Ships to Air Attack was presented to Parliament in November, 1936.[4] However, this did not come to much and in 1938 a parliamentary statement said little more than that experiments had continued to be made, and there was the fullest collaboration between the Admiralty and Air Ministry. Nor were later committees able to produce decisive conclusions.[5]

On operational intelligence, the Spanish Civil War had revealed deficiencies in communicating information. Nevertheless, the Royal Navy successfully tracked German naval movements.[6] The German navy for its part developed a system which allowed it to inform the Insurgents about movements of Republican warships.[7]

Grand Strategy: The Second World War Two

Italian activities in particular during the Spanish war created anxious speculation about the British role in the Mediterranean. Some thought that Italian sea and air power had made the Mediterranean unsafe for the Royal Navy. Although the general view was that to abandon the Mediterranean would cause an intolerable loss of British prestige, Singapore was considered more important and the Treasury opposed spending in the Mediterranean. This led to pressure for a rapprochement with Italy, which Prime Minister Chamberlain thought he had achieved by allowing Mussolini full licence in Spain.

Nevertheless, during the Second World War fears about Italian domination of the Western Mediterranean would amount to little.[8] Italy gained nothing from its costly support for Franco during the Spanish war. Apprehension that Franco Spain would be a danger to Britain also came to nought. The Spanish dictator did not take Spain into the Second World War, among other reasons because the Royal Navy's blockade, allowing only essential goods into Spain, was effective. Gibraltar, though in theory extremely vulnerable, remained a vital British base. As for Germany, apart from some Spanish facilities for its U-boats, admittedly threatening to Atlantic traffic, it profited little at sea from the aid it had provided for Franco's cause. The losers were, of course, the Spanish people, the countries occupied by the Nazis and the Soviet Union.

The reluctance of the British chiefs of staff, and especially of the Admiralty, to risk armed conflict with Italy over its intervention in Spain seems hard to understand from today's perspective. At a time when Germany's rearmament was rapid and British rearmament had barely got off the ground, British and French tolerance of German and Italian support for Franco played a major part in bringing about the collapse of the desirable but untried ideal of collective security. And yet, when Italian actions at sea became intolerable during August 1937, Rome caved in before there was even a need to take action. Italian and German support for Franco added to British unwillingness to press Rome and Berlin too far were the ultimate reasons for the result of the Spanish Civil War at sea.

Appendix I

Technical Details of Spanish Warships

REPUBLICAN				
BATTLESHIP				
	Launched	*Displacement (tons)*	*Armament (mm)*	*Max. Speed (knots)*
Jaime Primero	1914	15,452	8 × 305	19
CRUISERS				
Méndez Núñez	1923	4,650	6 × 152.4	29
Libertad	1925	7,850	8 × 152.4	33
Miguel de Cervantes	1928	7,850	8 × 152.4	33
DESTROYERS				
Alsedo	1922	1,145	3 × 101,6	34
Lazaga	1924	1,145	3 × 101.6	34
Sz.Barcáiztegui	1926	1,650	5 × 120	36
Ferrándiz	1928	1,650	5 × 120	36
J.L.Díez	1928	1,650	5 × 120	36
Lepanto	1929	1,650	5 × 120	36
Churruca	1929	1,650	5 × 120	36
Alcalá Galiano	1930	1,650	5 × 120	36
Alm.Valdés	1930	1,650	5 × 120	36
Alm. Antequera	1930	1,650	5 × 120	36
Alm. Miranda	1931	1,650	5 × 120	36
Gravina	1931	1,650	5 × 120	36
Escaño	1931	1,650	5 × 120	36
The following, of like characteristics, came into service during the war: *Císcar, Almirante Ulloa* and *Jorge Juan*.				
SUBMARINES				
B1–B6	1921–1923	556	4 × 435mm torpedos	16/8
C1–C6	1927–1929	915	6 x530mm torpedos	16/10*

* surface and submerged maximum speeds.

	Launched	Displacement (tons)	Armament (mm)	Max. Speed (knots)
In addition				
7 torpedo boats	1912–1919	177	3 × 47mm	26
1 gunboat and 4 coastguard cutters armed with 76.2 mm guns				

	Launched	Displacement (tons)	Armament (mm)	Max. Speed (knots)
INSURGENT				
BATTLESHIP				
España	1913	15,452	8 × 305	19
CRUISERS				
República	1920	5,502	6 × 152.4	26
(later *Navarra*)				
Al. Cervera	1925	7,850	8 × 152.4	33
Canarias	1930	10,668	8 × 203	33
Baleares	1933	10,668	8 × 203	33
DESTROYER				
Velasco	1923	1,145	3 × 101.6	34

3 modern minelayers, displacing 2,000 tons, with 4 × 120mm guns and speed of 18,5 knots
5 torpedo boats, displacing 177 tons, armed with 3 × 47mm guns and speed of 26 knots
3 gunboats and 5 coastguard cutters

Appendix II

Soviet Naval Officers in Republican Spain

This list is based on website http://wap.kortic.borda.ru/?1-3-0-00000060-000-10001-0, with additional help from Dr Boris Wolodarsky, to whom I am in great debt. See also Frank, Willard C., Jr., *Marinos Soviéticos con la Flota Republicana durante la Guerra Civil* (Cartagena, Divum & Mare, 2009), Appendix 1.

Only the more significant of the seventy-seven Soviet naval personnel who went to Spain are listed here as well as the most important information about them. All of them were awarded decorations (the submarine commanders were made Heroes of the Soviet Union). Most were promoted and served in important positions in the Second World War. In contrast to some of the army and air force advisers who went to Spain during the civil war, none of the navy men were 'purged' on their return.

1. Abramov, Nikolay Osipovich, Captain 3rd rank (equivalent to Captain RN), was in Spain December, 1937 – October 1938 as adviser to the commander of the Republican destroyer flotilla. In 1941 he became Rear Admiral and commander of the Danube fleet.
2. Alafuzov, Vladimir Antonovich, Captain 3rd rank, was in Spain from May 1937 to April 1938 as adviser on the flagship cruiser *Libertad*. He replaced Kuznetsov as chief adviser. In 1941, as Rear Admiral, he was Chief of the Operations Department and Deputy Chief of Naval Staff.
3. Aleksandrov, Aleksandr Petrovich, Captain 2nd Rank (equivalent to Commander RN), was in Spain from April until October 1937 as adviser to the commander of the flotilla in the Cantabrian Sea. In 1941 he was promoted to command the Novorossiisk naval base, becoming later commander of the Azov Flotilla.
4. Annin, Nikolai Petrovich, Commander, was in Spain from mid-September 1936 to May 1937 as adviser to the commander of the destroyer flotilla and to the commander of the cruiser *Libertad*. In 1941 he was appointed to command the Northern section of the White Sea. His aliases were 'Gregorio Fernández' and 'François'.
5. Arbuzov, Nikolai was in Spain from May 1937 to October 1938 in the torpedo boat detachment. In 1941 he was promoted Senior Technician and Lieutenant Commander.
6. Basistiy, Nikolai Efremovich, Commander, was in Spain between April 1937 and April 1938 as adviser to the commander of destroyer flotilla under the alias 'Juan Montenegro'. In 1941 he was appointed to command a cruiser in the Black Sea Fleet.
7. Batrakhov, Alexei Petrovich, Lieutenant, served in Spain from May 1937 to November 1938, being wounded on 30 July 1937. In 1941, promoted Lieutenant Commander, he served in the Intelligence Division of the Baltic Fleet. He was killed in Leningrad during the Second World War.

8. Bekrenev, Leonid Konstantinovich, Lieutenant Commander, was engaged in naval intelligence in Spain. In 1941 he became Head of the 2nd section of the Intelligence Department of the Staff of the Northern Fleet.

9. Belov, Ivan, Chief Petty Officer, was in Spain from May 1937 to October 1938 as Head of Communications in the torpedo boats detachment. In 1941 he was promoted First Lieutenant in the Black Sea Fleet.

10. Bogdenko, Valentin Lukic, Lieutenant Commander, was in Spain from May 1937 to February 1938 as gunnery adviser under the alias 'Julio Olivares'. In 1941, as Rear Admiral, he was appointed Chief of Staff of the Pacific Fleet.

11. Burmistrov, Ivan, Lieutenant Commander. In Spain since February 1937. He commanded submarines under the alias 'Luis Martinez'.

12. Bykov Ivan, Lieutenant Commander. He served in Spain from November 1936 to November 1937. He was gunnery adviser on the cruiser *Méndez Núñez*.

13. Drozd, Valentin Petrovich. Commander, he was in Spain in 1936–1937 as adviser to the commander of the destroyer flotillas under the alias 'Don Ramón Hernández'. In 1941, as Rear Admiral, he commanded a squadron in the Baltic Fleet. He was killed in January 1943.

14. Egipko, Nikolai Pavlovich, Lieutenant Commander, served in Spain from May 1937 to August 1938 in command of a Spanish submarine under the alias 'Don Severino de Moreno'. In 1941 he was the commander of the 1st Brigade of Baltic Fleet submarines.

15. Egorov, Vladimir served in Spain between May 1937 and November 1938, under the alias 'Valdés', commanding a submarine. In 1941, he led the 7th Division of the Baltic Fleet submarines. He was killed in August, 1942.

16. Eliseev Ivan D. Lieutenant Commander. In Spain he was adviser to the commander of the destroyer flotilla. In 1941, as Rear Admiral, he was chief of staff of the Black Sea Fleet.

17. Epishev, Gregory S. In Spain, under the alias 'José Gutiérrez' he was radio operator on the destroyer *Almirante Antequera*, taking part in the sinking of the cruiser *Baleares*.

18. Gavrilov, Victor M. Served in Spain, 1936–1938 as communications adviser at Fleet Headquarters. In 1941 he was Engineer Rear Admiral and head of communications.

19. Golovko, Arseniy G. Lieutenant Commander, served 1937–38 as adviser to the commander of the naval base of Cartagena (replacing S.S. Ramishvili), under alias of 'Don Simón García Gálvez'. His responsibilities included unloading transports, ship repairs and improvement of coastal and antiaircraft defence. In 1941 as Rear Admiral, he commanded the Northern Soviet Fleet.

20. Ivan Grachev, Lieutenant Commander. In Spain he commanded a submarine under alias of 'Juan García'. He was killed in June 1942.

21. Nikolai Ilyin, Commander, was in Spain from December 1937 to July 1938 as adviser to the commander of the destroyer flotilla.

22. Kanevski, Nikolai L., a torpedo boat commander, was in Spain from May 1937 to autumn 1938 as commander of the torpedo boat detachment. In 1941, he was base commander of the 2nd Brigade of torpedo boats.

23. Karandasov, Peter Lukyanovich, was a sub-lieutenant who was in Spain from October 1936 to April 1937. In 1941, he commanded torpedo boats and later participated in the defence of Sebastopol.

24. Katrichko, Mark Kupriyanovich, Commander, was in Spain from October 1936 to June 1937. In 1941 he commanded cruisers in the Black Sea Fleet.
25. Korobitsyn, Alekesey Petrovich. From May 1937 he commanded the Portman torpedo boats base.
26. Kruchenykh, Arkady V., Lieutenant Commander, he served in Spain from May to November 1937 as gunnery adviser. He became adviser to the chief of staff in the Cantabrian Sea. In 1941, he served in the Operations section of the staff.
27. Kuznetsov, Nikolai Gerasimov, Commander. In Spain, he was the naval attaché and chief naval adviser between August 1936 and July 1937, under alias of 'Lepanto'. He was later Admiral of the Fleet and People's Commissar of the Soviet Navy.
28. Kuzmin, Herman Yul'evich, Lieutenant Commander, served in Spain as submarine commander under alias of 'Murat'. In 1941, he led the 3rd section of the 1st Brigade of submarines in the Black Sea Fleet. He was killed in 1942.
29. Labudin, Aleksandr Petrovich, Lieutenant Commander, served in Spain from April to June 1937 as adviser to the commander of the battleship *Jaime 1*.
30. Lisin, Sergey Prokopovich, Lieutenant Commander. In Spain, from May 1937 to October 1938 he was the second in command of the submarine *C4*.
31. Likholetov, Vasily Petrovich, Lieutenant, arrived in Spain in January 1937 and commanded the torpedo boat detachment. He was wounded on 30 July 1937.
32. Pitersky, Nikolai A. was in Spain between November 1937 and November 1938 as chief adviser to the Republican fleet and Naval Attaché.
33. Ramishvili, Semen Spiridonovich, Lieutenant Commander, served in Spain between November 1936 and October 1937 as adviser to the commander of the naval base of Cartagena under the alias of 'Juan García'.
34. Sapozhnikov, Samuel G., Lieutenant Commander, adviser to the chief of naval staff.
35. Zaitsev, Eleazar Alexandrovich was in Spain from March 1938 until the end of the war. In 1941, he headed the 8th Division of the 1st (Intelligence) Department of the Navy.
36. Zhukov, Evgeny N., Lieutenant Commander. In Spain from June 1938 until the end of the war, he was adviser to the commander of the 1st destroyer flotilla. He was one of the last Russians to leave Spain. In 1941, as Captain 2nd Rank, he served on the staff of the Black Sea Fleet.
37. Zhukov. Gabriel V., Lieutenant Commander, served in Spain from October 1936 to July 1937 as Assistant Naval Attaché. In 1941, as Rear Admiral, he commanded the Odessa Naval Base.
38. Zybin, Alexander. In Spain between May 1937 and mid-1938, he was a mechanical expert in the torpedo boats flotilla. In the Second World War, he was Engineer Lieutenant Commander of the 1st Brigade of torpedo boats of the Pacific Fleet.

Notes

Preface
1. Latest edition London, Penguin, 2012.
2. This book uses the term 'Insurgent' to refer to the forces of General Franco, who called themselves *nacionales*, which became 'Nationalists' in English. 'Republican' here refers to the forces of the Spanish Republic, often called 'Government' or 'Loyalist', and *Rojos ('Reds')* by their enemies.

Chapter 1: Setting the Scene
1. See Brodie, B., *A Layman's Guide to Naval Strategy* (Oxford, Oxford University Press, 1943) and Graham, G., *The Politics of Naval Supremacy* (Cambridge, Cambridge University Press, 1965).
2. Kennedy, Paul, *The Realities behind Diplomacy* (London, Fontana, 1981), pp.273–274.
3. Barnett, C., *The Collapse of British Power* (London, Eyre Methuen, 1972), p.442.
4. Roskill. S., *Naval Policy between the Wars*, 2 vols., (London, Collins, 1976), ii, p.95.
5. Ibid, ii, p.86.
6. Ibid, ii, pp.170–172.
7. Ibid., ii, p.184.
8. See Alpert, M., 'The Spanish Civil War and the Mediterranean' in Rein, R.(ed.) *Spain and the Mediterranean since 1898*, (London, Frank Cass, 1999), pp. 150–167 (p.152 for Vansittart's comment).
9. Details of the history of Spanish warships have been taken from de Bordejé y Morencos, F., *Vicisitudes de una política naval: antecedentes, desarrollo de la Armada entre 1898 y 1936* (Madrid: San Martín, 1978), and Cerezo, R., *Armada española, siglo XX*, 4 vols. (Madrid: Poniente, 1983, i. pp.77 and ff.
10. Rodríguez Martín Granizo, G. and González-Aller, J.I., *Submarinos republicanos en la guerra civil española* (Madrid: Poniente, 1982).
11. The names of people and places are spelt in Spanish style, with accents, unless there is an established English name, such as Port Mahon or Seville.
12. Callejo Enciso, M., *Aproximación al estudio de una institución total: la armada* (Madrid; published by the author, 1981), pp.43–44. The prevalence of a limited number of frequently found surnames among the officers of the *Cuerpo General* gives the impression that this body was of very limited social extraction.

254 The Spanish Civil War at Sea

13. Hough, V.R., *The Potemkin Mutiny* (London, Hamish Hamilton, 1960); Getzler. I, *Kronstadt 1917–1921* (Cambridge; Cambridge University Press, 1983); Woodward, D., *The Collapse of Power: Mutiny on the High Seas Fleet* (London: A. Baker, 1973); Le Ramey, I.J., *Les mutins de la Mer Noire* (Paris: Editions Sociales, 1973).
14. Carew, A., *The Lower Deck of the Royal Navy 1900–1939* (Manchester: Manchester University Press, 1981) and Copeman, Fred, *Reason in Revolt* (London: Blandford Press, 148). In the Spanish Civil War, Copeman would command the British battalion of the International Brigades.
15. Cerezo, i. pp. 232–233.
16. The theory that the crews planned to isolate the army in Morocco, expressed by Rodríguez Martín-Granizo and González-Aller, p.17, cannot be defended without admitting that the army planned to bring its most professional regiments over the Strait of Gibraltar to the Peninsula to mount a coup and counted on help from the navy. Admiral F. Moreno, *La Guerra en el mar, hombres, barcos y honra* (Barcelona: AHR, 1959, pp.67–69) claims that discipline was maintained. For a more up-to-date, post-Franco and extended version of this book, see F. and S. Moreno, *La guerra silenciosa y silenciada*, five volumes (Madrid: Alborán, 1998). The authors are the sons of Admiral Francisco Moreno).
17. Cerezo, ii, p.30, though without stating his evidence for the figure.
18. José Regueira Ramos 'El radiotetelegrafista Benjamín Balboa y el paso del Estrecho del ejército de Africa (julio-agosto 1936)' in *Almoraima, Revista de Estudios campogibraltareños* (Algeciras), No.45, October 2016, pp.65–83 (specifically p.69).
19. Sueiro, D., *La flota es roja: papel clave del radiotelegrafista Benjamín Balboa en julio de 1936* (Barcelona: Argos Vergara, 1983), p.109.
20. Cerezo, ii, pp. 46 and 269–271.
21. For the situation in the army see Michael Alpert, *The Republican Army in the Spanish Civil War 1936–1939* (Cambridge: Cambridge University Press, 2007), pp.13–16.
22. Cerezo, ii, p.43.
23. SHEMA (Servicio Historico del Estado Mayor de la Marina) NC 211–3, 5 June, 1937.
24. Cerezo, iv, p.205.
25. Franco Araujo-Salgado, F., *Mis conversaciones privadas con Franco* (Barcelona: Planeta, 1976) pp. 110–111, as quoted by Sueiro, p.117.
26. Frank, W., 'Seapower, Politics and the Onset of the Spanish Civil War', unpublished doctoral thesis (University of Pittsburgh, 1969), whose evidence was probably taken from the tendentious, but probably reliable on this point, work of Arrarás, J, *Historia de la Segunda República República Española* (Madrid: Editora Nacional, 1956–1968), four volumes, i, pp.316–317.
27. See, for example, Bordejé cit.and Cervera Pery, J., *Alzamiento y Revolución en la Marina* (Madrid: San Martín, 1978).

28. These meetings are mentioned by Cervera, Sueiro and Cerezo, who refer to accounts given by surviving officers, to be found in the Colomina Report.
29. Sueiro, p.97.
30. Quoted in Cervera Pery, p.130.
31. Sueiro, p.96.
32. Balfour, S., *Deadly Embrace; Franco and the Road to the Spanish Civil War* (Oxford: Oxford University Press, 2002), p.271.
33. Quoted in Cerezo, ii, p.283.
34. Sueiro, pp.147–148.

Chapter 2: The Die is Cast
1. Cerezo, ii, p.226.
2. SHEMA NC 062-1.
3. SHEMA NC 14-39 and 284-1.
4. All details about Balboa's actions and the messages sent and received, are taken from Sueiro, Chapter One, who obtained them personally from Balboa in his exile in Mexico, and have been compared with the accounts of Cerezo and Cervera Pery.
5. Details in Cervera Pery, p.176, and Sueiro, p.148.
6. Cervera Pery, pp.89–91.
7. Cervera Pery, p.199.
8. F.and S.Moreno, i, pp.141–142.
9. Rodríguez Martín-Granizo and González-Aller, pp.39–40 and Appendix One for the orders received in the submarines.
10. Sueiro, p.132.
11. Ibid pp.160–161, who makes the point that later Francoist historiography insisted that the bodies had been flung overboard without ceremony.
12. On Azarola see M. García Bañales et al, 'Antonio Azarola Gresillón' in J. García Fernández (ed.) *25 militares de la República* (Madrid: Ministerio de la Defensa, 2011), pp.101–127.
13. Statement by one of the officers reproduced in Cerezo, ii, pp 153–156.
14. Cerezo, iii, p.42.
15. Ibid, ii, p.95 and Kuznetsov, N. In *Bajo la bandera de la España republicana* (Moscow: Progress Publishers no date [1967?], pp.135–136 (this work will be cited hereafter as *BLB*).
16. Figures from Frank compared with calculations in Cerezo, and Cervera Pery.
17. SHEMA *Historia Orgánica* 062-1; Cervera Pery, pp.147–148.
18. Text in SHEMA NC 284-8 and Cerezo iii, p.121.
19. Specific threats to sailors' families were made by Franco and General Queipo de Llano (Sueiro, p.160).
20. Details of the deaths of naval officers in the Republican zone come from Sueiro, pp.158, 161–162; Cerezo, iii, p.123 and 125.
21. Cerezo, iii, appendices XVI, XVII, XVIII, XIX, XX and XXI.
22. SHEMA NC 41-3.

Chapter 3: Tangiers and Gibraltar. Franco Crosses the Strait

1. '[el derecho] que asiste a España en relación con el Estatuto de Tánger. Barcos de esa escuadra pueden y deben aprovisionarse de cuantos elementos necesitan en esa plaza.' Quoted in Cervera Pery, p.241.
2. Rodríguez Martín-Granizo and González-Aller, Appendix 1.
3. Ibid., p.35.
4. Admiralty documents in National Archives, Kew (NA), ADM 116/3052.
5. All Franco's protests are textually quoted in Cerezo, iii, pp.63–67.
6. Rear Admiral Gibraltar to Admiralty, copied to Foreign Office in FO371 W/6754/62/41.
7. FO371 W 6987/62/41 of 22 July and W6989 /62/41 of 24 (from Mr Gye in Tangiers and Mr Monck-Mason in Tetuán) to London.
8. Quoted Sueiro, pp.219–220.
9. Admiral Peter Gretton, *El factor olvidado: la Marina británica y la Guerra Civil española*, (Madrid, San Martín, 1984), p.59.
10. According to F. and S. Moreno, i, p.155 note 93.
11. FO371 W6747/62/41 of 22 July 1936 from the Governor of Gibraltar to the Colonial Secretary in London.
12. Ibid., W6754/62/41 (Gibraltar to the Admiralty).
13. Ponce Alberca, J., *Gibraltar y la Guerra civil española: una neutralidad singular* (Seville, Universidad, Vice-Rectorado de Investigación, 2009) p. 71 (English edition *Gibraltar and the Spanish Civil War* (London: Bloomsbury, 2015).
14. Cerezo iii, pp.68–70.
15. FO371 W7171/62/41.
16. Gomá J., *La guerra en el aire* (Barcelona : AHR, 1958), pp.72–73.
17. Cerezo, iii, p.70.
18. Gomá, p.73; *The Times* (London) 30 July 1936.
19. Roskill, S., *Naval Policy between the Wars*, 2 volumes (London: Collins), ii. pp. 221–223.
20. See Preston P., *Franco* (London: HarperCollins), pp. 154–155 for a succinct picture of the situation in the Strait in late July and early August 1936.
21. For an account of this aircraft and its role in taking Franco's representatives to Germany to ask Hitler for aid see Michael Alpert, *Franco and the Condor Legion* (London Bloomsbury, 2019), pp. 25–26.
22. For the details of Hitler's decision see Viñas, A., *La Alemania nazi y el 18 de julio* (Madrid: Alianza, 2nd ed., 1977) pp.384–394.
23. Alpert, M., *Franco and the Condor Legion*, pp.49–50.
24. Tanner, S.W., *German Naval Intervention in the Spanish Civil war as reflected in the German Records*, doctoral thesis for the American University (Washington D.C., 1976), p. 56.
25. Faulkner, M., 'The Kriegsmarine: Signals Intelligence and the development of the B-Dienst before the Second World War', *Intelligence and National Security*, 25 (2010), Issue 4, pp. 521–546, specifically p.541.
26. FO371 W 9669/62/41 (Mediterranean Command to London) 3 August 1936.

27. Sueiro, p.229. The detailed orders for the aircraft are quoted in Martínez Bande, J.M., *La campaña de Andalucía* (Madrid: San Martín, 1969), Document 2.
28. Martínez Bande, *Andalucía*, pp. 43–44.
29. This episode has been reconstructed using Cerezo, iii, pp.76–80, Martínez Bande, *Andalucía*, pp. 40–43: *The Times* of 6 August 1936, and Sueiro, pp.235–236.
30. Alpert, *Franco and the Condor Legion*, p.36.
31. FO371 W9312/62/41.
32. Roskill, ii, p.373.
33. For a view of the situation in Málaga by a British sympathiser with the Republic, see Brenan, Gerald, *Personal Record (1920–1972)* (New York: Knopf, 1975), Ch. 22.
34. See ADM 116/3677 ; See also Anderson, P., 'British Government Maritime Evacuations in the Spanish Civil War 1936–1939', *War in History*, 26, 1, pp.65–85, who notes the Navy's lack of concern to evacuate Republican sympathisers in danger in Franco Spain.
35. Activities of *HMS Repulse* at Palma are described in ADM 116/3051.
36. For a vivid account of the evacuations see Edwards, Kenneth, *The Grey Diplomatists* (London: Rich and Cowan, 1938, Chapters 18 and 19).
37. Rubio, J., *Asilos y canjes durante la guerra civil española* (Barcelona; Planeta, 1979), pp. 282–287).
38. Cerezo, iii, p.186.
39. FO371 W6679/62/41.
40. Kindelán, A, *Mis cuadernos de Guerra* (Barcelona: Planeta, 1982), pp.82–84.
41. Admiral Pound to British Naval Forces in Western Mediterranean (ADM 116/3534). Many of these signals have been helpfully collected and published by Halpern, Paul, *The Mediterranean Fleet 1930–1939* (London: Routledge, for the Navy Records Society, 2016).
42. A Labour MP, Josiah Wedgewood, reported that a British officer had told him this (Ponce Alberca, p.76).
43. Ibid.
44. FO371 W9139/6700/41 of 21 August.
45. *Documents on German Foreign Policy 1918–1945*, Series D, Volume III, (London: His Majesty's Stationery Office, 1951), No.48 (Acting State Secretary to various German diplomatic missions).
46. Tanner, p.66.
47. Cerezo, iii, pp.89–90. *Documents on German Foreign Policy* No 52 of 22 August, 1936 (Chargé d'Affaires in Lisbon to Berlin).
48. Ponce Alberca, pp 100–101.
49. ADM116/3051, 29 August 1936.
50. Cerezo, iii, pp.93–104, Martínez Bande, J.M., *La invasión de Aragón y el desembarco en Mallorca* (Madrid: San Martín, 1970), Bayo, Alberto, *Mi desembarco en Mallorca* (Guadalajara, Mexico, 1944; Palma de Mallorca: Miquel Font, 1987).

Chapter 4: Reorganisation

1. Cerezo, iii, Appendix One.
2. SHEMA 062-1.
3. Cerezo, ii, p.31.
4. Cervera Pery, p.366. F. and S. Moreno, p.215 and note 256.
5. Salas, R., *Historia del Ejército Popular de la República* (Madrid, Editora Nacional, 1973, 4 vols. i, pp.287–289).
6. *Diario Oficial del Ministerio de Marina (DOMM)*, No 173.
7. Cerezo, iii, p.37.
8. SHEMA 062-1.
9. See *Gaceta de Madrid*, 16 and 17 October 1936 and Alpert, M., *Republican Army...*, pp.185–189.
10. SHEMA 062-1 and Cerezo iii, p.33.
11. Cervera Pery, p.269.
12. *BLB*, p.142.
13. Sueiro, p.262.
14. *Gaceta*, No.131.
15. These figures are taken from Cerezo, iii, pp.130–132.
16. *Gaceta* No. 73 of 14 March 1937.
17. SHEMA NC 41–3, folder 6.
18. Cervera Valderrama, J., *Memorias de Guerra* (Madrid, Editora Nacional, 1968).

Chapter 5: Off the Northern Coast

1. Appendix 5 of F. and S. Moreno vol. 1 lists the death sentences.
2. Moreno, p.87.
3. SHEMA 25-15 *Resumen de las principales acciones de guerra*.
4. Gretton, p.66. Without seeing Admiral Gretton's original English text, which was not published, the reader must rely on the Spanish translation, which may have been subject to censorship.
5. Ibid, pp.91–92. Gretton quotes the report of the commander of the *Veteran*.
6. Ibid p.103.
7. For the sinking of the *Blue Shadow, see The Times* 9 August 1936. For the Russian ships see Ibid, 17 September 1936 and 'Soviet Shipping in the Spanish civil war' (New York, Research Program on the USSR, 1954), p.8 note 2.
8. Rodríguez Martín-Granizo and Martínez-Aller, p.26.
9. Ibid. p.29.
10. Ibid. p.48.
11. Benavides, M.D., *La escuadra la mandan los cabos* (Mexico: Roca, 1944 and 1976), p.391. The relevant date is not reported.
12. DOMM, 4 September and 5 October 1936.
13. Alpert, *Franco and the Condor Legion*, p.76.
14. *BLB* pp. 163–164.

15. See Frank, Willard C., *Marinos Soviéticos con la flota republicana durante la guerra civil* (Cartagena, Divum & Mare, 2009), p.29.
16. Martínez Bande, J.M., *La Guerra en el norte*, (Madrid: San Martín, 1969), p.89.
17. Ibid, p.129.
18. Tanner, p.128.
19. Moreno, p.105.
20. The novelist Miguel Delibes was one of these. See his *Madera de Heroe* (1987; translated as *The Stuff of Heroes*, New York, Pantheon, 1990).
21. Emanuel, W.V, 'The Naval Side of the Spanish Civil War', *Fortnightly Review* (London, July 1938), pp. 83–91. ADM 116/3052 (Commander of Electra to Captain of flotilla), 15 September, 1936.
22. Cerezo, iii, p.60.
23. Ruiz Sierra, M., *Así empezó todo* (Valladolid, Ediciones AF, 2005), p.229.
24. ADM 116/3052.
25. Cerezo, iii, p.165.
26. SHEMA NC 284-1.
27. See Alpert, M., *Franco and the Condor Legion*, p.55.
28. SHEMA NC 202-3, fleet commander to Minister.
29. SHEMA NC 062-66 contains a Spanish translation of Piterski's report *Vospominanya na flote respublikanskoi ispanyii*.
30. Rodríguez Martín-Granizo and González-Aller, p.56.
31. SHEMA 211–1.
32. *The Times* (London), 10 and 16 December 1936.
33. F. and S. Moreno, ii, p.796.
34. SHEMA NC 41–61, as published in Rodríguez Martín-Granizo and González-Aller, appendices 3 and 4.
35. *BLB*, p.145.
36. The insulting message is in Rodríguez Martín-Granizo and González – Aller, appendix 1, No.68.
37. Benavides, p.385.
38. F. and S. Moreno, ii, pp.1002–1002.

Chapter 6: War Material Comes From Abroad. The Insurgents Try to Block Merchant Traffic

1. González Echegaray, R, *La Marina mercante y el tráfico marítimo en la Guerra civil española* (Madrid, San Martín, 1977), pp.43, 67–68.
2. Santander, later Valencia and Barcelona.
3. Cerezo, iii, p.192.
4. For a general account of arms traffic see Frank, Willard C., 'Logistic Supply and Commerce War in the Spanish Civil War, 1936–1939', *Commerce Raiding, Historical Case Studies 1755–2009*, (eds. Elleman, Bruce A. and Paine, S.C.M.), (Newport RI, Naval War College Press, 2013), pp. 165–186.

5. *Documents on German Foreign Policy, 1918–1945*, Series D, Volume iii (London, HMSO, 1951), Document 29.
6. The details of the Non-Intervention agreement can be followed in Thomas, H, *The Spanish Civil War*, (London, Penguin Books, 2012 edition), pp.382–385. There is more detail in Carlton, D., 'Eden, Blum and the Origins of Non-Intervention, *Journal of Contemporary History*, 6 (1971), pp.40–55. For a succinct account, see Alpert, M., *A New International History of the Spanish Civil War* (Houndmills, Palgrave Macmillan, 2nd ed. 2004), pp.44–46.
7. Alpert., M *Franco and the Condor Legion*, pp.27–28.
8. Shirer, W., *Berlin Diary*, pp. 58, 60.
9. Spain, Foreign Ministry Archives, Madrid. (AMAE), Azaña Papers RE144, C5 and C6; RE64, C88.
10. Frank, Willard C., 'Politico-Military Deception at Sea in the Spanish Civil War 1936–39', *Intelligence and National Security*, 1990, 5:3, 84–112, specifically p.86.
11. Tanner, p.105.
12. Raeder, E., *Struggle for the Sea* (London, Kimber, 1959).
13. Statement published by the Berlin correspondent of *The Times* on 28 December.
14. *Documents on German Foreign Policy*, No.182, 3 January 1937, Memorandum of Political Division I.
15. Ibid, No.183, 4 January 1937, Memorandum of Director of Legal Department.
16. For a fuller treatment, see Padelford, Norman J., *International Law and Diplomacy in the Spanish Civil Strife* (New York, The Macmillan Co. 1939, republished London, Forgotten Books, 2018).
17. Moreno, p.169; Cervera, and SHEMA 211–1 where the German ship *Albatros* communicates news of the destroyer *Gravina*'s departure from Casablanca.
18. SHEMA 2841–1.
19. Howson, Gerald, *Aircraft of the Spanish Civil War* (London. Putnam, 1990), pp.176–177.
20. Tanner, p.314.
21. FO371 W12797/62/41, Captain of HMS *Esk* to Admiralty.
22. ADM 116/3052.
23. FO 371 W184480/62/41 of 10 November 1936.
24. Archivo Histórico Nacional, Presidencia del Gobierno, Dirección General de Adquisición, Legajo (Bundle) 167.
25. *German Documents on Foreign Policy*, No.297, 10 June, 1937.
26. SHEMA 211–1.
27. Cervera, p.27 '[…] sin que jamás traspasaran los límites de la corrección y la cortesía.'
28. Quoted by Tanner, p.134.
29. According to the British Naval attaché in The Hague, plans for submarines were kept hidden in the Dutch capital. (Schofield, Admiral B.B., *British Sea Power. Naval Policy in the Twentieth Century*) (London, Batsford), p.127).

30. Alpert, M., *Franco and the Condor Legion*, p.43.
31. Rodríguez Martín-Granizo and González-Aller, pp.61–62.
32. Arias, Ramos. R. *La Kriegsmarine en la guerra civil española* (Valladolid, AF Editores, 2005), pp.5–9. Longer accounts of the episode of the sinking of the *C3* by the *U-34* can be found in Vega, J de la, *Operación Ursula (https://uboat.net/articles/59 html./*accessed 15 May, 2019), and in Frank, Willard C., 'German Clandestine Submarine Warfare in the Spanish Civil War, 1936', *New Interpretations in Naval History; Selected Papers from the Ninth Naval History Symposium held at the United States Naval Academy, 18–20 October, 1989* (eds. William R. Roberts and Jack Sweetman (Annapolis, MD, Naval Institute Press, 1991) pp.107–123).
33. The principal work in English on this subject is Coverdale, J., *Italian Intervention in the Spanish Civil War* (Princeton University Press, NJ.1975).
34. Alpert, M., *Franco and the Condor Legion*, Chapter Three.
35. Salas, J., pp.319–320.
36. FO425 (confidential prints) file 115.
37. *German Documents on Foreign Policy*, No 30, 6 August 1936.
38. Ibid, No. 60, 28 August 1936.
39. Mattesini, F. 'Il blocco aeronavale nella guerra di Spagna,' *Associazione Italiana di documentazione marittima e navale*, Bolletino 32, 2018, p.38.
40. Coverdale, p.103, Table 2.
41. ADM 116/4048, 28 October 1936.
42. Rapalino, Patrizio, *La Regia Marina in Spagna 1936–1939* (Milan, Mursia, 2007), p.170.
43. Cerezo iii, Appendix XXXI contains the *Torricelli*'s report of its action.
44. ADM 116/3053.
45. *The Times*, 25 November 1936. This claim was generally accepted, at least in pro-Franco accounts. See, for example Sencourt, R., *Spain's Ordeal*, (London, Longman's, Green, 1938), p.109.
46. Cerezo, Appendix XXXII.
47. Discussion in FO371, W16336/16334/16443/16576/9549/41 of 22 to 25 November 1936.
48. *ABC* (Madrid), 24 November 1936.
49. Coverdale, pp.156–159.
50. Rapalino, p.174.
51. Cervera, pp 28–29.
52. SHEMA 211–3.
53. *German Documents on Foreign Policy*, Nos. 142 and 157.
54. *The Times*, 21 November 1936.
55. Padelford, Appendix 111, reproduces the Act in full.
56. SHEMA 25-11.

Chapter 7: The War Against Traffic Continues as the Russians Send War Material to the Republic

1. *The Times*, 6 January 1937.
2. Ibid, 4 January, 1937.
3. Ibid, 14 January 1937.
4. Cervera, pp.53–54.
5. ADM 116/4084, information from the Directorate of Naval Intelligence on 22 October 1936.
6. Ibid 30 October 1936. The aircraft were German, and had been intended for the Abyssinian forces in their war against Italy (information from Gerald Howson). Reports in the same file concerning interviews with British shipowners were made on 3, 4 and 10 November 1936.
7. Viñas, A, *El oro de Moscú* (Barcelona, Grijalbo, 1979).
8. See specifically Kuznetsov, N., *Na dalekom meridiane* (Moscow, Nauka, 1988). I thank my late colleague Dennis Ogden for helping me to read this book. See also Frank, Willard C., 'The Soviet Navy and the Spanish Civil War', *Proceedings of the Citadel Conference on War and Diplomacy* (ed. White, D.) The Citadel, Charleston, SC, 1976, pp.67–73. More recent works consulted on the USSR and the Spanish Civil War include Howson, G., *Arms for Spain* (London, John Murray, 1998) and Frank, Willard C., *Marinos Soviéticos con la Flota Republicana durante la Guerra Civil* (Cartagena, Divum & Mare, 2009), and Kowalsky D., *La Unión Soviética y la Guerra civil española* (Barcelona, Crítica, 2003).
9. *BLB* pp. 132–133.
10. For more on Soviet intervention in Spain see Alpert, *A New International History*, Chapter Six.
11. Monakov, M., and Ribalkin, Y., 'Los marinos de la flota soviética y la asistencia a la España republicana' in *Revista de Historia Naval* (no.41, 1993), pp.61–77, gives a summary of Russian naval activities. Frank, Willard C. Jr. *Marinos soviéticos con la Flota Republicana durante la Guerra Civil* (Cartagena, Ediciones Divum & Mare, 2009), gives a longer account.
12. See Abrahamson, P. and A., *Mosaico roto*, (Madrid, Compañía Literaria, 1994) for a memoir of two interpreters.
13. See Volodarsky, B, *Stalin's Agent: the Life and Death of Alexander Orlov* (Oxford, Oxford University Press, 2015), p.232.
14. Frank, *Marinos Soviéticos...*, p.71.
15. *BLB* p.133.
16. *Na dalekom meridiane*, p.59.
17. Ibid, pp. 49 and 73–74. See also Kuznetsov's reports quoted by Kowalsky, pp.271–274.
18. *Na dalekom meridiane*, pp.48–49, 56–57.
19. Frank, *Marinos soviéticos...*, p.17.
20. *German Documents on Foreign Policy*, No.88.
21. Ibid, No.89.

22. See 'Soviet Shipping', p.3.
23. Minutes of meetings of the Non-Intervention Committee are to be found in the National Archives, Kew, FO849.
24. See Howson, G., *Arms for* Spain (London, John Murray, 1998), Appendix iii.
25. I follow Howson's dating and other details here.
26. See the description by Krivoshein in *BLB*, p.319. Gretton, p.146.
27. Mattesini, p.31.
28. Alpert, *New International History...* pp.64–68. See also the memoirs of the Soviet ambassador in London, Maiskii, I., *Spanish Notebooks,*(London, Hutchinson, 1966), p. 47.
29. For a complete list of voyages from the USSR to Spain, and their cargoes, see Howson, *Arms for Spain*, Appendix iii.
30. See, for example, *German Documents on Foreign Policy,* Nos. 107, 115 and 120.
31. Kuznetsov, *Nakanune* ('On the Eve'), (Moscow, Voene izdat, 1966, p.297, quoted by Herrick, R, *Soviet Naval Strategy; Fifty Years of Theory and Practice* (Annapolis, US Naval Institute, 1968, p.25).
32. Academy of Sciences of the USSR, *Solidarnost Narodov s Ispanskoi Respublikoi 1936–1939* (Moscow, Progress, 1972), p. 255.
33. SHEMA NC. 21–3, sub-folder 13.
34. SHEMA NC. 4-41.
35. Hadwin was identified to the author by Bill Alexander, one-time commander of the British battalion of the International Brigades.
36. Frank, *Marinos Soviéticos...* is useful for identifying Soviet personnel in the Republican navy. I have also been provided with much information translated for me by Dr Boris Wolodarsky, to whom I am most grateful. For a list of Soviet personnel who served in the Republican navy, see Appendix Two.
37. Kowalsky, pp. 273–274.
38. See Appendix Two for further details.
39. Cervera, p.64.
40. *The Times*, 16 and 19 November 1936, and 3, 5 and 11 January 1937.
41. Eden to Chilston, British ambassador in Moscow, in FO371 W744/23/41
42. *The Times*, 6 May 1937.
43. Kuznetsov in *BLB*, p.178. Frank, thesis, p.349. Sources agree on the figure of 21, 24 or 25 ships, although their conclusions about the content of the holds are often unreliable. There seems to be no reason, however, to doubt the statement of Ivan Maiskii, ambassador in London, when he claims that between October 1936 and September 1937 only 23 Russian ships carried war material to Republican Spain (Maiskii, p116). Kowalsky (p. 218) gives the figure of 30 voyages until May 1937 but not all were in Russian ships. See also Howson, *Arms for Spain*, Appendix iii.
44. Quoted by *Soviet Shipping* pp.13–17. This source seems to have been unknown to the Spanish historians of the war at sea and to Admiral Gretton.

45. Moreno, p.129.
46. According to F. and S. Moreno, ii, pp.916 note 147.
47. Gretton, pp.161–162.
48. F. and S. Moreno, ii, p.915.
49. Frank, Willard C., 'Politico-Military deception at sea in the Spanish civil war, 1936–39', (*Intelligence and National Security*, vol 5, no.3 (1990)), pp.84–112.
50. *Soviet Shipping…*p.13.

Chapter 8: Winter and Spring 1937 in The Mediterranean

1. Martínez Bande, *Andalucía*, Document 10 and p.95 note 123.
2. Ibid. p.148.
3. See the very full account of the Málaga campaign from the sea in F. and S. Moreno, iii, pp.1483–1522.
4. Martínez Bande, *Andalucía*, p.154, note 204.
5. SHEMA 284-1.
6. This was suggested by the later Admiral Pablo Suanzes, a personal friend of Buiza (F. and S. Moreno, iii, 1490, note 76).
7. SHEMA 284-1.
8. Report quoted by Cerezo, iv, appendix 10 and Martínez Bande, *Andalucía*, document 9.
9. A complete account of Málaga from the beginning of the war until it was abandoned, and of the role of Sanmartín, can be read in Cerdera, L.M., *Málaga, base naval accidental*, (Seville, Punto Rojo, 2015).
10. SHEMA -25-15.
11. Ibid.
12. FO371 W22587/23/41 of 3 December 1937.
13. See *Presidencia del Gobierno, Dirección General de Adquisición* (in the *Archivo Histórico Nacional*, Madrid) Legajo 4. Orders for SECN sent from El Ferrol dockyard for 13 July and 19 August 1938.
14. See the comments of Frank in his 'Naval Operations in the Spanish Civil War', *Naval War College Review*, Norfolk VA, No.37, 1, January-February, 1984, pp.24–55, in particular p.48.
15. *Na Dalyekom Meridiane*, pp. 73–74.
16. Moreno, p.82.
17. Fuentes, A., *El crucero 'Canarias' proa a la victoria* (Madrid, Espasa-Calpe, 1940), p.100.
18. FO371 W18181/62/41 of 13–17 November, 1936. Gretton (p.204) records other reports which suggest that the people responsible for the delays were not the British experts.
19. SHEMA NC21–2, folder 4, 15 February, 1937.
20. SHEMA 284-1, 10 June 1937.
21. SHEMA NC 21–36, folder 9.
22. SHEMA 2515-1.

23. ADM 116/3053.
24. *Gaceta de la República* of 30 December 1936.
25. SHEMA 21–35, document 3, 31 December 1936.
26. SHEMA 21–36, 18 November, 1936.
27. Ibid.
28. SHEMA 202-3, 20 December 1936.
29. Alonso's circular letter No.52 of 16 March 1937.
30. SHEMA 21–37, folder 7.
31. Cerezo, iv. p.63.
32. For complete details of the Vimalert deal, see Howson, *Arms for Spain*, pp.175–183, and Alpert, *A New International History of the Spanish Civil War*, pp.109–112.
33. Aguirre, J.M. de, *El informe del presidente Aguirre al Gobierno de la República*, (Bilbao, La Gran Enciclopedia Vasca, 1978), pp. 65 and ff.
34. Martínez Bande, J.M., *Vizcaya*, (Madrid, San Martín, 1971), p.50 note 71, and Aguirre, pp.67–68.
35. Cerezo, iv, 343.
36. This interpretation of the events is based on report No. 18 of the *Canarias*, signed by Captain Moreno in El Ferrol on 12 March 1937 and reproduced by Cerezo, iv, Appendix XIV, pp.337 and ff.
37. *The Times*, 30 March 1937.
38. Howson, *Arms for Spain*, pp.195–196. The head of the the German Intelligence Service or *Abwehr*, Admiral Canaris, may have been pulling an intricate web of strings behind these shipments.
39. Cerezo, iv, p.87.
40. Cerezo, iv. p.97.
41. *BLB*, p.199 and ff. (cp. Cerezo, iv.69 and F. and S. Moreno, iii, p.1647).
42. Ibid, p.210.
43. Arias Ramos, R., *La Kriegsmarine en la guerra civil española*, pp.58–59.
44. F. and S. Moreno, iii, p.1648.
45. This account has been pieced together from the versions of Cerezo, iv. pp.69–71 and Kuznetsov, *BLB*, pp.199–207.

Chapter 9: The Naval Campaign in the Cantabrian Sea

1. SHEMA NC 2.46. Post-war statement by Captain Raimundo Fidel Martínez.
2. Rodríguez Martín-Granizo and González-Aller, p.58.
3. F.and S. Moreno, i, pp.552–558 and 606–611, ii, pp.999–1003.
4. *The Times*, 6 March 1937. See also Howson, *Arms for Spain*, pp.195–197 for the role of the Nazi arms dealer, Veltjens, in selling useless material to the Republicans.
5. Steer, George L., *The Tree of Guernica*, (London: Hodder and Stoughton, 1937), p.146.
6. 'The *Nabara*', *The Penguin Book of Spanish Civil War Verse* (Cunningham, V., ed) pp.236–245.

7. Aguirre, pp.110, 122, 124.
8. Enrique Navarro Margati is not to be confused with Fernando Navarro Capdevila (see Chapter 3).
9. Sabatier de Lachadenède, R., *La Marine française et la guerre civile d'Espagne* (Paris, Service Historique de la Marine, 1993), p.482.
10. Rodríguez Martín-Granizo and González-Aller, pp.68–69.
11. Aguirre, p.407.
12. Rodríguez Martín-Granizo and González-Aller, p.164.
13. Jill Edwards, *The British Government and the Spanish Civil War*, (London: Macmillan, 1979), Chapter 4; Anthony Eden (Lord Avon), *Facing the Dictators* (London, Cassell, 1962), pp. 412–413.
14. Cable, James, *The Royal Navy and the Siege of Bilbao* (Cambridge, Cambridge University Press, 1979) p.35.
15. Thomas, p.605.
16. *The Times*, 31 March 1937.
17. FO371 W6302/23/41.
18. FO371 W6742/23/41.
19. FO371 W6309/23/41.
20. Halpern, pp.231–233.
21. Gretton, p.204.
22. ADM 116/3534, quoted Halpern, p.244.
23. On Hillgarth, see Hart-Davies, D., *Man of War: The Secret Life of Captain Alan Hillgarth, Officer, Adventurer, Agent.* (London, Century, 2012).
24. On bombing civilians, see Alpert, *Franco and the Condor Legion*, pp.123–125 and 173–175.
25. For conditions in Bilbao, see Steer, p.127 and ff. Also p.198.
26. Aguirre, pp. 265, 275 and 401.
27. ADM 116/ 3512.
28. Cable, p.52.
29. Ibid. p.53.
30. F. and S. Moreno, ii, p.1030, admit that Spain was almost alone in insisting on the six-mile limit.
31. Padelford, p.10.
32. Chatfield, E., *The Autobiography of Lord Chatfield*, (London, Heinemann, 1942–1947), ii, p.93.
33. Padelford, p.20.
34. Padelford, pp.12 and 15.
35. ADM 116/3917 Chatfield's minute of 20 June 1937. See several similar comments in Roskill, ii, p.380.
36. FO371/20527. W7781.
37. Quoted by Roskill, ii 380.
38. This meeting is discussed in Cable, pp.55 ff., Edwards, pp.114 and ff. The official record is in CAB 23/88 and 27/639 and in FO371 W6725/23/41.
39. Cable, p.57.
40. FO 371 W6684/23/41.

41. FO371 W6725/23/41.
42. CAB 23/86.
43. Cable, p.62, quoting Cabinet records. Italics are mine (MA).
44. Cable. p.62.
45. Ibid, p.66.
46. The debate can be read in *Hansard*, vol 322, columns 1029–145.
47. FO371 W7418/23/41.
48. Stevenson to Eden FO371 W7488/23/41 of 17 April 1937.
49. *The Times*, 20 April, 1937.
50. Cable, p.74. See also Heaton, P., *Welsh Blockade Runners of the Spanish Civil* War, (Newport, The Starling Press,1985), p.38. See also Davies, G., *Outwitting Franco: the Welsh Maritime Heroes in the Spanish Civil War* (Kindle Direct Publishing, 2019).
51. Steer, p.203.
52. Heaton, p.45.
53. Ibid., pp.39–41.
54. *The Times*, 5 May 1937.
55. Kennedy, p.269 and Schofield, Vice-Admiral B., *British Sea Power: Naval Policy in the Twentieth Century* (London, Batsford, 1967), p.181.
56. For a close discussion of the Guernica bombing see Alpert, *Franco and the Condor Legion*, pp.125–132. For the role of Steer see Rankin, N., *Telegram from Guernica* (London, Faber, 2003).
57. Cable, pp 8–13.
58. For an account of the background to the admission of Basque children to the UK see https://www.basquechildren.org/-docs/alpert
59. The *Almirante Cervera*'s officer who read the signal underlined the last few words in red.
60. F. and S. Moreno offer a full description of the sinking of the *España* (ii, pp.1135–1139).
61. FO 371 W8549 and W85801/23/41.
62. Cable, pp.143–144.
63. See Steer, p.193.
64. ADM 116/3678.
65. Heaton, pp.56–71.
66. Rodríguez Martín-Granizo and González-Aller, pp.73 and 118.
67. Prieto, I., 'Cómo y por qué salí del Ministerio de Defensa Nacional' in *Convulsiones de España*, (2 vols, Mexico City, Oasis, 1968), ii, pp.58–63.
68. From the oficial report of Lieutenant-Colonel Buzón, quoted by Martínez Bande, J.M., *El final del frente norte* (Madrid, San Martín, 1972), document 11.
69. There is confusion about the date of the exploit, but the press reported it on 20 September.
70. *The Times*, 20, 21 and 23 September, 1937, and 5, 17 and 23 March, 1938. See also *La Armada* (Cartagena), 16 October, 1937, for an account of the

case. Appendix XI of Rodríguez Martín-Granizo and González-Aller
contains a brief report by the consul of the Spanish Republic in Brest. A
full account in Barrruso Barés, P., 'La guerra del comandante Troncoso.
Terrorismo y espionaje en Francia durante la Guerra civil española', in
Diacrone: Studi di Storia Contemporanea, (online) No. 28, 4/2016, Document
10, No pagination.
71. FO371 W16541, W16668, W16669/165641/41 of 31 August 1937.
72. FO 371, W17408/16541/41.
73. FO371 W1681/16541/41 of 9 September 1937.

Chapter 10: Non-Intervention and the International Patrol
 1. For a more detailed discussion about the Naval Control plan see Alpert, *A New International History...* pp.113–119.
 2. *Documents on German Foreign Policy*, No. 224, 27 February 1937 (Chargé d'Affaires in London to Berlin).
 3. Hauner, Milan, L., 'Stalin's Big-Fleet Program', *Naval War College Review* 57 (2), 2004, pp.87–120,specifically pp.88 and 110.
 4. Alpert, *A New International History...* p.116.
 5. Gretton, p.254, quoting Merkes, M., *Die Deutsche Politik im Spanischen Bürgerkrieg* (Bonn, 2nd ed.1969).
 6. See Grisoni, D. and Herzog, G., *Les Brigades de la Mer* (Paris, Grasset, 1979).
 7. See list in Howson, *Arms for Spain*, pp.297–300. For the French frontier see ibid, p.160.
 8. ADM 116/3681, Halpern, p.356.
 9. Ibid, 7 September 1938.
10. Pritt, D. N., *Autobiography* (London, Laurence and Wishart, 1965, pp.156–174).
11. Alpert, *A New International History...*, p.116.
12. ADM 116/3521 reproduced in Halpern, pp.253–256.
13. Halpern, pp.196–197.
14. ADM116/11594, Gretton, pp.255–257, Cervera, p.164, FO 371 W12012 and W21969 /23/41, Cerezo iv, p 66.
15. Whelan, Paul, *Soviet Airmen in the Spanish Civil war* (Atglen PA, Schiffer, 2014) pp.52 and 66. Also Kuznetsov, *Na Dalyokom Meridiane*, pp.205–209.
16. Thomas, p.665.
17. *Documents on German Foreign Policy*, Nos. 267 and 268.
18. *The Times*, 31 May 1937.
19. *ABC*, Madrid, 1 June 1937.
20. FO371, W10500/1/41 of 31 May 1937.
21. See report of HMS *Hereward* in ADM 116/3519, reproduced in Halpern, pp.263–264.
22. Raeder, p.81.
23. *Documents on German Foreign Policy* No. 270, 31 May, 1937.

24. Ibid, No.273.
25. Ibid, Nos. 331 and 332, 16 June 1937.
26. Ibid, No.339, 19 June 1937, von Neurath to embassies in London, Paris and Rome.
27. Ibid, No.341, Ribbentrop to Berlin.
28. Ibid. No.343.
29. F. and S. Moreno, iii, p.1719.
30. *Documents on German Foreign Policy*, No.343, 20 June 1937, von Neurath to Ribbentrop.
31. Rodríguez Martín-Granizo and González-Aller, pp. 75–76.
32. *Documents on German Foreign* Policy, No.351.
33. Ibid, No.354.
34. Ibid, No.407.
35. FO 371 W1936/23/41.
36. ADM 116/3534. Ciano, p.8
37. Gretton, pp.312–315.
38. Ibid, p.310 quoting ADM 116/3917.
39. Eden, p.461.
40. ADM 116/3520, Halpern, p.268.
41. Gretton, pp.317–322. See the messages between the Admiralty and Mediterranean command in ADM116/3522, reproduced by Halpern, pp.276–284.
42. Gretton, pp.322–324.
43. *Documents on German Foreign Policy* No.417.
44. Ciano, p.9.
45. ADM 116/3523.
46. See ADM 116/3522 in Halpern, pp.311–313 for the allocation of zones.
47. Eden, p.467. See the records of the sessions in ADM 116/3522.
48. ADM 116/3525 in Halpern, p,316.
49. Ibid. Halpern, p.323.
50. Ciano, p.15.
51. SHEMA 99-1 of 29 September 1937.
52. Hillgarth to London in FO 371 W 21719/545/41.
53. Captain Tait, of the cruiser *Shropshire*, praised Hillgarth as a particularly valuable contact with Insurgent naval command on Majorca. See his report (Halpern p. 273).
54. FO 371 W18572/23/41 of 6 October 1937 (Hillgarth from Majorca to London).
55. SHEMA 99-1.
56. Salerno, R., 'The French Navy and the Appeasement of Italy 1937–9', *English Historical Review*, 112, 44 (February 1997) pp.66–104, specifically p.76.
57. SHEMA 9901–12.
58. ADM 116/3532 of 8 and 19 October 1937.

59. ADM 116/3525, 3 November 1937.
60. ADM 116/9948 of 4 November 1937 in Halpern, p.352.
61. Ibid, ADM 116/3533, Halpern p.353.
62. This list was the answer to a parliamentary question by the Communist MP W. Gallagher on 3 November (*The Times*, 4 November, 1937).
63. Cerezo, iv, p.46 and Appendix 7.
64. FO 371 W 1936/23/41.
65. Padelford, p.27 note 8.
66. Ibid, p.36.
67. See list in F. and S. Moreno, iv, Appendix iii.
68. *The Times*, 13 December 1937.

Chapter 11: Two Spanish Navies in Contrast

1. For the training of war-temporary officers for the Republican Army, see Alpert, *The Republican Army*. Chapter 6.
2. *Gaceta de la República*, No. 82, 23 March 1937 and *Diario Oficial del Ministerio de Marina y Aire*, 25 March 1937.
3. SHEMA 202-3, folder 17, 18 May 1938.
4. Benavides, pp.423–424.
5. FO 371 W13514/1/41 of 30 June 1937.
6. For commissars in the army see Alpert, *The Republican Army...*, Chapter 8.
7. *La Armada*, 30 July and 24 September 1938.
8. SHEMA 21–36, no date.
9. '*Nos encontramos alejados de nuestro hogar y faltos del cariño maternal, de la compañera, de los hijos, y siendo por lo tanto aves errantes nos obliga a buscar un medio donde compensar este amor [...] y adquirir una cultura [...] pues se ha llegado a la conclusión de formar el Hogar del Marino donde, alejados de la depravación y solamente puestos los sentidos en conversaciones, lecturas[...] se vaya robusteciendo nuestra mente con sanos principios.*' SHEMA NC 21–2.
10. See several files in SHEMA NC 21–36.
11. SHEMA 062-1, folder 383, p.118.
12. Ibid, NC 21–2, folder 4, 13 December 1937.
13. *La Armada*, 7 May 1938.
14. Alonso, pp.88–89.
15. Ibid, p.91.
16. Quoted from *La Armada*, 5 June 1937.
17. *BOE* (*Boletín Oficial del Estado*), the official gazette of the Insurgents, 3 November 1937.
18. Gárate, J.M., *Alféreces provisionales* (Madrid, San Martín, 1976), p.365.
19. SHEMA 211–3.
20. Cervera, p.327.
21. Cerezo, iv, p182.
22. SHEMA 211–3.
23. Ibid., 12 August 1937.

24. Cervera, pp. 182 and 266.
25. SHEMA 143-2 of 2 October 1938. The note is unsigned but would seem to have been written by Cervera
26. Moreno, p.170.
27. Ibid, p.211.
28. For these decisions see Cervera, pp. 183–184, 207 and 215.
29. Moreno, p.170.
30. SHEMA 216-5.
31. Alcófar Nassaes, J.L., *La Marina italiana en la Guerra de España* (Barcelona, Euros, 1975), p.124.
32. SHEMA 216-5.
33. Alcófar Nassaes, p. 236.
34. Cervera, p.255.
35. SHEMA NC 143-2, 17 March 1938.
36. FO371 W21719/545/41.
37. Cervera, p.224.
38. SHEMA 216-5.
39. Ibid, 25021 of 20 November 1937 and 25–11 (Orders for 'legionary' submarines of 2 October 1937).
40. Cerezo, pp.185–186.
41. These casualties are discussed in F. and S. Moreno, iii, p.1674.
42. Cervera, p.64.
43. Howson, *Arms for Spain*, Appendix 3.
44. Report from HMS *Resource* in ADM116/3529.
45. Cerezo, iii, p.216 and 219. Kuznetsov, *Na Dalyekom Meridiane*, p.201, adds V. Larionov.
46. Cerezo, iv. p.73.
47. Moreno, p.211.
48. Gretton, p.274m.
49. Moreno, p.201, Alonso, p.69.
50. Kuznetsov, *Na Dalyekom Meridiane,* pp.57–58.
51. Cerezo iv, pp.114–115.
52. FO 371 W21136/23/41.
53. Rodríguez Martín-Granizo and González-Aller, pp. 85–96.

Chapter 12: 1938, Testing the Limits of British Tolerance
1. *The Times* 1, 7, 13, 21, 25 and 27 January 1938.
2. Cervera, p.227. Harper, Glenn T., in *Historical Dictionary of the Spanish Civil War* (Westport, CT, Greenwood Press, 1982), p.40.
3. ADM 116/3532.
4. Gretton, pp.285–286.
5. Ibid.
6. SHEMA 9901.
7. *The Times,* 1 March 1938.

8. ADM 116/3532.
9. Cerezo, iv, pp.204–205.
10. *The Times*, 9 May 1938.
11. ADM 116/3532 of 11 May 1938.
12. See *The Times*, 16 and 25 May and 1 June.
13. See *Hansard* of 21 June 1938, and Philip Noel-Baker's pamphlet 'Franco bombs British Seamen' (London, Labour Party 1938).
14. Gretton, p.413.
15. See Griffiths, R., *Fellow Travellers of the Right; British Enthusiasts for Nazi Germany 1933–1939* (London, Constable, 1980), pp.261–287, Pamphlets published by the *Friends of National Spain* (British Library press mark 8042.f.38) and in particular Page-Croft, Sir H., 'The Massacre at Castellón and Desolation at Bielsa' (British Library press mark 8042. M. 5).
16. *Documents on German Foreign Policy*, Nos. 617–125.
17. ADM 116/3892.
18. SHEMA 2500, 28 September 1938.
19. Coni, Nicholas, 'A Tale of Two Ships: the Spanish Civil War reaches the British Coast', in *International Journal of Maritime History*, Vol. 26/1 (January 2014), pp. 44–63.
20. S. and F. Moreno, iii, p.2181, note.
21. This account is based on Cerezo's very detailed text, iv pp.188–197, and on Gretton, pp.418–429.
22. 'Vospominaniya na flote respublikanskoi ispanyii' in SHEMA NC 062-66.
23. Ibid.
24. Hart-Davis, D., *Man of War, the Secret Life of Captain Alan Hillgarth*, (London, Century, 2012), pp.171–172. Quoting Hillgarth's account of the actions of the *Kempenfelt*.
25. Ibid, p.171.
26. SHEMA NC 143-2. Report on loss of the *Baleares*, dated 17 March 1938.
27. F. and S. Moreno, iii, pp.2223–2224 discuss in depth the causes of the loss of the *Baleares*.
28. SHEMA 25-12.
29. 30 April 1938, quoted Cerezo, iv.pp.203–204.
30. Rodríguez Martín-Granizo and González-Aller, Appendix XVI.
31. Letter in *Historia y Vida* (Barcelona), No.115.
32. Frank, Willard C. Jr. 'Submarinos Republicanos bajo mando soviético (1)', Revista de Historia Naval (Madrid), No.64 (1996), pp.7–51;. ''Situación de la Flota republicana y de sus submarinos a 25 de septiembre de 1938 (2)', Ibid. No.69 (2000) pp. 37–55. 'Submarinos republicanos bajo mando soviético (3)', Ibid. No 70 (2000), pp.25–46.
33. Zugazagoitia, J, *Guerra y Vicisitudes de los españoles*, (Buenos Aires, 1940; Barcelona, Crítica, 1977), pp. 458–461. This book publishes Salvador Moreno's letter and instructions on how to surrender the *José Luis Díez*.
34. SHEMA NC 257-11.
35. Moreno, p.267.

36. SHEMA 995-01. ADM 116/3949 from Rear-Admiral Gibraltar to the Admiralty at 0549 on 27 August and *The Times* of 29 and 30 August 1938.
37. Cerezo, iv, p.212.
38. ADM 116/3947.
39. Cerezo iv, p.214.
40. Commander of HMS *Isis*, in ADM 116/3947.
41. Ibid.
42. ADM 116/3947 and SHEMA 25-14 and 257 of 29 November (telegrams from Azcárate, ambassador in London, to Negrín and the chief of staff in Barcelona).
43. Castro's report is in Cerezo, iv, Appendix 23.

Chapter 13: Surrender, Evacuation and Flight
1. Alpert, *Franco and the Condor Legion*, pp.185–186.
2. Benavides, p.500.
3. The account of the surrender of Minorca is based on a letter of 22 June 1974 which the author received from Captain Hillgarth, on documents in FO 371 W314 and in ADM 116/3896. The latter have been published in Halpern, pp.476–489.
4. San Luis's report is quoted in Martínez Bande, J.M., *El final de la Guerra civil* (Madrid, San Martín) 1985.
5. Message from Buiza to González de Ubieta in SHEMA 061-1, 254C.
6. Zugazagoitia, p. 545.
7. For these events see Preston, Paul, *The Last Days of the Spanish Republic* (London, William Collins, 2016), Chapter Nine.
8. See Egea, P., 'La visión comunista sobre la Armada republican. El informe de 1938', in Avilés, J., (ed.)., *Historia, Política y Cultura: Homenaje a Javier Tusell* (Madrid, Universidad Nacional de Educación a Distancia, 2009), pp. 307–356 (for Alonso's comment see p.338).
9. For a succinct and detailed account of disloyalty and the Fifth Column in Cartagena, based on evidence from both sides in the war, see M. Egea Bruno, 'La quinta columna y la derrota de la II República: la Base naval principal de Cartagena, una fortaleza minada (1936–1939)', in *Cuadernos de Historia Contemporánea*, (2020) 42, 241–262.
10. Zugazagoitia, p.547.
11. Cervera, p.378.
12. Cerezo, iv, p.266.
13. Benavides, p.545 and Romero, Luis, *El final de la Guerra* (Barcelona, Ariel, 1976), p.304.
14. Romero cit., pp.305–306.
15. Rolandi Sánchez Solis, M. and Franco Fernández, F., 'Las últimas acciones de la Marina republicana', part 2, in *Cuadernos Republicanos* (Madrid, No.95, 2017), pp.11–70, specifically pp.64–65.
16. Preston, p. 239.
17. Ibid, pp.286–287.

18. Mainar, E., and others, *Gandia i el seu port, març 1939* (Gandía, Alfons el Vell, 2010), p.131.
19. Graham Davies, *Outwitting Franco: the Welsh Maritime Heroes in the Spanish Civil War*, no place, author, 2019.
20. See Casado, S., *The Last Days of Madrid* (London, Davies, 1939). This is the unreliable English account with which Casado defended his actions soon after arriving in Britain. ADM 116/3896 contains the report of the Captain of HMS *Galatea* which is reprinted in Halpern, pp. 497–507. See also Mainar.
21. FO 371, W2082/2082/41 of 20 February 1939. See Alpert, M., 'La Diplomacia inglesa y el fin de la guerra civil española' in *Revista de Política Internacional* (Madrid), No.138, March-April 1975, pp.53–72.
22. Mainar, p.124.
23. ADM 53/110/723.
24. Report of Rear Admiral Tovey aboard HMS *Galatea* to London, 3 April 1939, in ADM 116/3896, reproduced Halpern p.502.
25. Goodden told the author this personally.
26. Mainar, p.129, who reproduces a list by name on pp.218–221.
27. Halpern, p.504.
28. F. and S. Moreno, IV, p.3237–3241, list the vicissitudes of many of the Republican naval officers. For the harsh conditions of internment, see the chapter on Buiza in García Fernández, J, (ed.) *25 militares de la República* (Madrid, Ministerio de Defensa, 2011), specifically pp. 180–181.
29. *Historia y Vida*, August 1971.
30. Cervera Pery, Appendix.
31. F. and S. Moreno, i, Appendices 5 and 6 include an incomplete list with penalties imposed both in 1936 and after the war.
32. Egea Bruno, Pedro, *La represión franquista en Cartagena (1945–1945)* (Cartagena, 1987, private publication), pp. 51–52.

Conclusion
1. Roskill, ii, pp.221–222.
2. Schofield, pp.134–135 and 156–157.
3. Roskill, ii. p.390.
4. Command Paper 5301.
5. For these discussions and reports see Roskill, ii., pp.221–222 and 329.
6. Moretz, J., *The Royal Navy and the Capital Ship in the Interwar Period: an Operational Perspective* (London, Frank Cass, 2002), p.162 and note.
7. Faulkner, M., 'The Kriegsmarine Signals Intelligence and the Development of the B-Dienst before the Second World War', *Intelligence and National Security*, 25 (2010), 4, pp.521–546.
8. Pratt, L., *East of Malta, West of Suez: Britain's Mediterranean Crisis 1936–1939* (Cambridge, Cambridge University Press, 1939) pp.45–46.

Bibliography

Unpublished Sources
Admiralty (ADM) and Foreign Office (FO) papers held at British National Archives, Kew
Spanish naval history archives held by the Servicio Histórico del Estado Mayor de la Armada (SHEMA)

Published Official Material
Boletín Oficial del Estado (Burgos and Madrid) Insurgent
Diario Oficial del Ministerio de Marina (Madrid) Republican
Diario Oficial del Ministerio de Marina y Aire (Madrid and Valencia) Republican
Diario Oficial del Ministerio de Defensa Nacional (Valencia and Barcelona) Republican
Documents on German Foreign Policy, Series D, Volume III (*The Spanish Civil War*) (London, HMSO), 1951

Books And Articles
Aguirre, J.A. de, *El informe del presidente Aguirre al Gobierno de la República sobre los hechos que determinaron el derrumbamiento del frente del norte, 1937* (Bilbao, La Gran Enciclopedia Vasca, 1978).
Alcófar Nassaes, J. L., *La marina italiana en la guerra de España* (Barcelona, Euros, 1975).
Algarbani Rodríguez, J.M., 'El "SIPM", el servicio de información nacional en el Campo de Gibraltar 1936–1939', *Almoraima* (Algeciras) No, 29 (2003), pp.497–508 and 509–525.
Alonso, Bruno, *La flota republicana y la guerra civil de España* (Mexico City, Grafos, 1944).
Alpert, Michael, 'La diplomacia inglesa y el final de la guerra civil', *Revista de Política Internacional*, No. 138 (1975), pp.53–72.
Alpert, Michael, 'The Spanish Civil War and the Mediterranean', in (Rein, R. Ed.), *Spain and the Mediterranean since 1898* (London, Cass, 1999), pp. 150–167.
Alpert, Michael, *La guerra civil española en el mar* (Barcelona, Crítica, 2008).
Alpert, Michael, *A New International History of the Spanish Civil War* (Houndmills, Basingstoke, Palgrave-Macmillan, 2nd ed. 2004).
Alpert, Michael, *The Republican Army in the Spanish Civil War 1936–1939* (Cambridge, Cambridge University Press, 2007).

Alpert, Michael, *Franco and the Condor Legion: the Spanish Civil War in the Air*, (London, Bloomsbury, 2019).

Anderson, P, 'British Government maritime evacuations during the Spanish Civil War', *War in History*, 26, 1 (2017), pp. 65–85.

Arias Ramos, R., *La Kriegsmarine en la Guerra Civil Española* (Valladolid, AF Editores, 2005).

Balfour, S., *Deadly Embrace, Morocco and the Road to the Spanish Civil War* (Oxford, Oxford University Press, 2002).

Bargoni, Franco, *L'Impegno navale italiano durante la guerra civile italiana 1936–1939* (Rome, Ufficio Storico della Marina di Guerra italiana, 1992).

Barroso Burés, P., 'La guerra del comandante Troncoso. Terrorismo y espionaje en Francia durante la guerra civil española', *Diacrone. Studi de Storia Contemporanea*, No. 28 (2016), Document 10.

Bayo, A., *Mi desembarco en Mallorca* (Guadalajara, Mexico, 1944, no Publisher; 2nd edition Palma, Miquel Font, 1987).

Benavides, Manuel D., *La escuadra la mandan los cabos* (Mexico City, Roca, 1976).

Bordejé, F. de, *Vicisitudes de una política naval, desarrollo de la Armada entre 1898 y 1936* (Madrid, San Martín, 1978).

Brenan, Gerald, *Personal Record, 1920–1972* (New York, Knopf, 1975).

Brodie, B., *A Layman's Guide to Naval Strategy* (Oxford, Oxford University Press, 1943).

Cable, Admiral J., *The Royal Navy and the Siege of Bilbao* (Cambridge: Cambridge University Press, 1979).

Campo Rizo, J.M., 'El Mediterráneo, campo de batalla español: la intervención naval italiana; una primera aproximación documental', *Cuadernos de Historia Contemporánea*, No. 19 (1997, pp. 55–87) (Madrid, Universidad Complutense).

Coni, Nicholas, 'A Tale of Two Ships: the Spanish Civil War reaches the British Coast', in *International Journal of Maritime History*, 26, 1 (January 2014), pp. 44–63.

Cerdera, Luis Miguel, *Málaga, base naval accidental* (Seville, Punto Rojo, 2015).

Cerezo, Ricardo., *Armada española siglo veinte*, 4 vols (Madrid, Poniente, 1981).

Cervera Cabello, M. and Chereguini, R., *Crucero 'Baleares' 1936–1938* (Madrid, Editora Naval, 1948)

Cervera Pery, Juan, *Alzamiento y revolución en la Marina* (Madrid, San Martín, 1978).

Cervera Valderrama, Juan, *Memorias de guerra* (Madrid, Editora Nacional, 1968).

Chatfield, Admiral A., *The Navy and Defence*, 2 Vols., (London, Heinemann, 1947).

Coverdale, John, *Italian Intervention in the Spanish Civil War* (Princeton NJ, Princeton University Press, 1975).

Davies, Graham, *Outwitting Franco; the Wesh Blockade Runners in the Spanish Civil War* (KPD, 2019)

Eden, Anthony, *The Eden Memoirs: Facing the Dictators* (London, Cassell, 1962).

Edwards, K., *The Grey Diplomatists* (London, Rich and Cowan, 1938).

Faulkner, M., 'The Kriegsmarine Signals Intelligence and the Development of the B-Dienst before the Second World War', *Intelligence and National Security*, 25 (2010), 4, pp.521–546.

Franco Salgado-Araujo, F., *Mis conversaciones privadas con Franco* (Barcelona, Planeta, 1976).

Frank, Willard C.Jr, 'The Soviet Navy and the Spanish Civil War', *Proceedings of the Citadel Conference on War and Diplomacy* (ed. White, D.) The Citadel, Charleston, SC, 1976, pp.67–73.

Frank, Willard C. Jr. 'Naval Operations in the Spanish Civil War', *Naval War College Review*, Norfolk VA, No.37, 1, January-February, 1984, pp.24–55.

Frank, Willard C. Jr. 'Politico-Military deception at Sea in the Spanish Civil War,1936–39', *Intelligence and National Security*, Vol 5, No.3 (1990), pp.84–112.

Frank, Willard C. Jr., 'Misperception and Incidents at Sea; the *Deutschland* and *Leipzig* crises, 1937', Norfolk VA, *Naval War College Review*, 1990, pp.31–46.

Frank, Willard C. Jr. 'German clandestine submarine warfare in the Spanish Civil War, 1936', in *New Interpretations in Naval History. Selected papers from the Ninth Naval History Symposium held at the US Naval Academy, 18–20 October 1989* (Roberts W.R. and Sweetman, J. eds.) Annapolis, US Naval Academy, Naval Institute Press, 1991.

Frank, Willard C. Jr. 'Submarinos Republicanos bajo mando soviético (1), *Revista de Historia Naval* (Madrid), No.64 (1996), pp.7–51.

Frank, Willard C. Jr. 'Submarinos Republicanos bajo mando soviético (2)'Situación de la Flota republicana y de sus submarinos a 25 de septiembre de 1938', *Revista de Historia Naval* (Madrid), No.69 (2000) pp. 37–55.

Frank, Willard C. Jr. 'Submarinos republicanos bajo mando soviético(3), *Revista de Historia Naval* (Madrid), No 70 (2000), pp.25–46.

Frank, Willard C. Jr. '¿ Un peso muerto o una fuerza frustrada? Las dificultades estratégicas de la marina republicana durante la guerra civil 1936–1939', *Revista de Historia Naval* (Madrid), No.105 (2009), pp. 7–38.

Frank, Willard C. Jr, *Marinos Soviéticos con la Flota Republicana durante la Guerra* Civil (Cartagena, Divum & Mare,2009).

Frank, Willard C. Jr, 'Logistic Supply and Commerce War in the Spanish Civil War 1936–1939', in Elleman, Bruce A. and Paine, S.C. M., (eds.), *Commerce Raiding, Historical Case Studies 1755–2009* (Newport, RI, Naval War College, 2013).

Fuentes, A., *El crucero "Canarias" proa a la victoria* (Madrid, Espasa Calpe, 1941).

Gomà, J., *La Guerra en el aire* (Barcelona, AHR, 1958).

González Echegaray, R., *La marina mercante y el tráfico marítimo en la guerra civil española* (Madrid, San Martín, 1977).

Gretton, Admiral P., 'The Nyon Conference; the Naval Aspect', *English Historical Review*, 90, 1 (1975), pp.103–112.

Gretton, Admiral P., *El factor olvidado: la Marina británica y la guerra civil española* (Madrid, San Martín, 1984).

Grisoni, D. and Herzog, G., *Les brigades de la mer* (Paris, Grasset,1979).

Hart-Davis, D, *Man of War: the Secret Life of Captain Alan Hillgarth* (London, Century, 2012).

Heaton, P. *Welsh Blockade Runners in the Spanish Civil War* (Newport, Wales, The Starling Press, 1985).

Holland, R., *Blue-Water Empire; the British in the Mediterrannean since 1800* (London, Penguin, 2012).

Howson, G., *Arms for Spain* (London, John Murray, 1998).

Kennedy, G., 'The Royal Navy, Intelligence and the Spanish Civil War. Lessons in Air Power', *Intelligence and National Security*, No. 20 (2005), pp.238–263.

Kennedy, P., *The Realities behind Diplomacy* (London, Fontana, 1981).

Kennedy, P., *The Rise and Fall of British Naval Mastery* (London, Penguin, 2016).

Kersh, J., *The Influence of Naval Power on the course of the Spanish Civil War 1936–1939* (US Army War College, Carlisle Barracks, PA, 2001).

Kowalsky D., *La Unión Soviética y la Guerra civil española* (Barcelona, Crítica, 2003).

Kuznetsov, N., *Na Dalyekom Meridiane* (Moscow, Nauta, 1966).

Kuznetsov, N. *Nakanune* (Moscow, Voennoe izdat, 1969).

Kuznetsov, N, 'Con los marinos españoles en su guerra nacional-revolucionaria', in *Bajo la bandera de la España republicana* (Moscow, Progreso, no date), pp.131–215.

Mallett, R., *The Italian Navy and Fascist Expansionism 1935–1940* (London, Cass, 1998).

Martínez Bande, J. M., *Andalucía* (Madrid, San Martín, 1969).

Martínez Bande, J. M., *La invasión de Aragón y el desembarco en Mallorca* (Madrid, San Martín, 1970).

Martínez Bande, J. M., *Vizcaya* (Madrid, San Martín, 1971).

Martínez Bande, J. M., *El final del frente norte* (Madrid, San Martín, 1972).

Martínez Bande, J.M., *Los cien últimos días de la República* (Barcelona, Luis de Caralt, 1973).

Mattesini, F., 'Il blocco aeronavale italiano nella guerra di Spagna, agosto-settembre 1937' (Rome, Bolletino d'Archivio dell'Ufficio Storico della Marina Militare, 32, 1997).

Military Effectiveness, Millett, Alan R. and Williamson Murray (eds.), 3 Vols. Allen and Unwin, 1988,Vol.2, 'The Interwar Period'.

Monakov, H., and Ribalkin, Y., 'Los marinos de la flota soviética y la asistencia a la España republicana', Madrid, *Revista de Historia Naval*, No.41 (1993), pp.61–77.

Moreno de Alborán, Admirals F. and S., *La guerra silenciosa y silenciada*, 5 vols. (Madrid, n/p 1998).

Moreno Fernández, Admiral Francisco, *La guerra en el mar* (Barcelona, AHR, 1959).

Moretz, J., *The Royal Navy and the Capital Ship in the Interwar Period: an Operational Perspective* (London, Cass, 2002).

Naval Policy and Strategy in the Mediterranean, Past, Present and Future (Ed. Hattendorf, J.B.) London, Cass, 2000.

Navy Records Society, Vol. 163, *The Mediterranean Fleet 1930–1939* (ed. Halpern, P., 2016).

Padelford, N., *International Law and Diplomacy in the Spanish Civil Strife* (New York, Macmillan, 1939).

Paterson, L. *First U-Boat Flotilla* (Barnsley, Pen and Sword, 2001).

Payne, S. G., 'Fascist Italy and Spain 1922–1945', in Rein, R. (ed.), *Spain and the Mediterranean since 1898* (London, Cass, 1999), pp. 99–116.

Ponce Alberca, J., *Gibraltar and the Spanish Civil War* (London, Bloomsbury, 2009).

Pratt, L., *East of Malta; West of Suez. Britain's Mediterranean Crisis* (Cambridge, Cambridge University Press, 1975).

Preston, P., 'Italy and Spain in Civil War and World War 1936–1943' in Preston and Balfour (eds.), *Spain and the Great Powers in the Twentieth Century* (London, Routledge, 1999), pp. 151–184.

Preston, P. *Franco* (London, HarperCollins, 1993).

Preston, P., *The Last Days of the Spanish Republic* (London, William Collins, 2016).

Raeder, Admiral E., *Struggle for the Sea*, (London, Kimber,1959).

Rankin, N., *Defending the Rock* (London, Faber, 2017).

Rapalino, P., *La regia marina in Spagna 1936–1939* (Milan, Mursia, 2007).

Requeira Ramos, J., 'El radiotelegrafista Benjamín Balboa, y el paso del Estrecho por el Ejército de Africa, julio-agosto 1936', *Almoraima* (Algeciras), No. 45, octubre de 2016, pp.65–83.

Rodríguez Martín-Granizo, G. and Martínez-Aller, J, *Submarinos republicanos en la guerra civil* (Madrid, Poniente, 1982).

Romero, L., *Desastre en Cartagena* (Barcelona, Ariel, 1971).

Roskill, S., *Naval Policy between the Wars*, 2 vols. Vol.2.*The Period of Reluctant Rearmament 1930–1939* (London, Collins, 1976).

Rubio, J., *Asilos y canjes durante la guerra civil española*, (Barcelona, Planeta, 1979).

Sabatier de Lachadenède, René, *La marine française et la guerre civile d'Espagne (1936–1939)* (Paris, Service Historique de la Marine), 1993.

Sadkovich,J., 'The Indispensible Navy: Italy as a Great Power 1911–1943', in Rodger, N.A.M. (ed.) *Naval Power in the Twentieth Century* (Annapolis, Naval Institute Press, 1996), pp. 66–76.

Salas, General J., *La intervención extranjera en la guerra de España* (Madrid, Editora Nacional, 1974).

Salerno, R., 'The French Navy and the Appeasement of Italy', *English Historical Review*,Vol. 112, no.445 (1997), pp.66–104.

Saz, I., 'Fascism and Empire; Fascist Italy against Republican Spain' in Rein, R. (ed.), *Spain and the Mediterranean since 1898* (London, Cass, 1999), pp. 116–134.

Schofield, Admiral B., *British Sea Power: Naval Policy in the Twentieth Century* (London, Batsford, 1967).

Sola, V. de, and Martel, C., *Estelas gloriosas de la Escuadra Azul* (Cádiz, Establecimientos Cerón,1937).

'Soviet Shipping in the Spanish Civil War', Research Program on the USSR (New York, East European Fund, Inc.,1954). Typescript.

Spain Betrayed: the Soviet Union in the Spanish Civil War (Radosh, R., Mary Habeck and Sevostianov, G.) eds., (New Haven, Yale University Press, 2001)

Steer, G.L. *The Tree of Gernika: a Field Study of Modern War* (London, Hodder and Stoughton, 1937).

Sueiro, D., *La flota es roja* (Barcelona, Argos Vergara, 1983).

Tanner, S, *German Naval Intervention in the Spanish Civil War as reflected in the German Records*, doctoral thesis for The American University, Washington DC, 1976.

Thomas, Hugh, *The Spanish Civil War*, (Penguin, 2012 ed.).

Vega, J. de la, *Operación 'Ursula'* (htpps://uboat.net./articles/59html). Accessed 15 May 2019.

Veinticinco militares de la República (García Fernández, J., ed.), (Madrid, Ministerio de Defensa, 2011).

Viñas, A., *La Alemania nazi y el 18 de julio* (Madrid, Alianza, 1974).

Viñas, A., *Franco, Hítler y el estallido de la guerra civil* (Madrid, Alianza, 2001).

Wolodarsky, B., *Stalin's Agent: the Life and Death of Alexander Orlov* (Oxford, Oxford University Press, 2015).

Zugazagoitia, J. *Guerra y vicisitudes de los españoles* (Barcelona, Crítica, 1977).

Index